If other theatres such as ours across America had the opportunity to work with Jim Volz, there would be a flowering of American theatre unparalleled in our history. Following Jim Volz's suggestions for planning, marketing, budgeting, and the Board of Directors, New Orleans' Southern Rep has already reached extraordinary success.

Rosary H. O'Neill
Founding Artistic Director, New Orleans' Southern Rep

Jim is more knowledgeable about the pragmatics of running a major successful theatre than virtually anyone I've encountered. Orlando Shakespeare Festival is happening now, in large part, because of Jim Volz.

Stuart Omans, Founding Artistic Director, Orlando Shakespeare Festival

In the course of The Rep's 13-year existence, I have had the opportunity to work with numerous national consultants. None has been as helpful as Jim Volz. His expertise in organizational planning, board of director development, marketing, and most particularly, personnel management have made him an invaluable resource.

Cliff Fannin Baker
Founding Artistic Director, Arkansas Repertory Theatre

Jim Volz's administrative skills rate with the best that I have seen in the arts or any other business. He continually amazed the Board with his ability to solve difficult problems in an entirely professional and exemplary manner.

Austin K. Letson, Former President and Chief Executive Officer
Roper Hospital and Health Services, Inc.

I have used Dr. Volz's consult on matters of board development, marketing, personnel and fundraising. He is a unique, knowledgeable professional with the perspective and experience to provide effective results.

Dr. Mac Groves
Professor/Former Chair, Northern Arizona University

Jim is the most completely organized and objective-oriented executive I believe I have ever had the pleasure of working with, either in the public/charitable sector, or in the business world. In all circumstances, he anticipated the needs of the organization, the Board of Directors, and the Treasurer. Problems were solved before we knew problems existed.

James M. Scott, Attorney at Law
Former Board Treasurer, Alabama Shakespeare Festival

Jim's wide range of knowledge—from marketing to development, financial management to facilities coordination—give him a particular perspective which is vital to an organization in transition.

Alexandra Urbanowski, Vice President Development & Marketing,
New Hampshire Public Radio,
Former Managing Director, San Jose Repertory Theatre

Simply stated, he knows how to organize, how to manage, how to motivate, how to assign priorities. In short, he knows how to get the job done, and how to do it with grace and style.

Abe J. Bassett, Former Dean, Indiana University/Purdue University

Thanks to Jim's wisdom, his vast fund of professional information and experience, and his impressive ability to bring people of clashing opinions and viewpoints into agreement, the difficult path was chosen by a unanimous vote of all concerned. The problem was solved – and Jim became everyone's friend forever.

John Jakes, Author, Arts Board Member and Patron

The value of Jim's vision, leadership and expertise is recognized by institutions across the country which seek his advice on their performing arts centers and programs. Dr. Volz has been a major asset to the cultural life of Alabama and a dedicated professional who knows how to get things done.

Mary P. Richards
Former Dean, Auburn University

Dr. Volz's greatest achievement as Managing Director is that he almost single-handedly transformed a state of rabid football fans into avid Shakespeare theatre-goers. In the Heart of Dixie, this is no small accomplishment.

Lisa Walsh Shivers
Past Director, Bureau of Tourism and Travel, State of Alabama

Jim's work with the Board on planning issues, including clarification of the company's mission and organizational structure, was critical to our development and to our ability to present those plans to the public and our potential contributor base.

Robert E. Carroll
Former Chairman and Chief Executive Officer, Sedona Cultural Park

Jim's professionalism, expertise and love for the Arts is without peer and puts him in a uniquely favorable position to help arts organizations facing growth management issues. As a former CEO and Chairman of several publicly traded healthcare information companies, I have participated in many executive searches. Jim Volz is by any standard at the top of my list.

John W. Lawless
Former Chair, Cultural Council of Hilton Head Island

By merit of my position with the Chamber of Commerce, I am fortunate to work with civic and business leaders of the highest caliber. However, none has surpassed the consistent professionalism, untiring enthusiasm and undaunting energy of Dr. Jim Volz. For me, working with Dr. Volz has been a luxury and a privilege.

Marianne Thompson
Former Vice President, Convention and Visitor Division,
Chamber of Commerce

Jim is a consummate professional whose work with the Alabama Shakespeare Festival verged on the miraculous. In all his work as a teacher, board member, panelist, and writer, he continues to uphold the highest standards of professional competence and service.

Edmond Williams, Former Chair,
Department of Theatre and Dance, University of Alabama

Jim saved us time and thousands of dollars as we evolved from a vision to a reality as an organization. I have been continually impressed with his intelligence, exceptional experience, very special people skills and total intellectual integrity. This man is a rare gem.

Al Wolfe, Former Board Member, Sedona Cultural Park

As an administrator, Jim is beyond reproach. His code of professional ethics enables him to make hard decisions but with the openness and fairness important to build a team of colleagues. The four years that I worked with Jim were among the most productive and enjoyable years of my professional life. I cannot speak highly enough of this man as a teacher, administrator and human being.

Will York, Head of BFA and MFA Professional Training Programs

His vision pointed us in the right direction, his style and patience got us to where he knew we had to be and has given us a sense of ownership. It is important to understand the lengths to which Jim will go to help people who are serious about the arts in their community. Without Jim's intervention and his towering reputation in the field, we would not have stood a chance. We will always be in his debt.

Sidney D. Clark, Former President, Board of Directors, The Hilton Head Playhouse

HOW TO RUN A THEATRE

A Witty, Practical and Fun Guide to Arts Management

JIM VOLZ

Bloomsbury Methuen Drama
An imprint of Bloomsbury Publishing Plc

BLOOMSBURY
LONDON • NEW DELHI • NEW YORK • SYDNEY

Bloomsbury Methuen Drama
An imprint of Bloomsbury Publishing Plc

Imprint previously known as Methuen Drama

50 Bedford Square	1385 Broadway
London	New York
WC1B 3DP	NY 10018
UK	USA

www.bloomsbury.com

**BLOOMSBURY, METHUEN DRAMA and the Diana logo are trademarks of
Bloomsbury Publishing Plc**

First edition published in 2004 by Back Stage Books, an imprint of
Watson-Guptill Publications, a division of VNU Business Media, Inc.
Reprinted by Bloomsbury Methuen Drama 2011, 2013, 2014

British Library Cataloguing-in-Publication Data
A catalogue record for this book is available from the British Library.

ISBN: PB: 978-1-4081-3474-0
ePDF: 978-1-4081-5505-9
ePUB: 978-1-4081-5506-6

Library of Congress Cataloging-in-Publication Data
A catalog record for this book is available from the Library of Congress.

Typeset by Country Setting, Kingsdown, Kent
Printed and bound in Great Britain

Acknowledgements

Special thanks go to my Methuen Drama Publisher Jenny Ridout and Managing Editor Inderjeet Garcha, as well as my myriad consulting friends and longtime colleagues who do so much for the American theatre through the National Theatre Conference, Shakespeare Theatre Association of America, American Theatre Critics of America, League of Resident Theatres, Association of Theatre in Higher Education, Theatre Communications Group, Institute of Outdoor Drama, National Association of Schools of Theatre and *Back Stage*. Special recognition goes to Mark Glubke, Michele LaRue and treasured colleagues Scott Parker, Robert Fass, Milton Gordon, Joseph Arnold, James R. Taulli, Bruce Goodrich and my many associates at California State University, Fullerton, who were invaluable in providing professional advice and/or support.

Most importantly, I would like to thank my wife and award-winning educator, Evelyn Carol Case, and children, Nicholas Volz and Caitlin Volz, who have helped me with book ideas, editing, research and resources during the fifteen years that this book has been in the making.

This edition is dedicated to my longtime friend and colleague Darline Sacquety Wilson.

"The very thought of this fair company
Clapp'd wings to me."

William Shakespeare

Contents

CHAPTER 6
FUNDRAISING FOR THE ARTS:
BASIC STRATEGIES FOR THE 21st CENTURY   129

CHAPTER 7
MARKETING THE ARTS IN THE 21ST CENTURY   146

CHAPTER 8
BUDGETING AND FINANCIAL MANAGEMENT   167

Preface

The first edition of *How to Run a Theatre* sold out within months of initial publication and it took the cries of the field and pleadings of professors who use the book in their university classes to encourage me to search for a publisher for this second edition. Fortunately, publisher Jenny Ridout with London's esteemed Methuen Drama/A & C Black Publishers Limited took time to review the book and take it to her Board. The results are before you – an updated edition with new sections, new contacts and new teaching tools.

Friends, students, and professional colleagues nudged me for over two decades to commit to a common-sense manual that could be used by professional theatres and in the classroom, combining:

1) Basic arts management procedures and strategies;

2) Time management, life management, and personnel management tips that address interpersonal and group skills crucial for executives and entry level employees; and,

3) Life-long career planning skills.

As a consultant to many of the nation's theatres, arts centers, cultural parks and universities, I've been privileged to coach, lead, direct, or assist board members, CEOs, marketing directors, directors of development, managing directors, general managers, artistic directors, producers, and presidents of non-profit operations while continuing as a working manager, workshop leader and Professor of Theatre at California State University, Fullerton.

From past experience, it's clear that the information contained in this book has the power to:

1) Improve your organization by building audiences, bolstering fundraising performance, and tightening financial controls;

2) Solidify relationships with your board, volunteers, community, and colleagues;

3) Contribute to your future earnings power through savvy career strategies; and,

4) Change your life with ethical, straightforward procedures that put you in control of your destiny, eliminate endless front-line "fire-fighting," and

allow you to anticipate and plan for your future and the future of your institution.

How does this book differ from other Arts Management books? It's simple. This book focuses on *you* and doesn't ignore *the heart* of your institution – the artists, craftspeople, staff, volunteers, and board members who make it all possible. There are other sources available that do an excellent job offering the "nuts-and-bolts" of marketing, fundraising, and business management. Unfortunately, few offer the strategic techniques and *immediate advice* that you need to organize your time, run a decent board meeting, chart out your fundraising strategy, communicate your audience development plan, and follow through on these wildly important areas.

This book is designed to assist producers, artistic directors, and managing directors, and to educate and prepare middle managers for moving into executive positions. Other theatre management handbooks do a fine job providing box office forms, sample contracts, and house management guidelines. This book offers you the strategic leadership tools you need to create, build, nurture and succeed as an arts executive.

Do write and let me know what you'd like included in the next edition!

Jim Volz
President, Consultants for the Arts
Professor, California State University, Fullerton
Editor, Shakespeare Theatre Association of America's *quarto*
jvolz@fullerton.edu

CHAPTER I

Life Management and the Arts

"Can you look someone straight in the eye, deliver a firm handshake,
stand up straight, dress appropriately, make someone laugh, comfortably
conduct a one-on-one interview, and participate in a group discussion?
If so, you are on the right track!"

UNDERSTANDING HUMAN BEHAVIOR
IS THE KEY TO SUCCESSFUL ARTS ADMINISTRATION

The ridiculous rate of theatre unemployment coupled with the sheer ferocity of a life in the American theatre should be an obvious indicator of the need for careful and consistent organizational, life, and career planning. Producers and artistic directors are often amazed that the same individuals who spend many years and a small fortune on actor training, voice work, singing lessons, and dance training have trouble investing a few days and a modest financial investment to organize and/or polish their career skills. Similarly, actors are sometimes dumbfounded to discover that individuals who have risen to the executive ranks of arts organizations are, all too often, rude, non-communicative, poorly organized "leaders" with questionable ethics, unpolished people skills, erratic behavioral traits, and modest expertise in either the arts or organizational planning.

Professional trade publications brim with offers to train the perfect actor; re-create lips, eyes, busts, thighs, chins, and cheeks; and then snap the definitive photograph to mail to a brilliant agent list in hopes of securing the breakthrough audition. Unfortunately, few publications, support organizations, or universities train arts administrators to be savvy concerning the realities of life in the nonprofit world and the terrifying myriad tasks that they will be expected to accomplish during the first year on the job. In the same way that young actors quickly grow to realize that the person with the cutest nose and thinnest thighs is not necessarily the actor who wins the role, arts executives soon discover that prestigious schools, MBAs, and a warm smile don't guarantee survival in the deficit-laden, tough-to manage world of the arts. In training arts executives, clear interpersonal communications skills, group-process understanding, and savvy strategic skills are every bit as important as training in marketing, accounting, contracts, business, and production management.

There is a reason why producers and artistic directors joke that the closest anyone comes to perfection is when applying for a job. Smart executives know to take care with their cover letters, resumes, recommendations, and support materials. Experienced administrators understand that nurturing potential employers and enticing CEOs and board members to review their written materials is the most important step leading to an interview. So how does this nurturing process happen?

"Acting is a matter of giving away secrets," hints actress Ellen Barkin. The same is true of the arts executive's career-planning process, and in order to fully comprehend the rigors of the field, it is important to understand theatre psyches, performer egos, employer needs, and the changing trends in the ever-evolving American arts environment. Even after twenty-five years of career planning, four college degrees, attending or conducting over 10,000 auditions, working as an executive search consultant for nonprofit clients, studying over 15,000 resumes, conducting countless personal interviews, and talking to many of America's arts leaders – only now have I begun to grasp the intricacies of the process.

Communication

For the past thirty years, at national conventions, in professional theatres, and on college campuses, I have taught seminars titled "Assertive Personal Marketing," "The Business of Acting," and "Introduction to Regional Theatre." Almost every session begins with counselor basics: teaching actors and administrators how to establish a rapport, make connections, and carry on a conversation outside the interview or audition. Seminar participants are prodded to risk establishing a more personal relationship by reaching out to potential employers with a sense of humor and disarmingly honest, straightforward talk that is appropriate to the situation. To help with this, participants are encouraged to identify the basic traits that attract them to people. For example, when questioned about first impressions and friendships, many participants acknowledge that they tend to like people who are kind to them – flattery! In addition, "warmth," "unselfishness," "friendliness," and "a giving, fun-loving personality" always top the "people we like most" list.

Keeping this in mind, doesn't it follow that hassled, overworked arts administrators, artistic directors, and board members might admire and respect similar traits if they were communicated in a phone call, letter, or interview? Knowing this, doesn't it make sense to learn how to communicate positive personality traits through an enjoyable conversation, and even to rehearse, role-play, or otherwise prepare for one of the most important parts of career building? Can you look someone straight in the eye, deliver a firm handshake, stand up straight, dress appropriately, make someone laugh, comfortably conduct a one-on-one interview, and participate in a group discussion? Do you understand the difference between assertive, passive, and aggressive behavior? Answer these questions and integrate them into your institutional leadership and career planning, and you will stand out in any pool of arts executives.

The bane of one's existence in most arts environments centers on petty politics, gossip, and innuendo. Understanding that the kind of people whom producers and board members wish to work with have all the personality traits of a faithful dog may propel you to the front of the employment line. Individuals with integrity, honesty, loyalty, warmth, and a sensitivity to others stand out in a crowd. A strong sense of ethics offers a comprehensive personal framework for living a professional life worth living. Mark Twain said it best: "Always do right . . . this will surprise some people and astonish the rest."

Understanding and Empathy

Ego and a remarkably fatalistic attitude regarding employment are two major obstacles for many administrators. "If I'm right for the job, they'll hire me," states one staff member. "They know who I am and what I can do, and if they don't want me, it's their loss," complains another longtime regional theatre actor. These naive comments fail to acknowledge the incredibly busy and complex lives of most board members, artistic directors, producers, and managing directors who respond favorably to friendly, consistent correspondence that reminds them that a potential employee is alive, still interested, and available.

Another administrative roadblock is ignorance – simply not realizing that employers are human beings who may indeed have the sensibilities, interests, concerns, and motivations of other living, breathing, thinking, feeling creatures. Many perceive the job search as a humiliating battle that they usually lose, while others seize an employment contact as an opportunity to endear themselves to a board member, artistic director, or fellow administrator, and, perhaps, even to make a friend. Many arts administrators I know are quick to fondly remember the individual who recalls their opening night – or better yet, their daughter's birthday. Producers' desks are lined with the photographs of actors who stuck by them through a life crisis, sent a bottle of wine to celebrate a particularly brilliant review, or let them know how much they enjoyed their production (after the critics savaged it)!

Of course, inspiring company members, strategic planning, and career sensitivity are about more than sending birthday cards, nurturing egos, and making friends.

A commitment to polishing personnel supervision skills, understanding board needs, attaining communications basics, perfecting financial planning, maximizing audiences and earned income, and streamlining fundraising efforts is a must for the savvy arts executive. Preparing the total career package, and working to understand human nature and the forces that guide the actions of executives and nonprofit board members, is exciting and rewarding work that hopefully will lead to an increased world perspective, personal satisfaction, and ongoing employment. The chapters that follow offer insights into this developmental process.

> "There are three four-letter words ending in 'k'
> that are responsible for my success.
> The three words are work, luck, and risk."
> *Muriel Siebert*

STRATEGIC TIME AND LIFE MANAGEMENT FOR SAVVY ARTS EXECUTIVES

Time management is really life management, people management, office management, money management, and, for most arts administrators, stress management.

This chapter provides many tools that will help you organize your staff, your meetings, your board, your arts institution, and your personal life. Still, *you* have to decide to use them. There are some tough life-management questions that only you can answer, and these questions are crucial to your use of time management as a strategic tool. At the very least, time management calls for deciding *who* you are, *where* you want to be, and *how* you want to get there, and then for tackling *your* agenda with ferocity.

For example, ask yourself: Where do I want to be at the end of this year (in terms of personal relationships . . . financial planning . . . work projects)? In five years? At retirement? If you choose to plunge into time management as a strategic-planning tool, these questions are your homework for the next two weeks!

Next, work to set goals and plot out how to achieve your goals. My suggestion is that you organize your strategy on your calendar. Goal setting is freeing: it can improve your personal relationships, enhance your business relationships, and wildly increase your productivity. Time management may indeed change your life! Aldous Huxley said, "Ye shall know the truth and the truth shall make you mad!" Mad that you didn't get organized sooner.

Time and life management sometimes require a different way of looking at yourself and the world. What time of day are you at peak performance? What tasks do you absolutely dread doing? Are you comfortable with delegating? Do you have a quick temper? I'm not going to get into the "Zen of Time Management;" suffice it to say, it is important that you know yourself and, as Shakespeare would say, "to thine own self be true."

Time management is often values clarification – knowing what is most important to you and why. Do you value your career over family? Are you a team player? How important are money and fame vs. job satisfaction and competency? For the harried arts executive, time management involves assertiveness training, interpersonal skills, and organizational savvy. Passive executives tend to get run over, aggressive executives often alienate key partners in the non-profit world, and assertive executives usually manage to achieve institutional goals without stepping on people or violating the rights of others. When clear values, a strategic mind, and an assertive character merge in business, executives are generally successful at finding a *graceful* approach to the *ruthless* pursuit of their goals.

Tools for Time Management

There are many different approaches to time, life, and office management. I'm going to share just one: the system I use. It's a combination of many systems, and starts with setting aside part of one day. You could pick any day (perhaps your next long plane trip, or next Saturday). The important point is that you hide away, do some soul searching, and spell out your short- and long-range goals and how you plan to achieve them. The results don't have to be profound – but they should be specific, should be in priority order, and should be attainable. Mine are listed on my "To Do List" as a constant reminder:

- Nurture family
- Exercise
- Publish
- Generate income
- Position for retirement
- Excel as a teacher/administrator/consultant

These items represent the most important things in my life, remind me that my career is not my entire life, and inspire me to do my best at work and at home.

Let's review this tool: At the top of any good to-do list are "priority" projects. At the bottom of my list are "to do today" tasks. Including these acknowledges the need to accomplish smaller, timely tasks, but doesn't allow me to stray too far from my first priority.

In the middle of this to-do list are the telephone, email, account numbers, or other numbers I use most frequently, and those I may need for an emergency. This saves tons of time spent searching through phone books, calling a secretary for purchase order numbers, etc. It also means that I have crucial numbers with me when I travel and leave my computer behind. Make sure you "code" confidential numbers!

Most importantly, this to-do list (comprising priority projects, priority phone numbers, and to-do-today list) is all on one sheet, corresponds to my working calendar and file system, is in priority order regarding major tasks/minor tasks, and can be updated on a daily basis in two minutes. This one-page to-do list and my organisational planning calm me down, keep me from worrying, and propel me into each day. Ironically, they also allow me to be more spontaneous, as surprise pockets of "found time" inevitably surface as a result of a carefully organized schedule.

For my "Working Calendar," I prefer a *Week At-A-Glance Professional Appointments* book for three major reasons:

- It allows you to break up the day into fifteen-minute segments;

- It is large enough to accommodate 8½″ × 11″ papers (the going size for most arts and business correspondence);

- It is large enough to be easily found, yet small enough to carry around discreetly.

Finally, to complete the "Time Management Ensemble," I heartily suggest a zippered binder that can hold a half-dozen CDs/DVDs, a cell phone, iPod, pens, pencils, a wallet, a calendar, a checkbook, and, most importantly, key files related to your priority to-do list, and a "Distribution Folder." (This is a separate file folder for all of the tasks that are done and need to be mailed, filed, or handed to the appropriate person. Separating these documents from the morass of other papers in your possession keeps vital papers from being lost or misplaced – i.e. bills, contracts, personnel files.) The zippered binder is available in office supply and department stores everywhere. It protects computer disks, photos, etc.; and small items such as wallets, loose change, cell phones, and gift cards won't fall out of it as they would from a non-zippered binder, bag, or purse.

Okay, enough about the tools that you can hold in your hand to make you feel better. Let's talk about the strategies that use your brain power!

Ten Timely Tips for Savvy Arts Administrators

TIMELY TIP #1: Schedule the time it takes to prepare for an appointment, as well as the appointment, as well as time to follow up on the appointment. My experience is that this will cut your hurried, crisis-oriented scrambling in half. It will save you from running late for meetings, allow you to show respect for others by keeping your appointments on time, and enable you to complete projects at a time that is best for you – preferably when conversations and meetings are fresh in your mind!

TIMELY TIP #2: Authorize, empower, and delegate partners to facilitate your time management. Don't complain, don't blame, don't shame – simply explain the importance of your time to your friends, your co-workers, and/or your family. Make it personal and let them know that you will respect the time they give you and their thoughts on how to maximize productivity. Enlist their support, understanding, and help – and use it.

For example, in a conversation with your assistant or colleague, you might say:

"John, I have an incredibly busy September and I really need your help. I find I'm working eight hours in the office, going home, and working another eight hours there. I used to be able to catch up on weekends, but now I find that fundraising receptions, nurturing the board, community networking, and catching up on my 'must reading' has me drowning.

"I really don't mind the work, and I enjoy the progress we're all making, but I need to *work smarter – not harder*. I would really like to spend more time with the company members, board, and staff, but it seems I'm spending too much time each day dealing with nuts-and-bolts questions or problems that should or could be handled by someone else.

"I look at it this way: Every moment of time I spend on these tasks is time I could be spending more productively with the staff, artists, or board, or is precious time taken away from the few moments I have with my family. Can you help?"

TIMELY TIP #3: Be proactive and maintain control over your calendar. Publish your goals, objectives, meetings, and remarkably tight schedule, and put your goals on your calendar. Each week, schedule ten to twenty fifteen-minute blocks of time when you are available to visit staff members in *their* offices or a neutral spot. (Longer blocks of time may be scheduled if *absolutely* necessary.) Make appointments with yourself! Schedule one and one-half hours of "do not disturb" time each day to tackle priority goals. "Punch a hole" in tough projects by committing to a ten-minute outline that will get you started.

For example, allow your assistant to show a copy of your calendar to others, and consider posting your calendar when you are out of the office most of the day. This sharing process lets colleagues know you are in pursuit of larger goals (goals that even *they* may agree take priority over their spur-of-the-moment "last minute" crises). It also alleviates suspicions that you are really out golfing, and may make you feel better about "being away." Some people are simply oblivious, some won't care, but most will respect your time if you show leadership.

By scheduling a time when you are accessible each week, you allow individuals to save up agenda items, maximize time spent one-on-one, and eliminate many concerns that "magically" work themselves out without your participation. By meeting in their offices or in a neutral spot, you ameliorate "territorial" concerns and can easily exit without having to push someone out of your office.

If you need to get a haircut, put air in the tire of your car, pick up the children from day-care, or hide behind a *USA Today* and drink a café mocha – put it on your calendar! Make an appointment with an important person in your life: you!

TIMELY TIP #4: "Hall walk." By increasing visibility, you often serve as the director of crisis intervention vs. the crisis manager! You can head off many problems, inspire loyalty, show personal interest, and gain people's confidence through visibility and outreach vs. surprise, uncontrolled, and, usually, uncontrollable outbreaks of frenetic finger-pointing meetings, bitch sessions, and bouts of competition. Using hall walks to communicate allows you to touch lives in a positive way, and people appreciate it. Plus you can always retreat back to your office, thus managing your time and emotions.

TIMELY TIP #5: Instruct your assistant to schedule appointments during previously agreed-to meeting times only. Have an assistant explain to callers that you or your staffers are "Out of the office on business" vs. "They're all out." Or, if you are in the office but working on other projects, instruct your assistant to explain that the boss is "unavailable to take your call . . . but I will make sure he/she receives your message." Specifically instruct your assistant not to say, "I will have him/her call you." This implies that your assistant has control over your decision-making, and it commits you to a call that you could potentially delegate.

Ask your assistant to take a clear message with the full name, telephone number, date, time, and purpose of the call or personal visit. Also, consider asking for an email address to give you the option to respond after hours (or when a generally more time-consuming phone call isn't necessary).

Plan on interruptions. Emergencies happen – just expect them and manage them. Don't let them derail your plans. The rule of "the worst-case scenario" should be planned for and greeted with a calm sense of inevitability.

TIMELY TIP #6: Screen all calls, text messages and e-mails, and return phone calls, texts and e-mails en masse at specified times each day, at times that are convenient for *you*. This will eliminate three of the major time-wasters for most executives and put you in control of your e-mail, texting and phone life. This also allows you to prepare and be ready for negotiations, concerns, and problems, and to gather the necessary data so that it is in front of you when you place the call or e-mail. It also prevents ongoing disturbance of your work on priority goals, and saves a lot of time (since it is more appropriate for you to quickly end a call that you initiated). If you don't have a secretary, a good voice-mail system or excellent answering machine is worth its weight in gold. If you have a secretary who can't grasp telephone etiquette, find one who can.

TIMELY TIP #7: Write it down! Don't rely on your memory. Discipline yourself to jot down notes on important commitments, or carry a phone/computer or small tape recorder for later transcription. Ask your assistant to insist that individuals commit requests in writing so that you 1) "have a record of it," and 2) "don't forget about it."

TIMELY TIP #8: Clarify and disseminate your expectations regarding agendas and meetings that you run and that you are required to attend. Suggestions:

- Agendas should be delivered to participants twenty-four hours in advance of meetings;
- Put important agenda items first to encourage promptness;
- Don't waste people's time. Only individuals actively involved in the particular agenda items should be required to attend;
- Unless otherwise stated, meetings (or your participation in meetings) are scheduled for fifty to sixty minutes;
- Meetings begin on time and there should be no surprises in the agenda;
- Close the door when the meeting begins to focus attention on latecomers;
- Speak privately to offending parties.

TIMELY TIP #9: Get to know yourself. Goethe said, "He who seizes the right moment, is the right man." When are you at your best? When are your writing skills ready for peak performance? When are your analytical skills clearly accessible? When do your creative skills tend to blossom? Matching your goals and tasks to your highs and lows will keep you from spinning your wheels and will help you make the most of your time. How do you procrastinate? (When I reach for my fourth cup of coffee and it's not yet 9 a.m. I know I'm avoiding the day. And when I rearrange my to-do list more than once a day – I know I'm in serious trouble!)

TIMELY TIP #10: The future is now. Choose to spend time doing what you will remember ten years from now, and what you want other people to remember you doing. Learn to just say "no" based on your own priorities and the priorities of the institution you represent. For example, I am often called on to sit on yet one more board or committee, or to deliver a speech or host a visiting VIP. Generally speaking, I usually sit down with the requesting party and review the priority projects I have selected or been previously assigned. We don't fight – Kafka reminds us that "in a fight between you and the world, bet on the world." *Together*, we explore options and usually tend to agree that my time is much better spent on previously assigned strategic planning, fundraising, community outreach, teaching, audience development, and/or writing assignments.

"What one has to do usually can be done."
Anna Eleanor Roosevelt

Twenty Terrible Distractions That Erode Productivity

1) **Procrastination:**
   Solution – Force yourself to get the job done and reward yourself for completing priority tasks.

2) **Over-commitment/poor delegation skills:**
   Solution – Just say "no," or if you feel that's impossible, review institutional or personal priorities with those closest to you and seek their help in establishing a reasonable schedule. Hire people you respect and trust, and by delegating responsibility give them the opportunity to shine.

3) **Perfection problem:**
   Solution – Give each task your best shot for the amount of time you have to work on it, and move on knowing that you did your best under the circumstances.

4) **Endless firefighting:**
   Solution – Plan for normal interruptions, deal with them quickly, and get back to work. Always finish thoughts before dealing with interruptions, and quickly outline where you plan to go with a report, letter, or plan before you leave it.

5) **Short-sightedness/inflexibility:**
   Solution – Don't be so wed to your schedule that you are unable to perceive and grab hold of opportunities that relate to your key life and career goals. Realize that change is inevitable and that, as Charles Kettering once said, "If you have always done it that way, it is probably wrong."

6) **Lack of preparation:**
   Richard Nixon used to say, "Always be prepared to negotiate, but never negotiate without being prepared."
   Solution – To avoid straying from your work, and other distractions, bring to the table all of the tools you need to finish the product.

7) **Not choosing the right place and the right time:**
   Solution – Do easy tasks during high-interruption times in your office, and do priority difficult tasks at a site and during a time when interruptions are minimal.

8) **Poor staff training, supervision, and follow-up:**
   Solution – If your current assistant is top-notch, ask him/her to prepare an overview for work in your office, a realistic job description, a day-to-day breakdown of assistant responsibilities and activities, and a *Handbook to Organizing, Cooperating with, and Surviving Work with (your name here]*. If your assistant is generally useless, put this handbook on *your* priority list,

complete it, and use it for future orientation, training, and evaluation.
Update and revise as necessary.

9) **Open-door policies:**
An open door says, "I am available to you and I'm not working on a priority project." An open door for a short, consistent time per day may work for you and employees who know they can catch you between 2 p.m. and 3 p.m. daily.
Solution – The aforementioned hall walks tackle accessibility issues while allowing you to control the use of your office.

10) **The waiting game: losing time just hanging out:**
Solution – With your organizational binder in hand, you have myriad projects just waiting for you! Have your assistant take your mail out of the envelopes and save it to read when you are standing in lines, stuck in traffic, or waiting for meetings to begin.

11) **Searching for addresses, telephone numbers, etc.:**
Solution – Have your assistant type all of your important numbers onto your computer, then reduce the type so they can easily fit into and be found in your notebook. This should include birthdays, anniversaries, holidays, etc. Important note: code any financial numbers to prevent theft!

12) **Instant gratification syndrome:**
Solution – Reward yourself only when priority projects are completed, and chastise yourself for dealing with little tasks just to get them off your list.

13) **Listening and reacting to the squeaky wheel:**
Solution – Reward individuals who respect your time and work plan; and penalize individuals who waste your time, by assigning them a less-than-desirable task every time they needlessly distract you.

14) **Bad attitude/fear of failure/jealousy/anger/depression:**
Solution – Let go of the past, look to the future, forgive, forget, and seize the joy that is available to you. Inventory your strengths and blessings, and be grateful for all you have accomplished. Consider seeking assistance and outside support for persistent emotional problems.

15) **Mealtime madness:**
So often, your prime time for working on priority projects is pre-empted by long, unproductive breakfast, lunch, or dinner meetings that don't engage or involve you for more than a few minutes.
Solution – Consider setting a fifty-minute limit on all morning meetings (including your own meetings and your participation in outside meetings). Avoid lunch dates and meal meetings that can drag on unproductively for hours without any graceful means of escape. Delegate!

16) **Proofreading, signing checks, and signing letters:**
Solution – Hire reliable assistants who can proofread, write, and edit materials. When you can't delegate check and letter-signings, save them for quiet TV vegetation times, for times you are waiting for meetings to begin, for waiting in line, etc.

17) **Handling the same projects, papers, and memos over and over and over and over and . . .**
Solution – Put #1 at the top of each new piece of paper that crosses your desk and add #2, #3, etc., each time you rehandle this paper. Resolve to complete the project, delegate it, or toss the project out, the third time you handle it.

18) **Handling correspondence on a piecemeal basis:**
Solution – Resolve to save up minor correspondence and respond to all of it during preset times during the week. Utilize the fastest means of dispensing with bureaucratic correspondence (fax, phone call, letter, e-mail, etc.) and don't waiver. Delegate whenever possible.

19) **The black hell of TV:**
Solution – Use the time you must spend in front of a television to review reports, sign checks, do push-ups, clean up your to-do list, compose or dictate basic correspondence, and delegate smaller projects to subordinates.

20) **Reading junk mail:**
Solution – Don't do it.

Thirty Wonderful Ways to Seize Control of Your Own Life

1) **Enjoy the time off!**
Never fret, worry, or fume about "waiting" for anything. Consider the extra minutes an absolute gift that may be used to pursue activities you enjoy (such as reading a newspaper, sipping a cup of coffee, or working on your to-do list).

2) **Happy birthday to me!**
Make a list of every birthday, anniversary, graduation date, holiday, and special event that is important to you, and put them on one computer list that may be easily updated. The week that you buy your new calendar, write each date on it (or ask your assistant to do so). If you plan to send a gift, also schedule on your calendar the time to buy and mail the gift.

3) **You are special!**
Take advantage of computer "mail merge" capabilities to keep in contact with friends and colleagues. Personalize letters, but use a consistent body of text as appropriate.

4) **Way to go!**
Send thank-you notes and congratulations notes as a way of showing appreciation, nurturing subordinates, encouraging cooperation, and sharing credit. As one smart team player notes, "It's amazing how much may be accomplished when we don't care who gets the credit." Richard Nixon would have said it in a different way: "Always do as much for our friends as our adversaries would do for our enemies."

5) **Teamwork pays off!**
When assembling committees, consider a strategist, a creative thinker, a financial wizard, and a "can do" facilitator to get things done.

6) **Massage time?**
Avoid stressful situations prior to important meetings or work sessions. Schedule aggravating situations and people at times that are best for you (and schedule time after the session to unwind and regain perspective). For example, don't review budget cuts, sexual harassment litigation, and Workers' Compensation claims just prior to a board meeting or a speech to the Rotary Club.

7) **Stay fit for life!**
Reduce stress by exercising regularly, playing soothing music to drown out office distractions, dressing comfortably, and taking a break from the grind.

8) **A little perspective, please!**
Ask yourself: What will matter most to me, my family, and/or my colleagues a week from now? At the end of the year?

9) **This really is important work!**
Consider ethical "codes" when scheduling on your calendar. For example, "stress reduction management" could serve as a calendar listing for a basketball game, a picnic on the beach, a mid-afternoon nap, or time to finish a new play from *American Theatre*. "Professional development hour" could be a code for listening to your favourite symphony or watching an important opera on video. "Long-range planning" provides the time and opportunity to read the latest journals and articles that shape your planning and learning process. The strategy is that an individual perusing your calendar will be more likely to barge in on your reading or attempt to usurp your picnic than to bother your "stress reduction" or "artistic planning" sessions.

10) **Lead by example!**
Demand ethical standards and make sure that you set the pace in the way you treat co-workers, board members, and janitorial staff. Columnist Ann Landers suggested that "the standard by which you will be judged is how you treat the people who can't do anything for you."

11) **Those dang dilemmas!**
When faced with a difficult dilemma or a confusing ethical decision, ask yourself: A) Is it legal? B) Is it fair? C) Does it fall within the guidelines of my institution? D) How would I feel if my decision were printed on the front page of my hometown newspaper tomorrow morning?

12) **Pick up the phone and talk to me!**
Surround yourself with positive-thinking, competent people. Here's a test: call your office. How many rings before someone picks up? Does the individual who answers represent the professional image you want for your office? Does the person take careful messages? Is anyone even answering the phones, or do you have an oftentimes frustrating voice-mail system or poorly functioning answering machine? How can you be well organized if those individuals who represent you aren't well trained and organized?

13) **Way to go . . . and you're fired!**
A leadership and team-building tip: help your company and staff build their personnel files and feel better about their work by sending short notes of congratulations or a thank-you on behalf of your institution. Put good news in writing . . . deliver bad news in person!

14) **Read the newspaper and fundraise!**
A leadership and community outreach tip: scan (or ask your assistant to scan) business publications and local newspapers, and send notes of congratulations to people who have been promoted, honoured, or otherwise recognized. You never know when you will be sitting on a Chamber of Commerce committee or community board with another leader from your city. How does this save time and help you control your life? It's amazing how outreach creates and solidifies allies that can help you cut red tape and save valuable time in planning and committee work. It's also a very small world, and someone you congratulate today will most likely be on your fundraising list next year.

15) **Leave my family alone!**
Instead of asking yourself, "Is it fair or appropriate for me to assertively end this non-productive meeting or cut off this rambling, inconsiderate individual who pushed his way into my office?" ask yourself, "Is it fair for me to deprive my children of their mother/father, my spouse of my companionship, or my institution of this crucial planning time because of this individual's lack of foresight or planning?"

16) **Write it down, or just forget it!**
Let those closest to you (spouse, children, faculty, staff, etc.) know that you need key tasks and requests in writing – even scribbled on a Post-it note.

This saves you from forgetting, and having to dealing with guilt and the wrath of others when you forget hasty requests screamed over balconies, on your way to work, in the hallways, when pulling out of the driveway, etc.

17) Watch where you grab me!
Remind individuals who grab you in hallways that personal matters and personnel issues should be discussed behind closed doors, and not in front of other staff and the world at large.

18) Don't put your clothes on; just pull them out!
Begin your morning the evening before. Pack up everything you need to take to work and put it in the same place each night. Pull out your clothes the night before and consider a programmable coffee maker.

19) Just file it under "T" for "trash!"
Experts insist that we spend 20% to 30% of our time looking for things. Toss out clothes you haven't worn in the last year, store everything in your desk that you haven't used in the past year, sift out files that are no longer necessary, and move them out of your office (preferably into a garbage can).

20) But I spent 88 hours on this press release!
Work smarter, not harder. Remember that results count – not the time you spend on a project.

21) Welcome, and get out now!
When interrupted in the office, do a half-standing, uncomfortable-looking crouch in front of your desk, and ask, "What can I do for you?" Don't remain seated with a friendly smile – it's an invitation for the other party to sit down.

22) Why am I talking to you?
When you inadvertently end up on the phone with someone you have no interest in talking to, let the caller speak for a moment, then quickly let him/her know you are "in the middle of a project" or "surrounded by people," and ask for the number so that the call may be returned. Then delegate it. A ruthless approach recently suggested by *Working Woman*: "Let the person talk for a minute or two. Then, when you're in mid-sentence, hit the disconnect button. No one thinks you would hang up on him when *you* are talking. If the person calls back, have your assistant say that you have "just taken another call."

23) Make memos count!
When writing memos, place your main point before your rationale, unless you feel your reader will disagree with you or lacks understanding of the issue

and you need to offer an explanation first. If you desire a response or a course of action, be specific and set a deadline. Never commit to letter or memo form what should be discussed face-to-face.

24) Boo! Your letters are haunting you again!
Letters, e-mails, and memos should be used to confirm new plans or policy, not to surprise, irritate, or announce a new policy. Consider the consequences of the letters you write, and understand that they may come back to haunt you.

25) We are so good!
Use an "Annual Report" to list your institution's success stories, achievements, and progress. Being proactive enhances your image and saves valuable time defending your programs later. It also allows your staff an opportunity to share their accomplishments and communicate their ideas and concerns with you. Keep it simple – short paragraphs and lists – or few people will ever read it. A personal annual report, detailing your own achievements for your direct supervisor, positions you more effectively for merit increases and future contract negotiations.

26) What would you do?
Always approach your supervisor with solutions, as well as with the problem. Ask those who report to you to do the same. As Richard Moran points out in *Never Confuse a Memo with Reality*, " . . . you are getting paid to think, not to whine." Moran also advises, "Don't get drunk at the company holiday party; never in your life say, 'It's not my job,' and always have an answer to the question, 'What would I do if I lost my job tomorrow?'"

27) Here's what I want from you! Please?
Executives who bring out the best in people treat their company members and employees with respect and dignity while communicating clear-cut expectations.

28) And you think you have storage problems now?
Take a world view and plan ahead. Stockpile birthday and Christmas/ Hanukkah/holiday presents in an empty closet; have generic greeting cards on hand; call stores and businesses before driving across town to find out they are closed; and stock up on groceries and office items you use a lot, to save seemingly endless shopping trips. Use your assistant or a mail house to wrap and send mail and packages.

29) **Could you repeat that?**

Listen carefully! Time, energy, and massive frustration (for you and others) may be saved if you pay attention the first time. For example, have a pencil in hand when listening to telephone messages so you don't have to listen to the entire message again just to retrieve the phone number. Writing down travel instructions will save you from missing appointment times or having to stop and call for new directions.

30) **Don't you dare knock on my door!**

Put a sign on your door that says, "In Conference," "Timely Work Session," or "Available 1–2 p.m. Today," to discourage interruptions.

"We haven't the time to take our time."
Eugene Ionesco

CHAPTER 2

Producers, Artistic Directors and Managing Directors: Executive Staff Strategic Planning

"Every artist dips his brush in his own soul,
and paints his own nature into his pictures."
Henry Ward Beecher

THE ARTISTIC VISION AND PRODUCING IN AMERICA'S NON-PROFIT THEATRES

An Introduction to America's Non-profit Theatre Movement

"Vision: the art of seeing things invisible," writes the brilliant Jonathan Swift. Throughout history, most great artistic enterprises, whether a single play, symphony, dance, or painting, have tended to reflect the vision of one individual. Perhaps not surprisingly, the same is usually true for America's theatres, orchestras, museums, and dance companies. But who were the early visionaries of America's non-profit theatre, and where did these theatres first surface?

To quote from Stephen Langley's *Theatre Management and Production in America*:

> *"The comparatively sudden existence of nearly three hundred non-profit professional theatres located from coast to coast – most founded after 1960 –*

has radically altered the map of the American theatre, in terms of both where and how theatre is produced. While many of these theatres may resemble the resident stock companies of the 1800s, they sprang out of a completely different tradition; indeed, they have created their own tradition in American theatre. The non-profit theatres are governed by boards of trustees and artistic directors who, unlike the actor-managers of yesteryear, have their sights fixed on artistic rather than commercial goals."

The 1934 guidebook *B'way Inc.! The Theatre as a Business* is one of the earliest published books on theatre management in America. Its author Morton Eustis offers a look at producing in America prior to the emergence of the non-profit theatre movement:

"Anyone who has money – or the ability to beg, or borrow it – can become a theatrical producer. Talent, background, theatre training, common or garden business sense, he need not have. . . To see his name in electric lights glimmering above that of the star and the play, he has only to take an option on a script, any script will do; engage a cast, director and technical staff; post a bond with Actors' Equity; sign a few standard contracts; rent a theatre; and order the curtain to be raised on another glamorous Broadway first night . . . producing a play can be a delightfully remunerative pastime."

That same year, *Theatre Arts* Editor, Edith J. R. Isaacs wrote:

"Any living theatre must have five essential qualities:

- *It must have an entity, an organism that can be recognized, as you recognize a human being, by certain traits of character and of physical presence that are marks of a personal life.*

- *It must have permanence in some one or more of its fundamentals. It may be a permanence of place or of leadership, as in the Moscow Art Theatre, or the Vieux Colombier or the Neighborhood Playhouse; of repertory, of course, of company, or of idea, as in Meiningen or the Theatre Libre or the Provincetown, or of any two or three of these combined; but they must have something that stands firm and rooted, something not too transitory, in that transitory world of the theatre where performances die as they live, each day, as a production is set up, played through and struck.*

- *It must have the power of growth, of progress, both in its permanent and its impermanent factors, because times change and it must change with them . . .*

- *It must bear within itself, the power of generation, the element of renewal, a force that, having flowed out of its own inner strength and integrity, can bring back fresh strength from a newer, younger world.*

- *And finally it must have a goal that is essentially a theatre goal. There is no reason under the sun why the leader of a fine theatre should not hope to gain money, or power, or preferment from the enterprise. But these are by-products of theatrical success, not essential theatre goals, which must always be in some way related to the performance of good plays by actors of talent, and the consequent development of the theatre's innate power of entertainment, edification, exaltation, escape and social persuasion.*

There has probably never been an organized theatre of importance that did not have, to some extent, these five qualities."

Beyond Broadway

Predating the regional theatre movement by almost three decades, these views of the American theatre are both wonderfully visionary and, in today's world, absolutely laughable. Producing a play as a "delightfully remunerative pastime" is a concept that would elicit a chuckle from most Broadway producers, while non-profit theatre producers might be rolling in the aisles. Although Broadway has arguably been the longtime center of America's commercial theatrical universe, many would argue that, today, America's true national theatre lies in the artistically, aesthetically, culturally, ethnically, socially, and politically diverse non-profit resident theatres that are spread from coast to coast. This would no doubt please the many pioneers of the non-profit theatre who were dedicated to artistic excellence and the production of creative work that was being overlooked in favor of more financially promising commercial shows on Broadway.

Still, it's important to note that little theatres and community theatres were a part of the American fabric long before the American regional theatre movement began to fully blossom in the 1960s. Boston's Toy Theatre (1912), Chicago's Little Theatre (1912), New York's Neighborhood Playhouse (1915), Massachusetts' Provincetown Players (1915), Ohio's Cleveland Play House (1917), New York's Washington Square Players (1918), California's Laguna Playhouse (1920), and Chicago's Goodman Theatre (1925), were just a few of the more than 2,000 theatres established throughout America by the mid-1920s, according to Drama League of America and Theatre Communications Group records.

Eva Le Gallienne's Civic Repertory Theatre (1926) and the Group Theatre (1931) in New York were important artistic forces, but important work was also being developed outside New York in Virginia's Barter Theatre (1933) and the Pittsburgh Playhouse (1933). As a means of battling unemployment, Hallie

Flanagan Davis headed up the Federal Theatre Project in 1935 and employed more than 10,000 people in forty states in hundreds of productions. Legendary theatre continued to surface and flourish in New York and throughout the country. The Mercury Theatre (1937); Actors Studio (1947); Dallas' Theatre '47 (founded by Margo Jones in 1947); Houston's Alley Theatre (founded by Nina Vance in 1947); Washington, D.C.'s Arena Stage (founded in 1949 by Edward Mangum, Zelda Fichandler, and Thomas C. Fichandler); Circle in the Square (1951); Actors' Workshop in San Francisco (1952); Stratford Shakespeare Festival in Ontario, Canada (1953); New York Shakespeare Festival (1954); Milwaukee Repertory Theatre (1954); Williamstown Theatre Festival (1955); and the American Shakespeare Festival in Stratford, Connecticut (1955), were just a few of the theatres established to produce new work and the classics.

Non-profits Nationwide

The "golden age of musical comedy" on Broadway in the 1940s, '50s, and '60s seemed to coincide with a decline in both classical play production and the production of many of America's best new plays on the "Great White Way" due to financial and marketability concerns. The cost of producing on Broadway was skyrocketing, and ticket prices were also spiralling.

Partly fuelled by Broadway production concerns, the non-profit theatre movement was experiencing unparalleled growth by the late 1950s and '60s. Many of the theatres that would provide opportunities for new playwrights, employment for actors, training programs for eager students, and astute leadership to help shape the resident theatre movement were emerging. Texas' Dallas Theatre Centre (1959), Florida's Asolo Theatre Company (1960), Ohio's Cincinnati Playhouse in the Park (1960), Minnesota's The Children's Theatre Company (1965), and the Utah Shakespearean Festival (1961) were a few of the early companies. Maryland's Center Stage (1963), Connecticut's Goodspeed Opera House (1963), Minnesota's Guthrie Theatre (1963), Washington's Seattle Repertory Theatre (1963), and Rhode Island's Trinity Repertory Company (1963) soon followed.

The growth of non-profit theatres in America was nothing short of startling. There was a pressing need to communicate, collaborate, and share information among the many theatre leaders, especially those who set up shop far from the bright lights of Broadway. Fortunately, the Theatre Communications Group (TCG) was founded in 1961, providing a national forum and communications network for the rapidly expanding non-profit professional theatre field.

To further illustrate the immense growth of the field, between 1964 and 1974, at least ninety new non-profit companies surfaced nationwide, and between 1975 and 1985, over ninety more companies jumped on the bandwagon. Today, more than 400 non-profit theatres are signed up as Theatre Communications Group members, and hundreds more operate as community, youth, college, and university theatres.

Dramatic Developments

With the help of the Federal Theatre Project, the Civilian Conservation Corps, and President Roosevelt's New Deal, the citizens of Roanoke Island, North Carolina, first produced Pulitzer Prize-winning playwright Paul Green's famed outdoor historical drama *The Lost Colony*, in 1937. Intended to run only one summer, the production was such a success that it continued each summer thereafter (except during World War II), and spawned the U.S. Outdoor Drama movement, which currently numbers nearly fifty productions across America. Designed to preserve and celebrate the heritage of the country and to increase tourism, the historical plays are based on significant events and performed in amphitheatres on or near the sites where those events occurred.

Other dates of great importance to the non-profit theatre movement would include the commitment of the Ford Foundation to provide millions of dollars of philanthropic support to the arts (1957), the establishment of the National Endowment for the Arts (1965), the first League of Resident Theatres and Actors' Equity Association contract (1966), and the creation of the now-defunct Foundation for the Extension and Development of the American Professional Theatre (FEDAPT) in 1967.

It's outside the scope of this book to even begin to mention the many leaders, pivotal players, and supporters of the non-profit arts movement in America. This brief summary is intended to simply indicate the youth, ambitions, and needs of a resident theatre movement that has long been ill-defined and poorly compared to its mainstream, commercial counterpart, Broadway. See Chapter 9, "Surviving in a Competitive Field," for listings of non-profit theatre associations, unions, and guilds; and a summary review of the Theatre Communications Group (TCG), League of Resident Theatres (LORT), Institute of Outdoor Drama (IOD), and Shakespeare Theatre Association of America (STAA).

Artistic Visioning, the Artistic Director and the Artistic Team

Certainly, the artistic director is the individual charged with crafting the vision, shaping seasons, hiring artistic personnel, and fully realizing the artistic mission of the institution. For artistic directors or institutions working to define, develop, or redefine their institution's mission, artistic ambitions, and strategic plans, the next few sections may come in handy.

In most non-profit theatre operations, the following areas or individuals directly report to the artistic side of the institution (i.e., to the artistic director/producing artistic director, etc.):

- Directors
- Associate artistic directors
- Choreographers

- Musical direction (composers/musicians, etc.)
- Designers (scenery, costumes, lights, sound, etc.)
- Actors
- Stage management
- Dramaturgy/literary management
- Production/technical direction (production manager, technical director, production crews, stage operations crews, etc.)

Since many of the standard non-profit professional theatre positions are outlined on the "Sample Organizational Chart" that follows, I won't repeat them all here. However, three key individuals who have strong connections to both the artistic direction of the theatre and the management, budget, and income side of the theatre deserve special mention and clarification:

THE PRODUCTION MANAGER: The production manager of larger professional theatres works closely with the artistic director, directors, designers and craftspeople, and usually supervises all production and technical areas of the theatre. On the management side, the production manager is crucial for budgeting, personnel hiring/supervision, and financial controls. Aside from the expense of salaries and benefits, production (scenery, costumes, lights, sound, properties, etc.) tends to be the highest annual budget allocation. With these realities in mind, it is recommended that the production manager report to the artistic director on artistic matters, and work closely with the managing director on financial and personnel matters.

THE COMPANY MANAGER: Company managers are most often involved with the coordination and implementation of travel, housing, and contract commitments, with an emphasis on meeting union agreements with the Actors' Equity Association (AEA), the Stage Directors and Choreographers Society (SDC), United Scenic Artists (USA), and other out-of-town independent contractors. In many theatres, the company manager is also encouraged to assist with company communications, company morale, and special events for the company. Since the bulk of the work is usually artist related (even though the day-to-days are largely management oriented), it's recommended that the company manager maintain very strong ties and reporting responsibilities to both the artistic and management sides of the theatre.

THE DIRECTOR OF EDUCATION: The director of education is often called on to conduct artistic research, tie productions to educational outreach efforts, and represent the artistic side of the theatre. At the same time, the director of education is often considered a pivotal player in group ticket sales, consumer relations, and the development of earned income. With these dual responsibilities, it's recommended that the director of education nurture strong relationships and report to both the artistic and management sides of the theatre.

The Managing Director

The managing director of most professional theatres is generally charged with the financial, fundraising, marketing, front-of-house, and general day-to-day management of the theatre. Working in partnership with the artistic director, the managing director is often called on to take the lead regarding community relations, personnel management, media relations, budget planning, and board of trustee development and planning.

In most non-profit theatre operations, the following areas directly report to the management side of the institution (i.e., to the executive director/managing director/general manager, etc.):

- Development (fundraising/advancement/unearned income) [See Chapter 6]
- Marketing (audience development/sales/earned income) [See Chapter 7]
- Finance (business management/accounting/contracts/financial reporting) [See Chapter 8]
- Front-of-house (box office/house management/concessions/gift shops, etc.)

The Artistic Director/Managing Director Partnership

One of the most important decisions that a new arts enterprise has to make relates to the overall hierarchy of the institution. The organizational chart of a non-profit theatre outlines basic lines of authority and responsibility so that the board of trustees and all employees understand reporting lines.

From a staffing point of view, it all starts with the executive staff. In the commercial theatre, there are producers and investors. In the non-profit theatre, there are usually artistic directors and managing directors (or, following more recent trends, producing directors, producing artistic directors, and executive directors).

Many professional theatres have found that the hiring of an artistic director and managing director provides checks and balances that are crucial to the credible operation of the non-profit arts organization. Unfortunately, with any series of checks and balances, there may be institutional stress points related to artistic ambitions and financial realities. In the best of all worlds, a respectful partnership between the artistic director and managing director contributes to an institution that lives up to its mission *and* the community's expectations of financial and management integrity.

In my consulting experiences, I have heard many board members lament the concerns of the "two-headed monster" in reference to the artistic director and managing director partnership. As part of this partnership, both the artistic director and managing director report directly to the board and may represent very different points of view concerning the financial realities, priorities, forecasting, and budgeting for the institution. Often, board members point to the CEOs in for-profit corporations and yearn to avoid difficult decision-making and personality conflicts by appointing one leader who will report directly to the board. The one leader they select may be the artistic leader (usually termed the producing artistic director) or the management leader (usually labelled the executive director). In either case, the potential for conflicts of interest and the absence of checks and balances can be devastating to the long-term development of the institution.

Certainly, there are brilliant producing artistic directors and executive directors at the heads of professional theatres in America. These individuals balance their commitment to the artistic product and institutional mission while providing or coordinating savvy management, fundraising, marketing, financial programs and controls. Unfortunately, for those institutions who select the "one leader" approach without the appropriate checks and balances, the results can be (and have been) extremely damaging to the short-range and long-range health of the institutions.

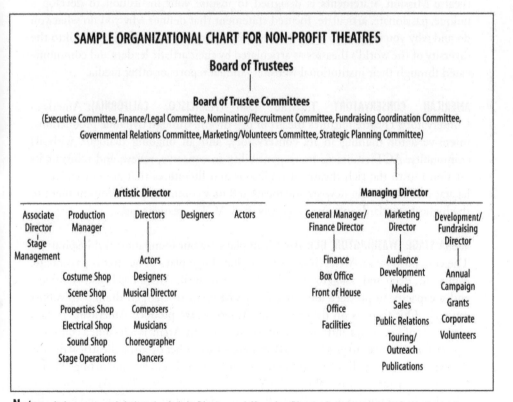

SAMPLE ORGANIZATIONAL CHART FOR NON-PROFIT THEATRES

Board of Trustees

Board of Trustee Committees
(Executive Committee, Finance/Legal Committee, Nominating/Recruitment Committee, Fundraising Coordination Committee, Governmental Relations Committee, Marketing/Volunteers Committee, Strategic Planning Committee)

Artistic Director

Associate Director | Production Manager | Directors | Designers | Actors
Stage Management

Costume Shop | Actors
Scene Shop | Designers
Properties Shop | Musical Director
Electrical Shop | Composers
Sound Shop | Musicians
Stage Operations | Choreographer
| Dancers

Managing Director

General Manager/Finance Director | Marketing Director | Development/Fundraising Director

Finance | Audience Development | Annual Campaign
Box Office | Media | Grants
Front of House | Sales | Corporate
Office | Public Relations | Volunteers
Facilities | Touring/Outreach
| Publications

Note: It is recommended that the Artistic Director and Managing Director both have strong ties and reporting lines to the Production Manager, Company Manager, and Education Director to protect both artistic and fiscal integrity.

Ideally, artistic directors and managing directors can work out any and all disagreements and find solutions that are in the best interests of the overall institution long before they reach the board's attention. However, if there are significant financial, budgetary, or institutional concerns, shouldn't this information be available and discussed with the board of trustees – the body legally charged with the institution's financial integrity and the approval of the annual budget? It may be uncomfortable for a board to wade through differences of opinion or conflicting information, but if one important thing is to be learned from the S & L, Enron, and Wall Street scandals, it's that being uncomfortable in the short term is better than being bankrupt forever.

A Sampling of Mission and Values Statements from Prestigious International Theatre Companies and Select American Non-profit Theatre Institutions

INTRODUCTION: This sampling of international theatre and non-profit American theatre Mission Statements is designed to inspire your institution to develop a unique, passionate, articulate, focused statement that defines why you do what you do and why you deserve to exist. These premiere institutions offer insights into the diversity of the world's theatres as articulated by their artistic leaders and communicated through their institutional websites, annual reports or other media.

AMERICAN CONSERVATORY THEATRE (SAN FRANCISCO, CALIFORNIA): American Conservatory Theatre nurtures the art of live theatre through dynamic productions, intensive actor training in its conservatory, and an ongoing dialogue with its community. ACT embraces its responsibility to conserve, renew, and reinvent its relationship to the rich theatrical traditions and literatures that are our collective legacy, while exploring new artistic forms and new communities. A commitment to the highest standards informs every aspect of ACT's creative work.

ARENA STAGE (WASHINGTON, DC): American plays are our foundation and inspiration. The core purpose of Arena Stage is to produce huge plays of all that is passionate, exuberant, deep and dangerous in the American spirit. Arena has broad shoulders and a capacity to produce anything from vast epics to charged dramas to robust musicals. Our focus is on theatre of the Americas; we produce American classics, premieres of new plays and contemporary stories. Our Arena is a forum, a coliseum, a place for audiences to argue, discuss and meet each other over the theatrical divide. At the center is art; all other programs are in concentric circles supporting the art. We live by a set of core values which are tested every day. The Arena Stage is relentless in our pursuit of excellence, flourishes by building a dynamic and powerful artistic community, champions various diversities through our organization and in the community, leads in our educational efforts to create models for learning, and cultivates an engaged, diverse and responsive audience.

BELL SHAKESPEARE (SYDNEY, AUSTRALIA): The Bell Shakespeare vision is to create theatre that allows audiences of all walks of life to see themselves reflected and transformed through the prism of great writing. Shakespeare's legacy to successive generations is his firm faith in human potential. His writing challenges us to reach beyond our grasp and gives us the wherewithal to imagine our future. If we can learn anything from Shakespeare and the great writers of our past, it is that we hold within ourselves the power to make choices about who we want to be. Bell Shakespeare believes that our greatest resource is our capacity to imagine and to transform: to picture a different world, to know that it can be one of our own making – and that we can be both its creator and a character within it.

BERKELEY REPERTORY THEATRE (BERKELEY, CALIFORNIA): Berkeley Repertory Theatre seeks to set a national standard for ambitious programming, engagement with its audiences, and leadership within the community in which it resides. We endeavor to create a diverse body of work that expresses a rigorous, embracing aesthetic and reflects the highest artistic standards, and seek to maintain an environment in which talented artists can do their best work. We strive to engage our audiences in an on-going dialogue of ideas, and encourage lifelong learning as a core community value. Through productions, outreach, and education, Berkeley Rep aspires to use theatre as a means to challenge, thrill, and galvanize what is best in the human spirit.

THE CHILDREN'S THEATRE (MINNEAPOLIS, MINNESOTA): The Children's Theatre Company exists to create extraordinary theatre experiences that educate, challenge and inspire young people. The Children's Theatre Company seeks to be an international model for excellence in theatre. We strive to lead in the creation of new work for young people, in theatre training and generating initiatives for using theatre in education and community development. The Children's Theatre Company will create an urban cultural center for young people and families, where theatre is the centerpiece, out of which emerge programs and activities celebrating diverse art forms, ideas and cultures. We will utilize the power of theatre to open discussion, touch hearts and question accepted notions.

CIRQUE DU SOLEIL (WORLDWIDE BASED IN QUEBEC, CANADA): Cirque du Soleil is an international company from Quebec dedicated to the creation, production and distribution of artistic works. Our mission is to invoke the imagination, provoke the senses and evoke the emotions of people throughout the world. Cirque du Soleil is a generator of new experiences, a laboratory and platform for creators. We are constantly researching new artistic avenues and innovating within our organization – and we intend to carry on taking such risks and inventing with audacity. As we pursue our dreams and grow our business it is also our intention to position ourselves in the community as an agent of change. We will, as a matter of policy, treat our employees, clients, partners and neighbors with respect, and willingly operate our business according to the laws of every jurisdiction we work in. In all our relationships – internal and external – we will always go the extra mile as proof of our daring and creativity.

THE CLEVELAND PLAY HOUSE (CLEVELAND, OHIO): The Cleveland Play House is America's first permanently established professional theatre company. We are an artist-inspired theatre that serves our community by bringing to life stories that are entertaining, relevant and thought-provoking; whose core company is comprised of many of the nation's most accomplished theatrical professionals. The Cleveland Play House produces a wide-ranging repertoire that has particular relevance to this community. Cleveland Play House develops important new work for the American theatre, celebrates the creative impulse of the artist, delivers educational programs for all age groups, and provides comprehensive facilities to other community arts organizations.

THE DONMAR WAREHOUSE (LONDON, UNITED KINGDOM): The Donmar Warehouse has a diverse artistic policy that includes new writing, contemporary reappraisals of European classics, British and American drama and small scale musical theatre. Over the last sixteen years the theatre has created a reputation associated with artistic excellence: it has showcased the talent of some of the industry's premier creative artists, and built an unparalleled catalogue of work. As well as presenting at least six productions a year at its home in Covent Garden, the Donmar presents work nationally and internationally. Through our Education programme, we aim to introduce a new, young and diverse audience to our work. We have worked with over 1,000 young people, many of whom have never been to the theatre before, through post-show talks, in-school workshops, and our devising project 'Creating A Scene' where students have the opportunity to create their own pieces of original theatre, using Donmar productions as their inspiration.

EAST WEST PLAYERS (LOS ANGELES, CALIFORNIA): As the nation's premier Asian American theatre organization, East West Players produces outstanding works and educational programs that give voice to the Asian Pacific American experience.

THE GOODMAN THEATRE (CHICAGO, ILLINOIS): The Goodman Artistic Collective is a vibrant and diverse group of this country's most exciting directors, actors and writers. Artists with a national reputation, who make Chicago their home. Artists whose extraordinary work on the Goodman stage holds up a mirror to our hearts, our city, and our world.

THE GUTHRIE THEATRE (MINNEAPOLIS, MINNESOTA): The Guthrie Theatre serves as a vital artistic resource for the people of Minnesota and the region. Its primary task is to celebrate, through theatrical performances, the common humanity binding us all together. The Theatre is devoted to the traditional classical repertoire that has sustained us since our foundation and to the exploration of new works from diverse cultures and traditions. The Guthrie aspires to the highest levels of artistic achievement and to reaching the widest possible audience with our work. The Guthrie Theatre sees itself as a leader in American Theatre with both a national and international reputation.

LA JOLLA PLAYHOUSE (LA JOLLA, CALIFORNIA): La Jolla Playhouse advances theatre as an art form and as a vital social, moral and political platform by providing unfettered creative opportunities for the leading artists of today and tomorrow. With our youthful spirit and eclectic, artist-driven approach we will continue to cultivate a local and national following with an insatiable appetite for audacious and diverse work. In the future, San Diego's La Jolla Playhouse will be considered singularly indispensable to the worldwide theatre landscape, as we become a permanent safe harbor for the unsafe and surprising. The day will come when it will be essential to enter the La Jolla Playhouse village in order to get a glimpse of what is about to happen in American theatre.

THE MARKET THEATRE (JOHANNESBURG, SOUTH AFRICA): The mission of the Market Theatre Foundation is to create an authentic South African cultural experience which is committed to providing the highest level of artistic excellence in all aspects of the performing and visual arts in which the education and development of a diverse community of artists, audiences and technicians is assured.

- We are proudly South African and deeply conscious of our history and current social context.
- We value and protect our artistic independence and right of free expression.
- We produce and present authentic SA and international art that is innovative and of the highest quality.
- We value our clients and aim to delight them with our offerings and service.
- We are conscious of and accept our social responsibility to train quality artists and to use our art forms to improve people's lives.
- We are custodians of the Market and always act in its best interest within the parameters of the Constitution, Bill of Rights, legislation and the principles of good governance.

- We respect all our stakeholders and their needs.
- We treat all people with respect and act with honesty and integrity in all we do.

NATIONAL THEATRE (LONDON, ENGLAND): The National Theatre is central to the creative life of the country. In its three theatres on the South Bank in London, it presents an eclectic mix of new plays and classics, with seven or eight productions in repertory at any one time. It aims constantly to re-energise the great traditions of the British stage and to expand the horizons of audiences and artists alike. It aspires to reflect in its repertoire the diversity of the nation's culture. At its Studio, the National offers a space for research and development for the NT's stages and the theatre as a whole. Through the NT Education Department, tomorrow's audiences are addressed. Through an extensive programme of Platform performances, backstage tours, foyer music, exhibitions, and free outdoor entertainment it recognises that the theatre doesn't begin and end with the rise and fall of the curtain. And by touring, the National shares its work with audiences in the UK and abroad.

OREGON SHAKESPEARE FESTIVAL (ASHLAND, OREGON): Inspired by Shakespeare's work and the cultural richness of the United States, we reveal our collective humanity through illuminating interpretations of new and classic plays, deepened by the kaleido-scope of rotating repertory. These are the values we hold at the Oregon Shakespeare Festival. They are at the center of everything we do, and describe how we work together. While we recognize the need for balance among them, these values guide us in all our decisions:

- **Excellence:** We believe in constantly seeking to present work of the highest quality, expecting excellence from all company members.
- **Inclusion:** We believe the inclusion of a diversity of people, ideas and cultures enriches both our insights into the work we present on stage and our relationships with each other.
- **Learning:** We believe in offering company members, audiences, teachers and students the richest possible learning experiences.
- **Financial Health:** We believe in continuing our long history of financial stability, making wise and efficient use of all the resources entrusted to us.
- **Heritage:** We believe that the Festival's history of almost seventy-five years gives us a heritage of thoughtful change and evolution to guide us as we face the future.
- **Environmental Responsibility:** We believe in making responsible choices that support a sustainable future for our planet.

- **Company:** We believe in sustaining a safe and supportive workplace where we rely on our fellow company members to work together with trust, respect and compassion. We believe that the collaborative process is intrinsic to theatre and is the bedrock of our working relationships; we are committed to the Festival's Communication Credo. We encourage and support a balance between our lives inside and outside the Festival.

SEATTLE REPERTORY THEATRE (SEATTLE, WASHINGTON): Seattle Repertory Theatre produces plays that excite the imagination and nourish a lifelong passion for the theatre. This mission statement is supported by the following objectives:

- To keep theatre artists at the center of the work we do;

- To be an organization in search of ways to say "yes" – to artists, audiences and the SRT community;

- To engage audiences of diverse ages, cultures and economic backgrounds;

- To be a community gathering place for active exchange about culture and the power of creativity;

- To create world-class theatrical experiences while maximizing and responsibly managing available resources;

- To provide a working environment that fosters leadership, collaboration and mutual respect, recognizes effort that sustains excellence, rewards innovation and encourages honest dialogue.

SHAKESPEARE & COMPANY (LENOX, MASSACHUSETTS): Shakespeare & Company aspires to create a theatre of unprecedented excellence rooted in the classical ideals of inquiry, balance and harmony; a company that performs as the Elizabethans did – in love with poetry, physical prowess and the mysteries of the universe. With a core of over 120 artists, the company performs Shakespeare, generating opportunities for collaboration between actors, directors and designers of all races, nationalities and backgrounds. Shakespeare & Company provides original, in-depth, classical training and performance methods. Shakespeare & Company also develops and produces new plays of social and political significance. Shakespeare & Company's education programs inspire a new generation of students and scholars to discover the resonance of Shakespeare's truths in the everyday world, demonstrating the influence that classical theatre can have within a community.

SOUTH COAST REPERTORY (COSTA MESA, CALIFORNIA): South Coast Repertory was founded in the belief that theatre is an art form with a unique power to illuminate the human experience. We commit ourselves to exploring the most urgent human and social issues of our time, and to merging literature, design and performance in ways that test the bounds of theatre's artistic possibilities. We undertake to advance the art of theatre in the service of our community, and aim to extend that service through educational, intercultural, and outreach programs that harmonize with our artistic mission.

STEPPENWOLF THEATRE COMPANY, (CHICAGO, ILLINOIS): Steppenwolf Theatre Company is a Chicago-based international performing arts institution committed to ensemble collaboration and artistic risk through its work with its permanent ensemble, guest artists, partner institutions and the community. Steppenwolf has redefined the landscape of acting and performance by spawning a generation of America's most gifted artists. Founded in 1976 as an ensemble of nine actors, Steppenwolf has grown into an internationally renowned company of thirty-four artists whose talents include acting, directing, playwriting, filmmaking, and textual adaptation. No other American theatre ensemble has survived as long and thrived as much as the Steppenwolf company of artists. Steppenwolf celebrates the intelligence of the actor, the vision of the director, the words of the playwright and the power of the theatre.

STRATFORD SHAKESPEARE FESTIVAL (STRATFORD, CANADA): With William Shakespeare as its foundation, the Stratford Shakespeare Festival aims to set the standard for classical theatre in North America. Embracing our heritage of tradition and innovation, we seek to bring classical and contemporary theatre alive for an increasingly diverse audience.

For more than half a century, our mission has evolved to address the ever-changing, ever-challenging Canadian cultural landscape. What has remained constant, however, is our determination to create stimulating, thought-provoking productions of Shakespeare's plays, to examine other plays from the classical repertoire, and to foster and support the development of Canadian theatre practitioners.

By searching Canada and the world for the finest talent, and by providing the conditions and training that enable those artists to achieve their most courageous work, we will immerse our audiences in a theatregoing experience that is not only innovative, entertaining and unsurpassed anywhere in the world, but also deeply relevant to, and reflective of, their lives and communities.

THE TRICYCLE THEATRE (LONDON, UNITED KINGDOM): The Tricycle Theatre has established a unique reputation for presenting plays that reflect the cultural diversity of its community; in particular plays by Black, Irish, Jewish, Asian and South African writers, as well as for responding to contemporary issues and events with its ground-breaking 'tribunal plays', and political work. Education and community activities are an integral part of the artistic output of the Tricycle. The Tricycle's home in the London borough of Brent comprises a theatre, cinema, art gallery, café and bar, and it is open all year round. The Tricycle presents an eclectic programme which reflects London's increasingly changing community. It continues to stimulate and provoke its audiences. Each year some of the theatre programme is devoted to contemporary issues that are part of a social debate – and sometimes work that addresses global issues.

> "Passion, though a bad regulator, is a powerful spring."
> *Ralph Waldo Emerson*

A SUGGESTED ARTS PLANNING SCHEDULE:
SEASON PLANNING & BUDGETING FOR A FALL SCHEDULE

AUGUST/SEPTEMBER

- Research play titles and availability.

- Audit the previous year's earned and unearned income, and compile comparative summaries.

- Do expense variance analysis on the previous year, to determine spending concerns.

- Review union contract concerns that impact budgets.

OCTOBER/NOVEMBER

- Compile a draft of the season's prospective plays, and review financial and production feasibility with artistic and production areas.

- Specifically budget for the planned season and review progress with your board finance committee and board chair.

DECEMBER

- Finalize the season and win board approval for the budget that supports this season.

- Research marketing and public relations materials for the plays, and begin publications and subscription-renewal planning strategies.

END OF FEBRUARY

- All materials, processes, and sales personnel should be in place for subscription renewals.

MARCH

- Renewal brochures, audience reminders, telephone calls, and major marketing efforts begin for the fall season.

BRAINSTORMING AND STRATEGIC VISION

DEFINE THE DREAM: THE PERFECT THEATRE

- Mission/Vision
- Plays
- Actors
- Designers
- Directors
- Audience
- Educational programs
- Community Relationships/Partnerships, etc.

NECESSARY COMPONENTS

- Research
- Planning
- Agreements
- Involvements
- Marketing
- Fundraising
- Budgeting
- General management
- Evaluation

IMMEDIATE DESIRES AND NEEDS

- Cooperation
- Collaboration
- Visibility
- Money
- Staffing
- Communications

TWELVE TIMELY TIPS FOR TAKING CHARGE AND ENDEARING YOUR THEATRE TO YOUR COMMUNITY

It's nice to have marketing staff, fundraising staff, box office staff, general managers, associate artistic directors, a great company, and fabulous delegation skills. But in the twenty-first century, if you are an artistic director or managing director, you soon learn that "If it is to be, it's up to me."

You are the top dog, key person, community leader, crucial spokesperson. And everyone knows you are busy directing plays, choosing seasons, balancing budgets, putting butts in seats, and dealing with endless crises. Still (or perhaps, *therefore*), you are the one who must take the lead in endearing your company to your community. Your company tends to take its "we love our community" cues from the top leadership – that's you! And your community, if it's similar to most communities in America, looks to the artistic director and managing director to set the pace for positive relationships between your theatre and the city you live in.

With this in mind, here are "Twelve Timely Tips for Taking Charge and Endearing Your Theatre to Your Community:"

TIMELY TIP #1: Arrive for meetings prepared and on time. Show your community leaders that you respect their time through your approach to theatre board meetings, city tourism sessions, Chamber of Commerce breakfasts, and the myriad other meetings you attend to positively position your theatre in the community.

TIMELY TIP #2: Return phone calls and insist that your staff return phone calls and e-mails within twenty-four hours of receipt. You don't have to address the concerns of all phone calls and e-mails within twenty-four hours, but the courtesy of an acknowledgement is paramount.

If you are out of the office or simply can't return the call personally, have someone in your office communicate when you will return the call, or delegate the call/e-mail to the appropriate staff member. Take great care in "delegating" – lest subscribers, patrons, donors, and friends of your theatre begin "delegating" their dollars, time, and energies to other worthwhile non-profit organizations.

TIMELY TIP #3: City Walk. Consider increasing your endearing visibility in the community by eating in public places, visiting board members and donors in their offices, stopping by businesses that display your posters and brochures to say "thank you," etc. City walking inspires loyalty, demonstrates personal interest, and boosts the community's confidence that you may be a near-normal human being vs. the egotistical, tantrum-throwing artist/producer portrayed on television and in the movies.

P.S.: Drinking too much in public places doesn't count as "endearing visibility."

TIMELY TIP #4: Ditch the impersonal phone trees, horrific answering machines, and ineffective phone services. Endeavor to create clear, straightforward communications on your telephones that connect to the general public. Remember, *you really do want them to be calling you* (although you'd never know it from the obnoxious phone messages, obstinate call-waiting interruptions, complicated phone systems, and maze-like procedures that many patrons, donors, and board members are forced to endure every day). If having someone simply answer your phone is just too complicated, make sure you have a friendly message or assistant who will greet callers and communicate with them in an endearing way. May I respectfully suggest "What do you want?" "Who are you, anyway?" "He hasn't been in all week!" "She's in the bathroom," "She's terrible about returning phone calls," and "And I'm talking to . . . ?" are *not* particularly endearing responses to the friends of your theatre. (These are all responses I have heard when calling America's professional theatres.)

TIMELY TIP #5: Donate blood, read for the blind, participate in United Way, be a leader in AIDS-awareness fundraisers, and run to the walkathon to support breast cancer research. Chances are, if yours is similar to every other American theatre, you are constantly asking people to buy tickets, send contributions, and donate time. Now would be a good time to give back to the community, encourage your company to contribute to the life of the community, and let people know how much your artists, administrators, and craftspeople adore the community.

TIMELY TIP #6: If appropriate, make a list of birthday, anniversary, and graduation dates of every member of your board of trustees' families. Send a warm note from the company and executive staff to celebrate the day.

TIMELY TIP #7: Keep in contact with board members and community VIPs. Short notes or phone calls will do.

TIMELY TIP #8: Send notes of congratulations to members of the community who are promoted at work, recognized for special achievements, or singled out for contributions to the community. Have an assistant scan local newspapers, business publications, and annual reports to target prospects for a timely letter.

TIMELY TIP #9: Attend other arts groups' performances. Showing support will help you nurture support for your institution. Chances are, many of your board members, donors, and audience members are also supporting other area arts endeavors; they will appreciate your recognition of their other involvements and the community's other arts organizations.

TIMELY TIP #10: Use an "Annual Report" and well-timed news stories to list your theatre's success stories, achievements, and progress. Being proactive enhances your image and saves valuable time defending your programs later. It also allows your company members the opportunity to share their accomplishments and communicate their ideas and concerns with you. Keep it simple: use short paragraphs and lists, or few people will ever read it. Also, a personal "annual report" detailing your own achievements for your board chair and executive committee will position you more effectively for merit increases and future contract negotiations.

TIMELY TIP #11: A sense of humor and positive approach to your board, staff, company, and community will often win the day and identify you as a "can-do" person.

TIMELY TIP #12: Embrace saying "yes" to community projects based on your own priorities and those of the institution you represent. Obviously you don't want to fight with your community – but ignoring its cultural diversity, selecting only rich white men for your board, or choosing to hide in the theatre and do nothing regarding community service too often ends up provoking someone. You can make a difference to your institution and to your community. Choose your community endearment projects, attitudes, outreach, and communications carefully, and influence the future.

FIFTEEN FABULOUS WAYS TO INFURIATE YOUR COMMUNITY

1) Break promises, procrastinate, or forget to follow through on your community commitments.

2) Sell single tickets for $10 to $100; then offer free tickets to your friends or others in the community at the last minute.

3) Beg for money that you desperately need for your artistic product; then send expensive Fed Ex deliveries to your board regularly because you aren't planning far in advance for board meetings.

4) Talk about your theatre's substantial economic impact on the community; then send all of your major printing out of state.

5) Schedule your theatre's fundraiser on the same date as a longstanding community benefit that supports another non-profit organization. Also, refuse to participate in your community's United Way campaign.

6) Forget to orient your office staff, box office staff, front-of-house staff, and switchboard operators regarding the names, photos, and contributions of the governor, mayor, board of trustees, etc., thereby embarrassing all of the above when VIPs visit your theatre.

7) Order supplies and services from your board members' or donors' major competitors, even though the board members' prices are competitive and they bend over backwards to support your business.

8) Be obstinate in refusing to offer discounts to seniors, students, active and retired military or other special interest groups.

9) Only call the press to complain about your last review . . . never to say "thank you" for a great feature, a positive review, or a special effort on the journalist's behalf. Write an odious letter to the editor and show the entire community that you don't know how to handle criticism.

10) With a long line at the box office, answer the phone and handle the patron who calls in, before dealing with the jerky patrons who had the audacity to drive to your theatre expecting fair and personal treatment.

11) Following poignant pleas to the community to help balance the budget, order expensive bottles of wine and five-course meals for the company executives, paying with the corporate credit card.

12) Send five copies of the same brochure to your customers on the same day.

13) Telemarket your own board members and VIP donors at dinnertime, and don't relay their giving history (or their VIP status) to your phone staff.

14) Sneak nudity, pederasty, and other X-rated "nasty" scenes into your season, and fail to warn your audience – even those who bring their young children, conservative parents, and easily embarrassed grandparents in order to support your theatre.

15) Forget to say "thanks, thanks, and ever thanks" to your subscribers, donors, board members, advertisers, and community supporters.

SEASON SELECTION: SAVVY STRATEGIES, SICK TALES & SAD STORIES

Introduction

How do you go about selecting a season? Certainly, the institution's mission drives the choices, and the artistic director's creative instincts and interests are paramount. Discussions with theatre leaders over the years reveal a long list of other determining factors (depending on the theatre's geographic location, political history, financial status, creative history, and myriad other details that come into play).

GET A VISION! Generally speaking, most artistic leaders and board members agree that it all begins with the "V" word – *vision* – as in, "You'd better have one if you are planning a season." Now this principle may seem obvious to most readers, but my favorite consulting call of all time was from an artistic director of one of the nation's Shakespeare festivals. Out of the blue one Sunday afternoon, I received an urgent call from the artistic director, who urged: "We just had our annual board meeting and the board is concerned that my vision isn't clear. I told them I would lay it out for them at the next meeting. But the truth is, I simply don't have one. Can you spend next week with me and *help me get a vision*?"

I do know that, in my experience, the number one reason boards give for disliking or firing artistic directors is that they don't have a vision. (The real reason, of course, is that the budget is a mess, strategic planning is nil, or the board simply doesn't like the artistic director – vision or no vision!)

A SAD STORY. CNN picked up this story and ran it nationwide. When I was the managing director of a Shakespeare festival, I was at one of the three-a-week black-tie fundraising dinners when one of our long-time corporate sponsors and board members informed me that she just loved Shakespeare, but I had to understand that there were two plays that we simply couldn't do – ever. Want to guess what they were? *Othello* and *The Merchant of Venice*!

A SICK TALE. It's great to have a vision, but marketing the vision may be another matter. I know I've written season brochure copy that made the plays sound absolutely riveting. When the productions didn't match the sizzling brochure copy, I had to face the perturbed subscribers who felt they had been misled. With Shakespeare, misleading marketing might entail something as simple as not informing patrons of a heavy-handed directorial concept, or of any production that deviates from Elizabethan costumes.

Sometimes the marketing is purposely misleading. One regional production of Chekhov's *Three Sisters* received angry national scrutiny when it described the play as something akin to "three babes yearning for hot times in Russia."

DON'T FORGET THE VISION! Professional theatres often use "economic coercion" to persuade freelance directors to direct productions for which they have little passion, no vision, or total disregard. Some professional, college, and university theatres are known to simply assign shows to guest directors, faculty, and directing students. This seldom serves the company, the audience, or the institutional mission.

DARE WE TACKLE CASTING CONCERNS? Back in the 1980s I remember one artistic director causing a stir when he sent a note to all of the other Shakespeare festivals, looking for an Othello. The wisdom of the time was that you don't set the show until you've committed the actor (for the *Lears, Othellos,* and *Hamlets* of the canon). Still, at least this artistic director was looking for the "right" Othello. What's with the balding Romeos, 40-year-old Juliets, Shaquille O'Neal-sized Pucks and diminutive Falstaffs we've all been subjected to in the theatre?

IT'S NICE TO KNOW YOU'VE BEEN ASKED! Some artistic directors lock themselves in a cave and emerge from the solitude with a season as if they'd returned with the new and improved Ten Commandments. As an associate artistic director once complained, "It's surprising how deeply an artistic staff is needed when we are being recruited, and how seldom we are consulted when season-selection issues arise." Even board members and audience members really appreciate being asked their thoughts about shows and seasons. You don't have to take their advice, but it's always nice to be asked. Set ground rules. Be honest. Care. Listen and lead.

ARE THERE FORMULAS THAT WORK? There was a time when many summer stock theatres opened with a comedy, followed with a mystery, and closed with a musical. Is there a formula that works? Research your community's interests as well as the season success of similar communities.

BE TIMELY! For every week one professional theatre delayed its subscription renewals, it lost approximately $40,000 in ticket income. Allow six months' to a year's lead time for subscription brochures, media impact, advertising, social networking, email blasts and friendly phone call follow-ups.

IT'S THAT VISION THING AGAIN! Finally, I'll always recall a highly sought-after and recruited production manager candidate who turned down a job offer in response to the interview process, feeling he would be treated as one more "functionary" in an already large company. "I want to be a part of creating *the* vision," he explained. "Not just a part of creating *your* vision." Food for thought.

This chapter is written in hopes that younger artistic leaders in America might benefit from the collective experiences of the many artistic directors and producing directors who have shared their stories over the years. As Earl Wilson so eloquently stated, "Experience is what enables you to recognize a mistake when you make it again."

ADVICE TO ARTS LEADERS EVERYWHERE: TWENTY-ONE WONDERFUL WAYS TO IMPROVE YOUR LIFE IN THE THEATRE

1) **Hide from the madness!**
   Avoid stressful situations prior to important meetings, performances, or work sessions. Schedule aggravating situations and people at times that are best for you (and schedule time after the session to unwind and regain perspective). For example, don't try to balance your checkbook or comprehend Equity rehearsal policies just prior to a board meeting, fundraising dinner,

or first play reading. Norman Mailer contends "the natural role of 20th-century man is anxiety." Don't believe it!

2) **Run from the madness!**
Reduce stress by exercising regularly, playing soothing music to drown out office distractions, dressing comfortably, and taking a break from the grind.

3) **Put the madness in perspective . . .**
Try prioritizing these items: children, David Mamet, money, board chair, Facebook, Stephen Sondheim, health, Twitter, Mom. Ask yourself: Where do my true priorities lie?

4) **Team build.**
You are the leader, you're in charge, your vision drives the theatre . . . got it. Now, if you want positive, ongoing, professional help to help you achieve that vision: enlist, charge, nurture, inspire, motivate, empower, support, thank, and build a theatre team.

5) **Ask for advice.**
Your voice should be the voice in season selection, artistic staff hiring, strategic planning, and so much more. Still, it doesn't have to be the only voice. People look to you for leadership and to promote "ownership" or "buy-in" for your theatre. When it is appropriate, consider asking your board/staff/community/patrons/subscribers for advice concerning community ties, artistic planning, outreach, personnel development – yipes, maybe even season selection.

6) **Appoint someone as a human resources director.**
Are non-profit theatres the last businesses in America to recognize the importance of focusing on the work at hand while separating out (or contracting out) the endless stream of personnel issues, and personal conflicts, phobias, and problems? Make sure your human resources are covered by trained professionals – hopefully, that's not you!

7) **Plan ahead for the people you love.**
Go ahead and plan something special for someone you love. Don't allow your life to turn into one big casting call or late-night rehearsal. Send flowers, book a reservation at that fabulous restaurant, or find a loved one something unique on eBay!

8) **Thanks, thanks, and ever thanks . . .**
When there's not enough time in the day to say "thank you," it's time to start looking for a new job. Let people know you appreciate them. Every day.

8) **Just say "no" to defensive behaviour.**
   Perhaps Josh Billings says it best: "Advice is like castor oil, easy enough to give but dreadful uneasy to take." Stay open to constructive suggestions and graciously ignore the rude remarks of ignorant people.

10) **There is room for one more appointment!**
    Consider making an appointment for cafe mocha, a shopping spree, or a nap with a very important person in your life: you!

11) **Lead by example.**
    Demand ethical standards and make sure you set the pace in the way you treat fellow theatre friends, employers, and employees. What are the names of the incredibly loyal and talented workers in your costume shop? When was the last time you had a chat with your box office staff? "Expedients are for the hour; principles for the ages," reminds Henry Ward Beecher.

12) **Stay out of trouble.**
    Racist remarks, sexist behaviour, crude gestures, off-colour jokes, and obnoxious banter may be fascinating on stage in a Joe Orton or Martin McDonagh play. They are less than fascinating, and are potentially devastating, if they impact your working relationships with your board, company, or community.

13) **Take risks.**
    "Our greatest glory consists not in never failing, but in rising every time we fall," contends Oliver Goldsmith. Remember why the non-profit theatre movement was founded in the first place?

14) **Put your personal stamp on your work.**
    "Individuality is either the mark of a genius or the reverse. Mediocrity finds safety in standardization," writes Frederick E. Crane. You don't have to be outrageous, just don't be consistently derivative.

15) **Prove Emerson wrong!**
    Pay attention to the people you love. The arts are demanding, but they don't need to rob you of your humanity. "Art is a jealous mistress," declares Ralph Waldo Emerson. "If a man has a genius for painting, poetry, music, architecture, or philosophy, he makes a bad husband and an ill provider." Prove Emerson wrong.

16) **Forgive and forget.**
    Move on and get over both real and perceived slights. Anatole France holds that "it is human nature to think wisely and act foolishly." Forgive your own occasional foolishness and the periodic idiocy of others.

17) **But when we get behind closed doors.**
   "Three may keep a secret if two of them are dead," quips Benjamin Franklin.
   Joking or not, old Ben certainly knew what he was talking about. Discuss
   salaries, grievances, and official business behind closed doors, and not in
   front of other theatre folk and the world at large.

18) **Do a good deed today.**
   Bring honor to your institution and satisfaction to your family as an ongoing
   "good-deed doer." Look around your company and change someone's life for
   the better. As a respected artist, you have the power to brighten days with a
   kind word, warm gesture, or expression of interest. Ben Jonson says it best:
   "When a virtuous man is raised, it brings gladness to his friends, grief to his
   enemies, and glory to his posterity."

19) **Dream on!**
   Take time to daydream, stay healthy, sleep well, and give yourself a fighting
   chance to tackle your dreams! "All men of action are dreamers," opines James
   G. Huneker. Consider sporadic five-minute "dream breaks" during the day.

20) **Focus on your vision and embrace the future.**
   "If art is to nourish the roots of our culture, society must set the artist free
   to follow his vision wherever it takes him," observes John F. Kennedy. Set
   yourself free for a day, a week, a month, or a lifetime.

21) **Climb a mountain and see the world.**
   Take a worldview and plan ahead. Take time each year to take stock of your
   life, pat yourself on the back for your progress and accomplishments, and
   thank those who have helped you along the way.

IN OUR OWN WORDS:
SEVENTEEN NOTES ACTORS WOULD LIKE TO OFFER ARTISTIC DIRECTORS

In the highly competitive, politically charged, sometimes ego-laden universe of
professional theatre, it is often difficult for actors, directors, and designers to offer
much-needed constructive criticism and suggestions to the artistic and managerial
leadership of theatres. Here is what a group of actors had to say, when asked to share
advice, concerns, and observations regarding the audition and casting process, and to
speak directly to directors, casting agents, and artistic directors "in their own words."

1) If you cut us we bleed, if you punch us we hurt. In other words, treat us
   respectfully, soften the harsh casting decisions, rude personal comments,

and inhumane communications (or lack of communication). Simply treat us as human beings and talk to us as collaborators or potential collaborators.

2) Know that many actors want to be everything for you, but in doing this we sometimes sabotage ourselves. We want to make strong choices and we want to stay neutral. We want to be distinct from everyone else and yet distinctly what you want. We try to be young and old, short and tall, black and white. But in doing this we drive ourselves crazy. (And probably drive you crazy, too.)

3) Like most anyone else, actors respond to constructive feedback, positive or negative, and when this is effectively conveyed, an actor will do just about anything for the director.

4) Actors are intimidated by you and they would like to be treated with respect and common courtesy.

5) Don't cast on image alone – an actor may be better suited for a part than you think.

6) The audition procedure is, in most cases, such an unnatural environment that it is hard to convey honesty. Work to make auditions more natural, and reap the rewards of recognizing the potential of your actors.

7) I have been in casting sessions where directors have been exceedingly cruel and where actors behaved as if they were entitled to the role – it seems to me that it is important to remember that we are all human.

8) My time is valuable, too!

9) My biggest wish is that casting directors take a second to say, "Thanks for coming in, Sarah." It's great when you use actors' names.

10) It should come as no surprise that many actors are highly stressed during the audition process. Actors would like the producers to know that all we really want to know is that they know we are talented.

11) I am responsible for arriving on time for my audition slot, and the director/person running the audition is responsible for sticking to that schedule as closely as possible.

12) If the people involved with the audition process don't present themselves as professionals, are rude, unorganized, or self-righteous, I might not accept the job even if it is offered.

13) We are nervous because we want it so badly. If we don't want it, you shouldn't want us.

14) Many actors are confused by the issue of small talk. If you don't wish to talk prior to auditions, don't ask, "How are you?"

15) I am going to give you all I have, and if you give me direction I can give you what you want.

16) I fear that asking a question or not asking a question may be read as not preparing adequately for the audition.

17) Make us feel safe and we're apt to be daring.

(Thank you to the following contributors: Kevin Beaty, Jason Buuck, Evelyn Carol Case, Janine Renae Christl, Danika Eger, Aimee Guichard, Emily Haase, Sarah Imes, Tiffanie Kilgast, Michael Kirby, James Knudsen, Dan Schaffer, Holly Jeanne Sneed, Rita Stevens, Matt Sullivan, Caitlin Volz, Terry Walcutt.)

CREATING OWNERSHIP: STRATEGIC TRICKS OF THE TRADE

Introduction

Endearing your theatre to your community involves personal attention, leadership, and active management both up and down the organizational structure. The goal is for artists, company members, staff, audience members, volunteers, university presidents, city council members, governors, etc., to feel a sense of ownership in America's non-profit professional theatre, thereby making it "their" theatre. Active participation, meaningful involvement, and personal contact can all help create a sense of necessity and pride. Celebrating your successes and letting people know that they are valued and appreciated keeps them committed.

The following resolutions evolved when a panel of Shakespeare leaders gathered together at an international Shakespeare conference to brainstorm successful techniques to "endear ourselves to our community." Leading the discussion was Nebraska Shakespeare Festival Artistic Director Cindy Melby Phaneuf; actress Annie DiMartino and I distilled and edited the group's suggestions. Obviously, not all of these ideas will apply to all theatres, but, hopefully, you will find some glimmer of an idea for yours. To remind ourselves that we serve many communities, we have divided the suggestions into four categories:

1) Artists/Company/Staff;

2) Audience/Education (students of all ages);

3) Patrons/Board members/Volunteers;

4) Community-at-Large (the community in which we live).

ARTISTS/COMPANY/STAFF

1) We will hire artists, company members, and staff interested in creating community – we will cast the company with people who are generous.

2) We will treat actors well and advocate for our local acting community.

3) We will acknowledge those who do a lot of work for very little money.

4) We will hire locally, when appropriate, and be honest in terms of salaries.

5) We will see possibilities when casting – offering actors diverse opportunities in our rep seasons.

6) We will say "yes" to other theatres in terms of sharing resources and creating programs.

7) We will honor our light board operators, volunteers, and technical staff.

8) We will ask, "What can we do for you?" or "How can we help?" or "How are you?" periodically throughout the process.

9) We will take time to celebrate our successes.

10) We will support other theatre and arts events in our community by attending and showing a real interest in their work.

AUDIENCE/EDUCATION

1) We will create an exciting "event" that turns observers into active participants.

2) We will make children welcome at our theatre and provide for family options, such as family day at the theatre or babysitting services for the plays.

3) We will provide golf cart pick-ups for patrons who are walking long distances or who need additional assistance.

4) We will allow audience members access to our process. For example, we will hold opening "readings" of the play as an event for the public.

5) We will be available after the performance to say "thanks" and "good night," and even more importantly, to accept thanks and compliments personally and with the glow of the theatre experience fresh upon us.

6) We will anticipate audiences' reactions, asking, "Who won't like this?" or "Whom might we offend?" and establish forums for discussion.

7) We will treat people well and know that our friends will emerge when times are tough. Also, we will let key people know that we appreciate them.

8) We will create opportunities for actors and audience members to interact in informal ways, such as receptions, dinners, or play readings with leading actors and audience members.

9) We will match educational programs to the community school curriculum.

10) We will do something for Shakespeare's birthday. (Perhaps in a new location such as a Borders bookstore – to attract a new audience).

11) We will remember that adults crave educational opportunities, and will consider "Camp Shakespeare" for adults.

12) We will sponsor sonnet writing, playwriting, and visual arts events that allow people to respond creatively to Shakespeare's work through other art forms.

PATRONS/BOARD MEMBERS/VOLUNTEERS

1) We will send Valentine's Day flowers to secretaries and assistants of sponsors, board members, etc.

2) We will send something on company members' and board members' children's birthdays.

3) We will sponsor a board appreciation night, brunch and/or luncheon put on by the company or staff.

4) We will throw dinner parties to make new "Friends of Shakespeare."

5) We will involve our volunteers with specific activities and responsibilities.

COMMUNITY-AT-LARGE

1) We will become the public face for the organization and embrace the fact that it is all about us. We will be friendly and useful.

2) We will visit personally with the mayor in his/her office, and inform him/her of our plans. We will listen to the mayor's platform and find things we can help the city accomplish.

3) We will find ways for our staff to be an example to the community, e.g., become donors by taking $1.00 per week from our checks, by turning in petty cash receipts for donations rather than reimbursement, or by simply writing a check.

4) We will do community or state altruistic work on causes that don't directly benefit our theatre or us. For example, this may include working on campaigns, or working for new facilities for other arts organisations.

5) We will open our facility for free use for community groups to get people into our venue.

6) We will have staff and company identify themselves while shopping and dining in the community.

By becoming an integral part of your communities, you are given the privilege of putting into practice the many "community lessons" in Shakespeare's plays!

"We know what we are,
but know not what we may be."
Hamlet

LOOKING FOR LEADERS IN THE TWENTY-FIRST CENTURY

Managers, oh managers. Wherefore art thou, managers?

Like Juliet, boards of trustees, search committees and artistic directors throughout America are searching for a serious partner (to produce), a dedicated lover (of theatre), and a *Romeoesque* or *Julietish* leading player with the training, diligence, charm and willingness to fight and strategize for their mutual long-term survival. Unfortunately, mirroring the fate of so many of Shakespeare's valiant characters, countless theatre leaders have succumbed to the pressures of leading a non-profit theatre while others have left the field for less stressful careers in business, academia, or more lucrative (yet still noble) non-profit operations. It's sad to say, but it's a reality nonetheless – so many key figures who helped shape the non-profit theatre field in the early years have moved on, passed on, or retired.

So who will fill the producing director, managing director, general manager, marketing director, development director, CFO leadership posts that are so important to the survival of America's twenty-first century theatres? Since the job description for most managerial openings in professional theatre might be summarized as a search for someone with the patience of Mother Theresa, the financial wizardry of Warren Buffet, the vision of Superman, and the resilience of Hillary Clinton, it's little wonder that ideal candidates are few and far between. One of regional theatres' success stories is the abundance of women in leadership roles in major professional theatres and pivotal League of Resident Theatre (LORT) and Theatre Communications Group (TCG) leadership positions over the years. Adversely, one of the failures of many of our larger institutional theatres is certainly the inability to attract and retain leaders of color to these same positions.

Where will we find the next generation of theatre managers, and exactly what combination of leadership and management skills are theatres seeking? Managing theatres has proven a perilous path for many would-be theatre leaders as natural disasters (Katrina), unnatural disasters (9/11), economic recession, "surprise" deficits, aging audiences, fundraising fiascos, board politics, and "human resource burn out" plague the profession. Are theatres mentoring future leaders who will rise through the ranks, or can we count on the nation's theatre management and arts administration training programs to supply the executives needed to create new audiences, mine new funding sources and strategically plan for more than just another year of survival?

In my experience directing both BFA Theatre Management and MFA Arts Administration programs, few students wander into faculty offices and declare their passion to work with non-profit boards of trustees and generally under-compensated colleagues to facilitate a theatre's fundraising, audience development, and strategic planning needs. Rather, it's those areas (acting and directing) with rampant unemployment and outrageous career demands (at least in for-profit 21st century business terms) that seem to charm most university students. Yale School of Drama Deputy Director Victoria Nolan speaks to the issue: "It is always the case that the acting applicants are far and away the largest pool of applicants to the school, by a factor of 8 or 10 to 1, at least."

Unfortunately, the results are obvious – way too many out of work actors and directors and a palpable shortage of professionally trained theatre managers. Perhaps this is why many boards and artistic directors are frustrated with their managers, why there has been a historical revolving door in top non-profit theatre management, marketing and fundraising offices, and why more boards seem to be relying on artistic directors to shoulder the management "burden" as producing directors.

In recent searches for artistic directors for American theatres, it's not unusual for 140+ applicants to tender their applications and for dozens of talented, experienced artists to emerge. Similar searches for managing directors often yield a mere handful of savvy, experienced candidates and multiple theatres are often vying for the same candidate. Check out a recent *ARTSEARCH* job bulletin that had ten pages of management positions open and *three* listings for artistic positions (and one of those was an internship)!

NOTES FROM BOTH SIDES OF THE FIELD:
IS THERE A CRISIS IN MANAGEMENT LEADERSHIP?

To answer the "crisis" question, it seemed logical to poll those who spend the greater part of their working lives pondering and addressing the question – so I touched base with over two dozen of the leading theatre management and arts administration program heads as well as artistic and administrative leaders in the field. The resulting dialogue is insightful, challenging and substantive.

"The crisis is related to compensation and governance issues and figuring out how to hold on to wonderful, talented people so they can have a life in the theatre," explains Brann J. Wry, head of the Performing Arts Administration program at New

York University. "If they were compensated even justly and to see an arc over the years, they might stay. The boards must be made aware of the crisis that we're talking about and we need to find better governance and board members to run our theatres."

So, is the concern in theatre management directly tied to theatre board issues? Do theatres dare address the too often hidden agenda of poorly prepared, uninformed, non-productive board members and their crucial role in developing and holding onto quality managers? Or is the "REAL CRISIS" related to many boards' inability to fully engage and provide the maximum financial resources when operations are purportedly going well (while micro-managing their executives in time of financial stress to make up for their own financial inattentiveness during the "good times?") Perhaps, most importantly, what role do theatre executives play in the recruitment, orientation and development of their board members, and is "scapegoating" the sad result of the theatre executives' own board development, audience development or fundraising ineptitude?

"One of the challenging aspects in training managers in an educational scenario is the exposure and knowledge needed to work with boards of directors and volunteers in the non-profit setting," explains David Rowell, former head of Florida State's MFA in Theatre Management program.

"*Today's* focus is on preparing folks to manage and lead *yesterday's* organizations," adds Virginia Tech former MFA director John M. McCann. "The solution," adds McCann, "is to focus more on leadership competencies and less on functional management training – challenge young potential leaders to be creative, intuitive, and open to new ideas."

Reaching out to a broader, more diverse group of theatre leaders seems more important than ever as so many of the original leaders of America's theatres are leaving the field. "We do have a generation of leaders who are looking toward their retirement and one hears expressed concerns about their replacements," offers Victoria Nolan, Managing Director of Yale Repertory Theatre. "I suppose if you consider how many theatres have open MD positions, one wonders if we, as a field, have systems that allow talent to rise to the top."

Cecelia Fitzgibbon, Director of Arts Administration at Drexel University, concurs: "I believe that my colleagues have forgotten the many opportunities we were given to reach beyond our qualifications when we got started . . . we are not making room for the brightest people to do important things soon enough."

"I think there are two crises," says Tom Parrish, Executive Director of Merrimac Repertory Theatre. "First, the retention of good people is a problem. A well-trained quality manager can be wooed easily by the commercial sector, which has much greater pay and benefits."

"The second crisis," explains Parrish, "is in the training itself. To be successful now, the arts leader must be skilled at both business and art. Our field has grown too fast relative to the supply of talent. We have created so many professional administrative and artistic positions that, without the quality people to fill them, we reduce ourselves to accepting a lower standard. I feel that collectively we have begun to accept mediocrity, which in the end, will hurt the entire field."

The impact of boards of trustees on the success, development and tenure of managers has been touched upon – but what role do artistic directors and board members play in the world of theatre managers? "The main crisis in training leaders of America's professional theatres is that NO ONE trains artistic leaders," says Anthony Lake, Head of the MFA in Theatre Management at Wayne State University. "No one REALLY allows students to be producers . . . the artistic director who can walk in both a management world and an artist's world is essential for the future. But no one is training them."

"We train leaders for these institutions, we provide them with a good understanding of the business and the arts, a sound perspective on the role of the arts in our society, and a set of real management skills, but when they get to these institutions, they too often see unchecked artistic leaders, boards who do not (and may not want to) understand the kind of institution they govern, and under-compensated staff with too few skills and little more than enthusiasm," explains Alan Yaffe, Director of the Graduate Program in Arts Administration at the University of Cincinnati's College – Conservatory of Music.

"The work is hard and the rewards are limited," adds Diane Claussen, former Managing Director of Paper Mill Playhouse and current Managing Director of Philadelphia Theatre Company. "As the industry has matured, the level of sophistication and experience needed to lead these major theatres has expanded. At the same time, the resources available to support and grow these institutions is shrinking."

"There's an emerging and essential debate going on about the nature of the leadership challenge in the arts, but I'd hope to nudge you away from the word crisis," adds Andrew Taylor, Director of the University of Wisconsin – Madison's Bolz Center for Arts Administration and President of the Association of Arts Administration Educators. "In a world of war, floods, famine, and massive international unrest, I don't think any particular challenge we face in the non-profit arts rises to the level of crisis. We have significant challenges and changes ahead, to be sure, well worthy of our energy and attention. But crises? Not so much."

Still, just try telling emerging prospective arts leaders facing mounds of student loan debt, sky high housing costs, other family economic woes, and the poverty level salaries often listed in *ARTSEARCH, Back Stage, Variety* and other trade publications that this isn't a *crisis* and their response is much more personal.

"We need to work together to identify the challenges to the sector and to collaborate on applied research in addressing them," says Dan J. Martin, Director of the Institute for the Management of Creative Enterprises at Carnegie Mellon University. He points to two major concerns including "the evolving, expanding challenges placed on theatre leadership" and "the lack of serious cooperation between the profession and the Academy."

"There is a disconnect between what arts organizations are asking for and expect to get, and what emerging leaders can give," says the University of Oregon's Lori L. Hager. She points to a "virtually non-existent" arts communications network for arts managers, arts organizations who don't offer stipends for internships, and other financial pressures that keep students from accepting "the really desirable internships."

What are the practical issues that are keeping potential managers out of the theatre? Recruiting and retaining quality managers is most often related to either financial or quality of life issues. "The cost of college tuition" and "burn-out among arts managers" are two of the key issues in the business, says Texas Tech's Head of Arts Administration, Linda Donahue.

Are the future theatre management leaders out there, and how do theatre leaders and educators nurture students whose primary early focus is acting or directing? "Educators must aggressively recruit the students who we find have a burning desire to make theatre happen and who want to ensure its success through marketing, development, and careful and critical management," says Thomas Adkins, a Theatre Development Fund Associate Director and former Director of the Theatre Management MFA Program at The University of Alabama.

But what about the artists with terrific organizational skills who have their eyes set on the somewhat fashionable Producing Director positions that are emerging in many theatres? "Someone had better start to look at developing a program that nurtures students in both managerial acumen and artistic/aesthetic leadership," contends Wayne State's Anthony Lake. "That program is going to be flooded with applicants. And if it is successful, it will put the rest of us out of business."

UNIVERSITY TRAINING OR PRACTICAL EXPERIENCE?

"The great difficulty in education," writes George Santayana, "is to get experience out of ideas." So, is a university route and formal academic training the best way to enter the field and train the future leaders of America's professional theatres? A university education isn't for everyone and many American theatre leaders have succeeded in professional theatre without a college degree. If a remarkable opportunity surfaces to learn from an outstanding producer, artistic director, managing director, marketing director or development director in a reputable theatre, I believe most university professors would urge their students to plunge in, as one can always enroll in a degree program and a student's stock generally rises with professional experience.

"My fear is that many training programs ignore the many intricacies of actually understanding what it takes to produce theatre," echoes Ithaca College Theatre Chair Lee Byron. Ithaca has one of the few undergraduate theatre management programs in America. "I believe it is more productive for students to seek entry level (or higher) positions before embarking on a graduate course of study," adds Byron.

"Real-world points of reference and practical experience in the field are absolutely critical ingredients in the training of successful arts managers," says Steven Morrison, former Associate Director of the Arts Administration Program at the University of Cincinnati. "As a practitioner, I believe that it would be naïve and even irresponsible of academia to profess that the qualified leaders of tomorrow's arts organizations can be trained in the classroom."

So, is it better for students to go to work or enroll in a graduate school program or both? "Certainly, new graduate students will do better in the MFA program if they have some actual work experience in the area," says Matt Neves, MFA Arts Administration Director at Southern Utah University. "Actually, we rarely admit someone that doesn't have some practical on-the-job training. Surely you can learn as you climb the arts management ladder, but how long will it take? Is formal educational training for everyone? Probably not, but in a world where an advanced degree is becoming required for almost all management positions, taking 24 months to prepare yourself is not a bad idea."

"Our best students are young professionals coming to us from regional theatres where they have occupied entry level or middle management jobs and are encouraged by their managing directors to seek graduate training," explains Yale School of Drama's Victoria Nolan. "It is a feeder system that works beautifully. It requires of the managing directors enormous generosity and a long view."

"Managers on-the-job don't always have the time to give one-on-one training to their subordinates or to each other," explains Tobie Stein, Director of Brooklyn College's MFA Program in Performing Arts Management. "A professionally oriented master's degree with a built-in multi-level mentoring program will help supplement the training that entry and mid-level managers get on-the-job."

Most reputable theatre management and arts administration programs offer both academic classes and professional experience in the arts through internships and apprenticeships. Mara Wolverton's recent research at Texas Tech reveals over 45 programs awarding more than a dozen types of graduate degrees with an arts administration emphasis in 29 different university graduate programs. The degrees include everything from over a two dozen variations of the MA and MS to MFAs (at Florida State, Brooklyn College, Texas Tech, Alabama, Virginia Tech, Wayne State, Yale) to MFA/MBAs (Yale) to MBA/MAs (Cincinnati) to MA/MBAs (Southern Methodist) to a straight MBA (Wisconsin) to PhDs with an emphasis in Arts Administration (Texas Tech, Ohio State, and Florida State). Ms. Wolverton makes special note of Goucher College's Master of Arts in Arts Administration Program, which offers a unique distance learning graduate degree allowing working professionals living anywhere an opportunity for professional development.

In addition, the Association of Arts Administration Educators (AAAE) lists over 39 universities (28 American and 11 international) with graduate programs; 13 undergraduate programs (9 American and 4 international); and myriad certificate programs in arts administration related areas. Fortunately, new graduate programs are surfacing every few years. Newcomers on the block include Southern Utah University's program (first class in 2001) linked with the Utah Shakespearean Festival and the North Carolina School of the Arts' Performing Arts Management Program (first class in 2004), focusing on the "future leadership of our nation's performing arts organizations."

Undergraduate programs at Columbia College Chicago, College of Charleston, Eastern Michigan University, Ithaca College, Salem College, Shenandoah University, State University of New York/Fredonia, University of Hartford, University of Kentucky and University of Wisconsin/Stevens Point (to name a few), offer many educational and geographical options for students who know early on that theatre management or arts administration is where they want to be.

For comprehensive lists of undergraduate and graduate programs, check out the website for the Association of Arts Administration Educators, to be found at www.artsadministration.org or the International Information Service for Culture and Management, at www.artsmanagement.net.

GRADUATE DEGREES PROVIDE FEW GUARANTEES AND ACADEMIA ISN'T THE ONLY OPTION

Even graduate degrees provide few guarantees of steady, fruitful, and satisfying employment, although the placement numbers are extremely high for many of the theatre management graduate programs.

"There is no prescribed course for advancing into the field," says John M. McCann. "The basics of accounting, human resources, production, etc. can be learned in a classroom, or on the job. The dilemma is that 'managers' do much more than manage, they are responsible for providing leadership to their board, direction to their staff, and partnership with the artists. These are learned by plunging in, examining the results you get, and then altering/refining your practice over a career."

Networking through college alumni, faculty, staff, friends and colleagues is one of the key reasons that parents, career counselors and theatre professionals often suggest students attend specific high-profile universities. Pulitzer Prize-winning playwright Robert Schenkkan addresses this issue: "I'm sure some training programs (professional or academic) are better than others and offer their graduates better connections and credits but I couldn't tell you who they are. And besides, they change drastically from year to year as people move from one program to the next. But certainly all Regional Theatres value talent and practical experience."

Sixteen months of research into over a thousand theatres over the past two years (for a book on working in regional theatre) has convinced me that practical experience may be attained through professional theatre internships and apprenticeships for individuals who can afford to travel to another state, work for free, and provide their own transportation and housing. Sadly, without any guarantees related to the quality of the experience and the future earnings potential of these positions, how many students can afford this gamble? Paid internships and grants for educational activities offer additional incentives but the experience still hinges on the quality of the institution, the institution's leaders, and the advancement and mentoring potential for the employee.

Opportunities in LORT, TCG, and other non-profit or commercial theatres offer a great alternative to graduate school if prospective leaders can negotiate the right match and avoid long-term ties to dead end jobs. To quote Diane Claussen, "Many students get lost in the academic world – not fitting into the particular focus of a University culture, resources and style of doing and thinking."

So what are the other pathways to leadership positions in professional theatre? Many managing directors and executive directors rise through the ranks of professional theatres by excelling in the marketing, development/fundraising or financial areas of the theatre. Institutions that provide solid mentoring programs and top managers who invest in and develop the talents of their junior managers certainly reap the benefits of their efforts. However, in the heat of producing, battling ferocious odds to meet annual income goals, and struggling to survive day to day, how many of America's theatres actually engage in formal professional development, in-service training or mentoring activities designed to move employees to another level of non-profit service?

A "known commodity" who rises through the ranks can certainly be assuring and there are plenty of examples of terrific LORT and TCG leaders who started in a box office. Still, fickle board hiring committees have dashed the hopes of many internal candidates and degrees, fresh ideas and external experience are often cited as key reasons to shun promotions from within. This is exacerbated by the fact that many management vacancies surface during troubled times at a theatre and that the entire management staff is often considered tainted by internal financial, leadership, or income producing predicaments.

Fortunately, many of the nation's arts service agencies are securing funding and developing programs to meet the need. "There is a wide spectrum of organizations and initiatives currently training theatre managers in various ways," explains Andrew Taylor (current AAAE President). "Given the scope and scale of the field, and the complexity of its challenges, theatre managers need a rich and varied set of opportunities to refine their craft and improve their effectiveness," explains AAAE President Andrew Taylor. "Theatre Communications Group is clearly a lead player in this capacity – through its conference workshops, leadership initiatives, and professional programs."

"The service organizations have elevated their game in this arena, with the Orchestra Leadership Academy of ASOL, and new initiatives by TCG, Dance/USA, Dance/NYC and Americans for the Arts putting a focus on the leadership competencies required to guide these highly complex, multi-constituent arts organizations," adds John McCann.

OPPORTUNITIES IN THE FIELD AND BEYOND

Despite the above-mentioned obstacles and gambles, practical experience may be gained in the professional theatre work environment through internships, fellowships, apprenticeships and grants. Few young theatre lovers (and potential future leaders of American theatres) realize that almost every League of Resident Theatre (LORT) and many Theatre Communications Group (TCG) theatres offer practical experiences and a taste of professional theatre through paid and unpaid work experiences. Thousands of annual educational experiences are available in prestigious theatres, coast-to-coast, and all over the map from Florida's Asolo Theatre Company to Washington's Seattle Repertory Theatre. These experiences allow prospective theatre leaders to learn on the job and experience the hell, heat, highs and realities of professional production. The links at www.lort.org and www.tcg.org provide quick access to over 400 professional theatre websites and a wealth of opportunities.

"Much has to be learned through observation and experience; text books are not going to prepare a manager for the myriad of situations that may arise," notes Arena Stage Executive Director Stephen Richard. For example, Arena Stage offers internships in marketing, fundraising, and finance, as well as an internship with the executive director to mention a few of the opportunities in areas that are prime paths to top leadership positions in professional theatre.

The shortage of savvy, experienced theatre managers is certainly evidenced by the number of longtime managing directors who have been recruited away from many of regional theatre's flagship theatres (including the Guthrie Theatre, Dallas Theatre Center, Cleveland Play House, Alley Theatre, and La Jolla Playhouse). Oftentimes, there's a demoralizing institutional toll (that's seldom talked about) when management leaders leave their theatres and it definitely has a snowball (or avalanche) effect on the board and the remaining personnel who are charged with recruiting and orienting a new manager while recalibrating strategic plans, fundraising and audience development initiatives.

Tired of the turnover and dealing with what many consider the "two-headed monster," many boards turn to an already beleaguered artistic director to "run the whole show." This often results in greater institutional stress as the financial checks-and-balances and human resource systems are thrown out of whack. "The need for qualified professional managers is greater now than ever," explains Orlando Shakespeare Artistic Director Jim Helsinger. "For the Artistic Director, every moment spent on business issues takes away from time spent envisioning the future, researching and reading plays, casting and hiring, designing, playwriting, directing, acting and teaching."

Turning to yet another conspicuous concern, how do we keep rising stars in theatre management areas from doubling their salaries overnight by "defecting" to either for-profit businesses (willing to share the wealth) or non-profits with more competitive compensation plans (most museums, symphonies, hospitals, social services, community foundations, colleges and universities)? Drexel's Cecelia Fitzgibbon advocates paying more attention to succession issues and, more radically, "examining the re-distribution of salaries to stimulate interest and viability, providing project based work for emerging professionals, and creating incentives for retirement of senior management."

Could the solution to the crisis be as simple as working to provide a "life worth living" versus the hurried, harried, under-compensated, "work for the love of the art" model that has served as the mantra for way too many non-profit theatre artists and managers since the movement began? What a concept! What hasn't been said is that there really isn't a shortage of brilliant leaders or managers in America – just a shortage of exceptional leaders who want to work in theatres where they are overworked, underpaid and subject to the devastating deja-vu of constantly retraining colleagues wooed away to professions who pay most of their employees a living wage.

"We need a new construct for the not-for-profit model that better fits today's definitions of community, philanthropy and what young people are looking for in their life balance between work, family, financial security and community participation," adds Diane Claussen. "A new funding and organizational construct for not-for-profits in the 21st century will address many of the threats and turn offs that are leading to an arts management crisis, particularly, among young professionals."

It's definitely time for theatre boards of trustees, artistic directors, service agency leaders, think-tanks strategists and university arts educators to put their heads together. The needs are great, the stakes are high, the future of our non-profit theatres hang in the balance, and the time is NOW.

Much of the information gathered for this story was included in an *American Theatre* article by Jim Volz entitled: *Where do Managers Come From?*

FIFTEEN DISTINCTIVE GRADUATE PROGRAMS IN THEATRE MANAGEMENT RELATED AREAS

There's room in this book for only a short list of distinctive American graduate training programs (leaning toward programs that emphasize professional theatre training and LORT connections).

Brooklyn College of the City University of New York

www.brooklyn.cuny.edu/pub/Department_Details.jsp?div=G&dept_code=95&dept_id=103

Students are taught and mentored by professionals in the classroom for this MFA in Performing Arts Management. Students attend classes in professional settings (such as the Roundabout Theatre, Brooklyn Academy of Music, etc.) and are required to take 60 hours of coursework, including three semester-long externships of a minimum of 200 hours each. Program Head Tobie Stein notes that "By the fourth semester, BC students are ready to assume a full-time job and to write their thesis about their job. In the nine years since taking over for Stephen Langley, almost all of my students landed full-time jobs before they graduated, and almost all are still employed in the field."

Carnegie Mellon Institute for the Management of Creative Enterprises, Pittsburgh, Pennsylvania

www.artsnet.org

This Master of Arts Management (MAM) Program is a two-year, full-time program designed for students interested in being executives in the arts and related areas. It is designed for students with significant experience in the arts. Director Dan J. Martin notes that "our programs are joint offerings of the College of Fine Arts and the Heinz School of Public Policy and Management at Carnegie Mellon" and "our students benefit from seeing how common challenges are addressed within other public and private sector industries." He also notes that "we infuse technology tools across the curriculum," "have a strong commitment to interdisciplinary" and encourage "entrepreneurial and forward thinking."

Columbia College Chicago, Arts, Entertainment & Media Management Graduate Program

www.aemmp.colum.edu

The 37-hour program focuses on both the non-profit and for-profit sides of cultural enterprise and offers the opportunity to specialize in Performing Arts Management and related areas. Each program combines a strong conceptual emphasis with practical professional education with a commitment to helping students learn to appreciate the value of the arts, to understand the economic, political and social climate in which the arts operate, and to anticipate future opportunities and challenges.

Columbia University Teachers College, Graduate Program in Arts Administration, New York

www.tc.columbia.edu/academic/arad

The Arts Administration program reflects the conviction that the management of cultural institutions and arts organizations requires strategic planning, artistic creativity and social commitment. Arts managers must possess integrated management and financial skills, knowledge of the artistic process in which they are involved and sensitivity to the dynamics and educational needs of the communities they serve. The Master of Arts degree represents an alliance of arts, education, business, and law and is designed to help professionals meet the challenges of the next decade. Joan Jeffri is the director of arts administration.

Florida State University Theatre Management Program, Tallahassee, Florida

www.fsu.edu/~theatre

FSU offers MA, MS, EdD, and PhD degrees through its Arts Administration Center and an MFA in Theatre Management, a three-year terminal degree consisting of two years in residence on the FSU campus and a third year spent in an internship at the FSU/Asolo and Ringling Center for the Performing Arts in Sarasota, Florida or pursuing internship opportunities in other theatres. Alumni of the program are working in professional regional theatres, major orchestras, performing arts centers, and related arts and culture organizations across America.

Indiana University Arts Administration Program, Bloomington, Indiana

www.indiana.edu/~artsadm

The program is a two-year, multi-disciplinary course of study leading to an MA in Arts Administration and strives to achieve a balance of artistic and management practices and theory and hands-on experience. Students complete three semesters of course work, on campus practicums, and a one-semester supervised internship off campus. Specialization is available in performing arts areas.

New York University Performing Arts Administration

www.steinhardt.nyu.edu/music/artsadmin

The NYU program is a cooperative program of both the School of Education and the School of Business and offers an MA in Arts Administration. Director Brann J. Wry notes that NYU's arts management program's faculty has "melded into a creative unit that's interested in the whole field of theatre arts, the music business, entertainment, visual arts and corporate art collection in an emerging creative fashion." "We talk about over arching issues all the time," adds Wry, "and we have a great laboratory from which to draw faculty and practitioners in the field and to provide internships and experiences for our students."

University of North Carolina School of the Arts

www.uncsa.edu

The NCSA MFA in Performing Arts Management Program emphasizes a responsible, hands-on approach to its training and expects the successful graduate of its program to be qualified to pursue theatre, dance or music careers in either a non-profit or commercial organization. Director Robert Wildman points to "the ever-growing need for well-trained executive leadership in the arts," and hopes the program will "help fill what many in the profession consider a void in the arts industry." The program requires two academic years in residence at NCSA, with a third-year internship of flexible length.

Southern Methodist University Meadows School of the Arts

www.smu.edu/meadows/artsadmin

Students are required to complete 75 hours (27 hours in the Meadows School of the Arts and 48 hours in the School of Business) over a two-year period. Students receive an MA in Arts Administration and an MBA from the School of Business. The SMU program, based in Dallas, Texas, is based on the philosophy that a successful career in arts management requires a thorough knowledge of contemporary business practices coupled with a deep appreciation for the arts. Course work continues for six terms and the sixth term is spent fulfilling an internship requirement.

Texas Tech University

www.theatre.ttu.edu

The primary focus of the Texas Tech program is to train leaders and advocates in the field of theatre administration/arts management. The program offers an MFA in Theatre/Arts Management as well as a Ph.D. in Fine Arts. "Our program at Texas Tech University is unique, not because we have an MFA in Arts Administration, but because we have a doctoral program – a PhD in Fine Arts, with major courses in Theatre, Art or Music," explains Arts Administration Head Linda Donahue. Within the doctoral program, a student can concentrate in the area of arts administration.

Southern Utah University

www.suu.edu/pva/aa

SUU's relatively new, two year, year round program allows students to work alongside arts management professionals in the MFA affiliates: the Utah Shakespearean Festival, the Braithwaite Fine Arts Gallery and the College of Performing and Visual Arts. According to MFA director, Matt Neves: SUU's 60-hour MFA program is different because "it relies heavily on mentored, supervised practice as well as rigorous educational standards." Every student that is accepted is given a full tuition waiver and an assistantship.

University of Cincinnati, College-Conservatory of Music

www.artsadminmba.com

The UC/CCM Graduate Arts Administration Program exists to prepare and train students to become successful CEOs and senior managers of non-profit arts and cultural institutions. Students may earn both the MA in Arts Administration and the MBA degrees in two full academic years. "Strong business training, excellent practical experiences and a knowledgeable, tough-minded faculty" are at the heart of all good programs, notes director Alan Yaffe, and former associate director Steven Morrison explained that the "program engages students to use their decision-making skills not only in the classroom, but in the practical real-world environment of arts organizations."

University of Wisconsin

www.bolzcenter.org

The Bolz Center for Arts Administration is one of North America's oldest graduate business degrees in arts and cultural management. The two-year intensive MBA degree program balances professional practice with high-level business thinking and includes extensive networking and close interaction with MBA classmates. Director Andrew Taylor notes that "our students take a full-on MBA degree, side-by-side in their classes with students heading toward the commercial world, adapted and enhanced by specialized coursework, hands-on work experience, and research in non-profit and public cultural enterprise."

Wayne State University

www.theatre.wayne.edu

Preparing graduates for advanced careers in theatre management is the primary focus of WSU's three-year MFA in Theatre with an emphasis in Theatre Management. The program is located in Detroit, Michigan. Students participate in the management of WSU's three producing theatres and graduate students may elect to teach an undergraduate course in theatre management in their third year. "We have a 100% placement rate into arts administration jobs – most go into mid-level management, and some start at salaries higher than their professors," notes MFA head Anthony Lake.

Yale University

www.yale.edu/drama

Yale has offered an MFA through the Theatre Management Department in the Yale School of Drama since 1965. The three-year program combines a full sequence of courses, a case study writing requirement, professional involvement in the management of Yale Repertory Theatre, collaboration in a full schedule of productions in the School of Drama and Yale Cabaret, and the option of a one-semester fellowship in a professional setting away from campus. Edward A. Martenson is the Chair. The Theatre Management Department also offers a joint MFA/MBA degree program with the Yale School of Management. "The most distinguishing aspect of YSD training is the collaboration between all disciplines," notes Deputy Dean Victoria Nolan.

NOTABLE NON-DEGREE PATHWAYS AND
ARTS LEADERSHIP FINANCIAL OPPORTUNITIES

Allen Lee Hughes Fellows and Intern Program, Arena Theatre, Washington D.C.

www.arenastage.org

The Allen Lee Hughes Fellowship Program was established to increase participation of people of color in professional theatre. One of the first theatre-run apprenticeships in the country dedicated exclusively to providing the highest standard of training to minorities, it is an attempt to break the cycle of exclusion and disengagement that has created a severe shortage of trained minority arts administrators, artisans and technicians. "We have been proud to see Fellows and Interns go on to leadership positions around the country," notes the Arena's Stephen Richard.

Americans for the Arts, New York and Washington D.C.

www.artsusa.org/networks/emerging_leaders/default.asp

An "Emerging Leaders in the Arts" program is central to Americans for the Arts' efforts to identify and cultivate the next generation of arts leaders in America. The program includes conference discounts, creative conversations, peer groups, interviews with leaders in the arts, and an emerging leader council to assist in developing resources to promote the growth, development, and sustenance of emerging arts professionals nationwide.

Federal/State/County/City Arts Councils & Foundations

Many theatre leaders have benefited from wide-ranging career development and arts support programs that come and go based on the politics and budgets of their local arts councils. A few examples are listed below.

Joyce Awards to Support Creation of Works by Minority Artists

www.joycefdn.org

One goal of the "Joyce Awards to Support Creation of Works by Minority Artists" is to strengthen the infrastructure and leadership of culturally specific and community-based arts organizations, primarily in Chicago.

New York Foundation for the Arts

www.nyfa.org

The New York Foundation for the Arts (NYFA) offers an extensive national directory of awards, services, and publications for artists with listings that include over 4,200 arts organizations, 2,900 award programs, 4,200 service programs, and 900 publications for individual artists across the country, including resources for immigrants and refugees and Leaders Circles® (peer-coaching groups of up to seven arts executives who meet to discuss leadership issues).

National Foundation for Advancement in the Arts

www.youngarts.org

Starting very early on is the National Foundation for Advancement in the Arts whose mission includes identifying emerging artists and assisting them at critical junctures in their educational and professional development.

Princess Grace Foundation

www.pgfusa.com

Also aimed at the aspiring young artist, the Princess Grace Foundation has awarded over $4 million to over 400 individuals since 1984 through fellowships and scholarships in non-profit theatres.

The Andrew W. Mellon Foundation, Doris Duke Charitable Foundation

www.mellon.org / www.ddcf.org

One objective of *New Generations,* a joint program of the Doris Duke Charitable Foundation (DDCF) and The Andrew W. Mellon Foundation, is to cultivate and strengthen a new generation of theatre leaders through mentorships with accomplished theatre practitioners, both within the United States and abroad. It is administered by Theatre Communications Group and detailed below.

The Fund Raising School, Indianapolis, Indiana

www.philanthropy.iupui.edu/TheFundRaisingSchool

A background in fundraising is music to the ears of boards of trustees who hire most of America's key non-profit arts leaders. Although it is true that this program is based at The Center on Philanthropy at Indiana University, the "Certificate in Fund Raising Management" recognizes and rewards a commitment to fundraising leadership through successful completion of *only four key courses* offered by the School in the Principles & Techniques of Fundraising, Planned Giving, Developing Major Gifts and Interpersonal Communication for Fundraising.

Kennedy Center Arts Management Programs, Washington D.C.

www.kennedy-center.org/education/artsmanagement

The Kennedy Center American College Theatre Festival (KCACTF) is a triumphant network of over 600 academic institutions involving 18,000 students. For many students, it is their first experience with theatre outside their home state and many theatre leaders consider it to be an early driving force in creating leaders for America's theatres. It is just one of the many Kennedy Center programs. Certainly, the most focused for managers would be the fellowship and internship programs in arts management. The Fellowship Program provides up to ten "highly motivated, disciplined, and creative artists and arts managers the instruction and experience they need to succeed." Fellowships are ten-month, full-time, September through June experiences. The Internship Program offers semester-long, full-time, on-the-job experiences for college juniors, seniors, graduate students, and recent graduates who are interested in beginning careers in arts management or arts education. Internships include advertising, development, education (local and national programs), National Symphony Orchestra, press relations, production, programming, technology, volunteer management, and finance.

National Arts Strategies, Washington D. C.

www.artstrategies.org

NAS has been around for over two decades providing leadership education for arts and culture, including executive education programs and residential programs studying cultural leadership in partnership with Stanford's Center for Social Innovation. Customized programs are created for individual communities or institutions and many of America's theatres have sent representatives to NAS for programs on strategic marketing, leading innovation, managing people, creative alliances, governance and financing the future.

TCG (Theatre Communications Group), New York

www.tcg.org

Certainly, TCG's Conversations in the Field, Managers Teleconferences, travel grants, and human resources training programs (including the TARGET co-sponsored Expanding the Theatre Manager's Repertoire program) have addressed timely leadership and professional development needs in the field. Perhaps, most importantly, the New Generations Program provides opportunities for "Future Leaders" with mentorships, stipends, and grants and "Future Collaborations" (TCG/ ITI International Fellowships) for theatre professionals to travel internationally and share ideas and techniques and/or collaborate. In addition, the Fox Foundation Resident Actor Fellowships supports both emerging and established actors and the Alan Schneider Directing Award goes to mid-career freelance directors who have established local or regional reputations. All of these programs have the potential to bolster the number of producers, producing directors, managers and other theatre professionals needed to lead America's theatres through the twenty-first century.

CHAPTER 3

Board of Trustee Management and the Arts

> "As long as you are going to think anyway, think big."
> *Donald Trump*

THE ROLE OF THE NON-PROFIT ARTS BOARD OF TRUSTEES

1) Keep the mission crystal clear, commit to it, and be able to articulate it to others.

2) Select the key executive(s), support the executive(s), and review executive performance.

3) Plan strategically and set institutional policy.

4) Preserve the organization's stability and ensure the institution's financial well-being.

5) Be an advocate! Serve as a positive networking agent between your organization and the community.

6) Participate actively in fundraising and audience development: be friend-raisers, fundraisers, and personal givers!

7) Conduct a self-evaluation and monitor the institution's programs and services.

BOARD OF TRUSTEE AND EXECUTIVE STAFF RELATIONS

Introduction
The non-profit arts partnership between artists, administrators, and board members is fundamental to the existence of most arts organizations. Since this is so obviously

true, one has to wonder why we so often fail to educate, train, or otherwise prepare any of the partners for their significant roles in the health of their arts organizations. Elaborate business plans, comprehensive marketing research, and volumes of fund-raising documents are a major part of the orientation and training of many staff and board members. Unfortunately, an unclear understanding of board and staff functions in regard to how these plans are to be researched, prepared, presented, and agreed to often results in upsetting communications, missed mutual expectations, finger-pointing, morale problems, and, eventually, costly resignations.

This chapter offers advice for executives and rising executives who haven't had the opportunity to work closely with board members over a long period of time, or whose experience is largely with one or more of the many dysfunctional non-profit arts groups which haven't found the key to clear organization, respectful communications, crisis intervention, and comprehensive planning.

General Tips on Board of Trustee and Executive Staff Relations

1) **Start smart!**
   Nail down your job description and clarify your expectations *before* you sign your contract. If you are already on board and you don't have a clear job description, create it *now* and review it with your board chair. Share your working style and expectations of the board, staff, administration, and the institution in a positive upbeat letter of acceptance or in an annual report that is reviewed and "stamped for approval" by the board chair. In other words, *get it in writing and cover your bases*!

2) **Make a pledge!**
   Pledge your commitment, dedication, and ethical, positive approach to your work, your patrons, your company, your board, and colleagues on the day you agree to take a new position. If your commitment isn't clear to the board chair and company, find the right opportunity to make it clear. Do it soon!

3) **Communicate often and in writing!**
   Communicate with your board chair and company in a positive, informal, "laundry list" fashion on *at least* a monthly basis. This update or monthly report should touch briefly on every item of real or perceived institutional, educational, or financial interest. Make sure that you are never accused of poor communication skills or deception through omission. Boil the information down into short, substantive bullets. "Perhaps you communicate too often," should be considered the ultimate compliment.

4) **No surprises!**
   "No surprises" should be a guiding rule. James E. Preston, President and Chief Executive Officer of Avon Products, used to say: "Bring me your troubles

early and you have a *partner* in finding a solution. Bring me a disaster late and you have a judge." Don't *unhappily* surprise board, staff, patrons, or audience!

5) Do I know you?

Talk to your board chair, board members and company members individually. Get to know their personal interests, professional standards, and expectations of you and your leadership role at your institution. Work to meet those expectations.

6) Quiet, please!

The fine art of silence may be one of the most useful tools an arts leader chooses to employ when it comes to cantankerous board meetings, disgruntled community gatherings, and free-for-all retreat sessions. Pensive silence and carefully considered responses beat "plunging in" 99% of the time. "Diplomacy is the art of knowing what not to say," says Matthew Trump in *Mother Earth News*.

RETREAT

1) A withdrawal, as from danger.

2) A safe, quiet place.

3) A period of seclusion, especially for contemplation.

4) The forced withdrawal of troops under attack.

Webster's New World Dictionary of the American Language

---

7) Don't kill the messenger!

Wise arts leaders deliver good news in writing, in person, or in any other way they choose. After all, who complains about good news? However, always deliver bad news in person. It may be more difficult for you in the short run, but in the long run, it will save you time, help you earn the respect of your colleagues, and assist you in working through crises.

8) Balance the budget!

Sounds easy, yes? For most arts leaders, balancing the budget is an endless nightmare of juggling salaries, fees, production concerns, educational needs, artistic sensibilities, and company, board, and administrative demands. For most arts leaders, balancing the budget, or living up to their financial agreements with their boards, begins the day they start work on *assembling* their budgets. Do your homework, build in flexibility, and get it right from the start. If you inherit someone else's budget, either make it yours and sign off on it, or make it clear that your responsibility for the budget begins on "this date."

9) **If it is to be, it is up to me!**
When it comes to finger pointing and blame ownership, go ahead and take responsibility for everything in your department. If not you, who? When it is time to concentrate on fulfilling your artistic/educational/cultural mission, take the lead now. If not now, when?

10) **Share the credit, claim the blame!**
Give credit where credit is due, inspire teamwork, promote board and company ownership and involvement. Be gracious when things go awry . . . there's always enough guilt to go around!

11) **No plan, no pay!**
In my experience, the lack of a strong strategic plan and clear mission is the number one reason given to most artistic and management leaders when they get the boot or are demoted from their leadership positions. Research, write, and organize a plan for your board of trustees and company to discuss, revise, promote, and enjoy.

12) **Don't sweat the small stuff . . . just take care of it!**
Strategic planning *and* attention to detail are marks of successful arts leaders. Remember to follow through on commitments and take care of the details!

13) **Better a saint than a martyr!**
Be a can-do person, leader, motivator, and well-rounded individual who inspires greatness. Also, find the time to be a team player, a follower, and a decent executive who rewards initiative!

14) **Take time to have a good time!**
Weak interpersonal skills, pessimism, and inadequate "people skills" are probably the real reason most arts leaders are fired, demoted, or shunned. "You're never too old to do goofy stuff," says Beaver's television dad, Ward Cleaver. Find opportunities for your board and company to get to know each other, to bond as a collaborative team, and to interact as enjoyable, non-competitive, responsible human beings. It's amazing how much may be accomplished when an institution isn't consumed with internal bickering, petty politics, and past territorial tragedies.

> **"Life is short; live it up."**
> *Nikita Khrushchev*

BOARD MEETING PLANNING

Since so many board/staff objectives and conflicts are articulated, planned, organised, and accomplished through board meetings, fundraising sessions, season planning, and budget planning debates, the following suggestions have been prepared to assist with the process.

In partnership with the board chair, executive staff (artistic and managing director) should prepare a clear and timely agenda. The managing director is usually the point person who coordinates the final drafting of the agenda. The agenda should include:

1) Artistic reports that combine current plans, future plans, and timely specifics mixed with upbeat anecdotal information that encourages and inspires volunteer participation, engenders "ownership," and reiterates the need for advocacy, fundraising support, and financial integrity. The board chair and staff should review these reports and interact with the artistic director's report in regard to the "good news" and institutional progress.

2) Financial reports offering clear, concise budget summaries that include this year's budget, year-to-date budget information, variances in the budget/year-to-date, the projected end-of-year figures, the projected end-of-year variances (in each category), and last year's end-of-year final audit summary. With proper planning, staffing, and computer support, this document should be able to be presented in columns on one page for quick comparison. Since condensing this information to one page may result in a tiny typeface, it is suggested that the page be blown up to 11" × 17" for meetings where the numbers are undergoing careful scrutiny. These reports should be available every other month.

3) The finance committee should meet with key staff prior to the meeting, agree on the report that is prepared by staff, and make suggestions. The board finance committee chair should make the report at the meeting, with staff support if needed to clarify specific points or to answer general questions. The staff person in charge of finance should also be given the opportunity to report or add to the process.

4) Ad hoc reports that detail timely current and long-range plans that are absolutely pertinent to board involvement, organization, and leadership issues. These reports should be organized with board and staff prior to the meeting, and should be delivered by board members at the meeting.

Organization of the Agenda

The board meeting agenda should be strategically arranged to balance reports and action items, board reports and staff updates, etc. Items are generally arranged in order of importance to allow greater participation from all in attendance (vs. saving problems for the end of the meeting, when some board members may have left for other commitments).

In summary, meetings should be well prepared in advance, with agendas sent to board members in time for a thorough inspection prior to the meeting. Communications should be clear in terms of the beginning and projected ending time of the meeting. Major issues and topics should be generally "scripted," although delivered with the ease that comes with familiarization and understanding of the reports. Advance meetings are suggested to ease tension, avoid unnecessary confrontation, and clarify information so that the board and staff are always partners in honest, straightforward communications. In other words, if everyone does their homework, there are few surprises; and board members are equipped to answer questions and ameliorate problems in the public board meetings, or to defer more problematic issues to the executive committee or the responsible overseeing committee.

Distribution of Board Meeting Minutes

It is suggested that carefully edited minutes should follow within one week of board meetings, and the board chair and designated staff should agree to the minutes before mass dissemination. Approval of the minutes should be the first order of business. There is an art to taking minutes, and board-staff preferences (regarding detail, quoting participants, identifying action items, and summarizing problem areas) vary from organization to organization. The chairperson of the board of trustees, your institution's legal counsel, and your financial auditor should be consulted for guidance, but "less is more" is generally a good rule. A guiding rule for many is, whenever possible, publish minutes that you would be proud to see on the front page of your local paper in the morning. (Because chances are, that's where they'll be!)

SEASON PLANNING, BUDGET PREPARATIONS AND BOARD COMMUNICATIONS

Introduction

It is often surprising that non-profits reach out to tap many of the best minds, warmest spirits, and most savvy individuals in their community, actively and passionately woo them onto their boards of trustees – and then ignore or dismiss them when it comes to communicating the essence of the institution on a year-to-year basis.

Whether a non-profit arts organization is producing musicals, operas, cutting-edge drama, Shakespeare, fine arts, or dance, it's the living, breathing heart of the organization that attracts most board members to an institution. In the board of trustee recruitment phase of institutional development, artists and managers work so hard to bond board members to the arts group's "Mission." Unfortunately, once board members sign on, many feel that they are alienated from the artistry and passion of the company and are relegated to discussions and tasks that exclusively address financial problems, fundraising needs, cash-flow concerns, and audience development ambitions.

Granted, the board holds the key to peer-to-peer fundraising, is an essential partner in the financial health of the organization, and approves the annual budget. Still, it's important for the board to have the inside story concerning the heart of the organization: artistic planning, program development, and everything that fulfils the all-important mission statement. Although few boards of non-profit arts organisations are involved in the artistic process (other than hiring and firing the key artistic executive, polishing the "Mission Statement," and providing advocacy for programs in the community), it is important for board members to feel informed, to be involved as VIP members of the institution, and to be the first to sign off on the budget and the program that fulfils the institutional mission.

Season Selection and Budget Planning

With this in mind, consider the following tips for board and staff communications in season selection and budget planning:

1) In partnership with the board chair, staff should prepare a process and timetable for season selection and budget preparation with the understanding that the two are absolutely tied to each other and that the budget process can not proceed on a timely basis without a firm handle on the season, programs, and overall artistic plan. To this end, I would suggest that the artistic director, in consultation with the staff – and with sensitivity to the theatre's mission, audience needs, and the myriad other artistic and institutional challenges – prepare a sample season that allows financial planning and guidelines that meet the board timetable for approving a budget with integrity in regard to planning and numbers.

2) Once the staff members designated to prepare the budget have roughed out a budget, appropriate staff should meet with the board fundraising committee to seek its support for all unearned (contributed) income projections, and with the finance committee to ratify all income and expense projections. The meetings reviewing the budget should include clear, understandable breakdowns of all income and expense items, with comparisons to actual end-of-year reports from the three previous years and a projection for the current year. In addition, a one-page summary reviewing strategies, concerns, and assumptions should preface the actual numbers and comparisons. Assumptions would include ticket prices and

seating breakdowns of all events; planned board fundraising participation; fundraiser event analysis; and any political, economic, or business forecasts that might impact the planned budget.

3) Once the finance committee and staff have agreed on a balanced budget with integrity, the head of the finance committee should present the budget to the board and be prepared to discuss it in depth with staff support. A copy of the budget draft should be mailed to board members at least one week prior to the meeting. Similarly the finance committee should have a draft of the budget suggested by the staff in time to adequately evaluate the draft prior to each of their meetings.

4) Realizing the importance of this key tool and their own responsibilities and liabilities in a not-for-profit corporation, the board members should carefully consider the budget, make sure they understand the assumptions and numbers, and approve it well in advance of the beginning of the fiscal year. In order to do this, it is suggested that a timetable with specific deadlines for season planning and budget preparation be delineated on an annual basis. Flexibility should be built into the schedule to allow for the typical not-for-profit planning issues and problems.

5) Remember that the budget is a "road map." The budget provides a guideline and should be monitored and evaluated on an ongoing basis with strategic contingency plans reviewed and discussed on a board-staff level.

6) Final note: carefully planning and approving the budget is only the beginning of that year's financial process. Evaluating budget variances, updating the budget, monitoring cash flow, and clearly reporting are key to year-round budget planning.

FUNDRAISING PLANNING AND BOARD COMMUNICATIONS

1) In partnership with the board fundraising committee chair (and consultants if needed), the staff should prepare a fundraising strategic plan, fundraising timetable, fundraising process, fundraising guidelines, and fundraising literature for the committee's consideration and approval. Once approved by the committee, the plan should be presented to the board at large for its approval and agreement to embrace and implement the plan with the staff's support. From the start, it should be acknowledged that fundraising is everyone's responsibility, and is a crucial aspect of budget fulfilment and season/vision fulfilment on an institutional level. Non-profit fundraising is challenging, exciting, and potentially complicated; and a number of handbooks, training programs, and consultant workshops are available. This

summary of board-staff interactions is an attempt to review basic fundraising processes, and to help you avoid the pitfalls that plague many fundraising campaigns and strain staff and volunteer relations. (Chapter 6 is devoted entirely to fundraising for the arts.)

2) To ensure confidentiality and the appropriate timing, solicitor(s), and number of fundraising requests, it is crucial that a well-organized "Prospect List" be developed and coordinated between board and staff. This list should include the prospect's name, address, telephone number, name of person to be contacted, the "Rating" (amount to be requested), and historical information that includes any past contributions, advertising history, subscriber history, and any other information that would be pertinent to the solicitation. This list must be carefully and confidentially prepared, monitored, coordinated, and used.

3) Ratings are usually accomplished by key board and staff members who know the history of area giving trends. They review the list together and agree on appropriate amounts, the key person to solicit, and any suggestions for solicitors.

4) After prospects are rated, they are generally divided up among the fundraising team members in a fair and equitable manner, with clear deadlines, timetables, and reporting requirements. (Often fundraising team leaders will do a "round robin," with each leader picking one prospect at a time for his or her team, to ensure that everyone has some options concerning the overall list). Reporting is usually set once a week or twice a month, to ensure that progress is being made and to alert the overall fundraising coordinator to any concerns. A set time frame for each aspect of the fundraising campaign is very important. The "United Way" format of seasonal fundraising with team captains, etc., is often recommended as a model for non-profit organizations.

5) The responsibilities of the board and the staff must be absolutely clear-cut to avoid confusion and to ensure cooperation and timely research and follow-up.

6) Generally speaking, in operations with sufficient staff, the staff person in charge of development will work closely with the board chair or designee to structure the various fundraising efforts and designate board leaders for each task (e.g., fundraisers, annual campaign, sponsorships, government grants, foundation grants). Especially in regard to the important annual campaign and corporate sponsorships, the staff generally organizes, researches, and prepares support materials while board leadership solicits volunteers for teams, organizes the forces, arranges the meetings, and leads the "ask." It is often helpful if a team of two board members and a staff member meets with the larger givers. It is fine for staff to schedule meetings at the request of a

board member. Staff should also be prepared to provide any necessary correspondence (letters confirming meetings, thank-you notes following meetings, reports, pledge cards, etc.) Most importantly, it is usually necessary for a staff member to be the "overall point person" in regard to prospects, meetings, etc., to avoid calendar mishaps, duplications of efforts, and prospects "slipping through the cracks."

7) Final Note: fundraising should never be considered an "Us vs. Them" proposition (e.g., board vs. staff, institution vs. community). Rather, raising money to support the vision and mission of your artistic endeavour should be considered a joint responsibility and an opportunity to "tell your story" and to "provide the opportunity" for the involvement of as many community members as possible.

> "The gratification of wealth is not found
> in mere possession or in lavish expenditure,
> but in its wise application."
> *Miguel de Cervantes*

A SAMPLE "BOARD OF TRUSTEE CONTRACT" AND "TALKING POINTS" OUTLINE FOR RECRUITING NEW BOARD MEMBERS

The Board of Trustees of [THE THEATRE] are valued partners in our non-profit theatre efforts to [THE MISSION]. Currently, the Board of Trustees of [THE THEATRE] includes the following dedicated volunteer leaders and supporters who serve rotating terms of one to three years, with renewal potential based on the needs of the institution, the deliberations of the Board Nominating Committee, and mutual consent:
[INSERT BOARD MEMBERS' NAMES & BRIEF BIOGRAPHIES AND BOARD POSITIONS.]

There is an annual meeting of the Board, typically held in October, prior to the opening of [THE THEATRE'S] season, and three other full Board meetings during the year. These meetings require approximately two hours, as much of the work of the Board is accomplished through committees.

- The standing Board committees include:

- The Executive Committee

- The Finance/Legal Committee

- The Nominating/Recruitment Committee

- The Fundraising Coordination Committee
- The Governmental Relations Committee
- The Marketing & Volunteers Committee
- The Strategic Planning Committee

Periodically, additional committees are formed for specific tasks and time frames. The Executive, Finance/Legal, and Fundraising Coordination Committees are the most active committees at [THE THEATRE].

Members of the Board of Trustees are expected to understand and contribute to the strategic planning process, financial oversight, financial well-being, and accomplishment of [THE THEATRE'S] Mission, Goals, and Objectives. Specifically, members of the Board of Trustees should be willing to contribute their time and expertise as follows:

- Attend at least three of the four quarterly meetings each year and offer guidance and expertise in regard to the issues under consideration;

- With the aid of the Executive Staff (the Artistic Director and Managing Director, who are ex officio members of the Board), determine the objectives and policies that will guide [THE THEATRE] toward the accomplishment of its mission;

- Act as advocates in communicating the mission, goals, and programs of [THE THEATRE] in the local and regional community, and, in turn, bring the community's concerns and interests to [THE THEATRE];

- Be responsible for the procurement and allocation of financial resources for [THE THEATRE];

- Be willing to make a personal gift at a level that demonstrates commitment, and to ask others to give to [THE THEATRE] at the highest appropriate level;

- Be able to involve others and expand [THE THEATRE'S] markets, attracting new subscribers, volunteers, and donors;

- Hold [THE THEATRE] season subscriptions and attend [THE THEATRE'S] performances and programs;

- Demonstrate sensitivity to the unclear line that sometimes separates functions related to Board and Staff responsibilities;

- Hold [THE THEATRE] in trust for the public interest.

SOOTHING SOULS, FUNDING DREAMS AND SAVING THEATRES: NATIONAL THEATRE LEADERS SPEAK OUT ON BUILDING AMERICA'S NON-PROFIT BOARDS

America's non-profit theatres are desperate for quality board members, and an experienced, resourceful, well-connected board of trustees is oftentimes the difference between bankruptcy and survival. Interviews with theatre leaders from New York to California illuminate the many obvious needs of non-profit theatres everywhere and pinpoint a few of the special challenges that theatre leaders face in recruiting, orienting, and nurturing quality board members.

"We are always looking for committed, compassionate, devoted board members who will stick with us through thick and thin and stand behind the organization no matter what," explains longtime arts leader Jacqueline Anne Siegel. "We are always looking for fresh voices and new energy to infuse the organization as we look to the next century."

So exactly who are these wildly committed individuals that all these theatres need, and what do they do? Theatre board members are volunteers who assist theatres in myriad ways, not the least of which include fundraising, ticket sales, policy making, strategic planning, financial monitoring, and the hiring and firing of the artistic director and/or managing director. What don't they do? Hopefully, they don't meddle in the artistic product or micro-manage the daily details of the theatre operation.

Throughout America, the search for exceptional board leaders for non-profit theatres is of major concern to artistic directors and managing directors charged with balancing budgets and forwarding the missions and goals of their theatres.

Dean R. Gladden, current Alley Theatre Managing Director and former Managing Director of The Cleveland Play House – the first permanently established professional theatre in America (founded in 1915) – offered these guidelines: "The first thing you look for in a great board member is a commitment to the art form. If they are committed to the art form and have a passion for it, then they will work in the theatre's best interests and give money to support the theatre. We sit down with our board and we say, 'Here is what it takes to be a good board member at The Cleveland Play House. Here are how many board meetings you need to attend, why we need you at the fundraisers, and what major contributions we expect (both personally and through your corporations). Our expectations are that everyone must be on the fundraising committee, raise money, and serve on other committees.' It's important to clarify your expectations – this is very, very important."

Paul R. Tetreault, current Director of Washington D.C.'s Ford's Theatre and former Managing Director of Houston's Alley Theatre, agrees. "The dialogue you have with your board must have clarity, and both the board and the staff must allow each other to do their job. The smaller the theatre, the more intimately involved the boards are. Smaller organizations rely on boards for more day-to-day activities, but as theatres grow, the boards must transform and develop into boards for oversight, long-range planning, and fundraising. The lines where management's job begins and ends and where the board's job lies must be cherished and respected."

"We want the board to have a clear understanding of where they can contribute individually and how the board functions as a whole," adds Ms. Siegel. "One of our board members always reminds us that we are looking for the 3Ws: wealth, wisdom, and work."

Tamar Copeland, formerly with New York City's Folksbiene Yiddish Theatre puts board development into perspective: "My advice is to think of building a theatre board as an evolutionary process. As a theatre company grows and develops, the needs will change. It's important for the board and staff to grow and develop together and to feed off each other. Strategic planning is paramount, so strong long-range planners, legal minds, and well-linked community members are so important for non-profit theatres."

"New York is a bit different because there is so much competition for board members," explains longtime arts leader Jessica L. Andrews. Ms. Andrews' perspective includes national service with the National Endowment for the Arts, the League of Resident Theatres, and myriad other non-profit theatres. "The first place you should go is to your audience. Find out who is coming to your theatre and research who they are. You may have the board expertise you are looking for in your own theatre! If you want people who are passionate about your work, what better place to look?"

Who Should Be on a Theatre Board?

A better question might be, "What does your theatre need and who can be of help?" With this in mind, many non-profit theatres work hard to recruit successful business CEOs with an entrepreneurial spirit and the ability to contribute and ask peers to contribute to their theatres. In addition, based on the unique needs of the theatre, lawyers, real estate professionals, educators, marketing experts, fundraising executives, bank trust officers, organizational planners, human resource specialists, and other individuals firmly committed to the theatre's mission, goals, and funding needs usually top the prospect list. Most importantly, they should be prepared to spend the time necessary to serve on the board, be willing to make a personal contribution, and actively fundraise to meet the growing financial needs of non-profit theatres in the twenty-first century.

"People with marketing savvy are essential for this technological age," suggests Ms. Andrews. "A willingness to fundraise is crucial, but it doesn't have to be the CEO of a major corporation. Someone who believes enough in your theatre to put a fundraiser together, sign letters, call friends, or make a curtain speech is great to have on board."

Certainly, board member needs and strengths vary from theatre to theatre. Whereas a small theatre may need board members to help with mailings, front-of-house work, and office assistance, larger theatres focus much more on board members' contributions to strategic planning, general advocacy, broad policy, and "the big picture." However, there are a few needs that all of the theatres interviewed for this article have in common. "Accounting and fiscal knowledge is important, and board members with access (social, small business, corporate, human resources, cultural diversity, etc.) can help you build bridges to the community," explains Ms. Andrews.

Margaret Chandler, former General Manager of New York's **Primary Stages**, helps illustrate board recruitment and orientation needs for smaller theatres: "We have twelve to fourteen board members who have been with us for a long time. They are friends of the company, they know our work, they are supportive, and they are very generous. We don't have major corporate contributors, but we have others who contribute through fundraisers, grant writing, accounting assistance, and play advocacy. They'll even stuff envelopes for us. One thing they never do is interfere with the artistic director's job.

"In New York, there are so many theatre lovers, so many people who support the arts, and so many people competing for funds," continues Ms. Chandler. "We look for board members who will oversee the financial stability of the company and assist the company in its growth by finding ways to bring us to a larger audience and funding community." According to a Primary Stages board handout, this includes attending the plays, attending board meetings, giving and getting a specific amount of money, and assisting in special projects (fundraisers, audience outreach, opening night galas, etc.)

"Every generic how-to guide for non-profit management includes the ubiquitous laundry list of professions we expect to see represented on a board: lawyer, investment banker, media rep, accountant, captain of industry, politician, fat cats, and people of influence, etc.," warns national arts consultant and former **Institute of Outdoor Drama** Executive Director Scott J. Parker. "In general, it's a fine list, but it does not speak to the essentials: attitudes, emotional attachments, commitment as an active participant in the life of the theatre and to its mission, and knowledge of the business and its standards."

What Is the Right Size for a Non-profit Theatre Board of Trustees?

In the 1960s, consultants usually recommended that boards stay lean and mean with approximately a dozen members; in the late twentieth century, the number rose to from fifteen to twenty. As many larger theatres' financial needs expand in the twenty-first century, the only appropriate answer seems to be "as large as you need to effectively service your mission and represent your intended audience and fundraising constituency." There are non-profit boards in America with forty, fifty, sixty, or more board members!

Art Manke, freelance director and former Co-artistic Director of Los Angeles' award-winning A Noise Within, contends that "it's not the numbers of board members we are concerned about – it's strong people who will support the theatre's mission. We have a large group of very busy people and we need to be respectful of their time and energies. We have three-year rotating terms for board members, and they may be re-elected. There is a tremendous value in long-term corporate memory among board members. We are always looking for individuals with strong leadership skills, good connections with funding agencies, diversity, and broad representation through our region and neighbouring regions, in order to expand audiences and funding."

How Do You Keep A Board Of Trustees Focused On The Theatre's Needs?

Secrets to successful non-profit theatre management include board of trustees' orientation, development, and team building. The best way to accomplish these tasks is to establish clear lines of communication, create carefully written institutional policies, and develop a fun, functional, and friendly forum for decision-making – otherwise known as board meetings. Too many non-profit board meetings are poorly conceived, ill-run, extremely boring sessions with a long list of "house-keeping trivia," incomprehensible financial reports, pleas for last-minute fundraising assistance, and little mention of the artistic product or theatre mission.

"Our ideal board meeting put the artistic director's report right up front, with financial, fundraising, and program updates to follow," explains Ms. Siegel. Board presidents lead meetings, see the big picture, bring the board and staff together, and stand behind the vision and mission of the organization in a way that makes everyone feel important."

Lesley S. Currier, Managing Director of the Marin Shakespeare Company near San Francisco, maintains that the greatest challenge for theatre executives is dealing with the board: "When your 'boss' is a many-headed hydra that must speak as one voice but that meets for two hours once a month, it is difficult to get clear direction." She offers this advice: "First, you can never thank people enough. Second, talking a board member, staff member, or volunteer into staying on the board or on the job when they have said they want to leave is always a mistake!"

R. Scott Phillips, Executive Director of the Utah Shakespearean Festival, implores colleagues to remember that "the very essence of live theatre implies that we touch the human soul. Don't forget to do that in your day-to-day dealings with your staff, patrons, board, volunteers, and community. Don't be afraid to talk with your board chair. Develop a relationship with board members, and attempt to make them see what you see. Be willing to put the time into it so that you will reap the rewards you expect. The board members are usually qualified business people who care about your theatre."

A SAMPLE BOARD MEETING AGENDA

BOARD OF TRUSTEES MEETING
San Jose Repertory Theatre
Silicon Valley Capital Club
Wednesday, September 24

I.	A Welcome from the Board President	Tom Denver
	Retreat Overview	Alexandra Urbanowski
	Mission Review	Timothy Near
	Consultant Introduction	Alexandra Urbanowski
II.	National Overview and SJRT	Jim Volz
III.	Investigative Reporting (Five-minute Breakout Sessions and Board Introductions)	All
IV.	SJRT Strategic Plan Review and Board Accomplishments	Alexandra/Timothy
V.	Strategic Planning Vs. Long-Range Planning Overview "Backward Thinking for Forward Motion"	Jim
VI.	An Artistic Look to the Future	Timothy
VII.	SWOT Discussion and Breakout Sessions (Strengths, Weaknesses, Opportunities, and Threats	All
VIII.	SWOT Reports Breakout Chairs	
IX.	The Board's Role and Future Strategic Planning	Alexandra
X.	Goals and Projects: Board Committee Overviews	
	Finance Committee	Nadine Priestley and Roger Smith
	Fund Development Committee	David Heiman
	Audience Development Committee	Peggy Lunsmann
	Nominating and Board Development Committee	Jeannie Duisenberg
	New Member Involvement Project	Sandra Moll
	Long-range Planning Committee	Alexandra (for Dean Bartee)
XI.	Brief Closing Note	Alexandra/Timothy/Tom

In Conclusion

Savvy staff and board members may want to heed the advice of author Robert Heinlein: "A human being should be able to change a diaper, plan an invasion, butcher a hog, design a building, write a sonnet, set a bone, comfort the dying, take orders, give orders, solve equations, pitch manure, program a computer, cook a tasty meal, fight efficiently, die gallantly." The challenges of running the world's theatres may demand skills far different from those in Heinlein's list, but our exciting and demanding environment requires flexibility, ingenuity, and ability to adapt to ever-changing audiences, patrons, artists, and volunteers.

> "Leadership:
> The art of getting someone else to do something
> you want done because he wants to do it."
> *Dwight D. Eisenhower*

IS IT LONELY AT THE TOP?
GIVE YOURSELF A GRADE FOR BOARD-STAFF COMMUNICATIONS

1) Do you have a *written* contract that covers all the pertinent aspects of your employment, including your compensation, specific responsibilities, and guidelines related to your annual evaluation?

2) Have you thanked your board members individually for their volunteer work and special contributions to your institution in the past six months?

3) Have you written your board, individually or collectively, in the last thirty days to detail your most recent institutional, financial, artistic, and community successes, plans, projects, and concerns?

4) Have you ever heard these words in a board meeting: "Why didn't I know about that?" "When did that happen?" "We're doing what?" "Why didn't you tell me?" "We have a deficit." "We need money."

5) Do you know the first and last names of each of your board members (and the names of their spouses . . . and the names of their children)?

6) Have you failed to balance your budget in the last five years?

7) Do you share credit with other members of your institution in formal board meetings? Do you introduce your company members to your board? Do any of your staff members attend board meetings?

8) Do you have an *up-to-date* strategic plan in place for your institution?

9) Does your board enjoy board meetings? Do you enjoy board meetings?

10) Do your board meetings start on time? Is there a clear agenda for every meeting? Does the board follow the agenda?

11) Do your board members feel you are accessible to them? Do your staff members feel you are accessible to them? Are you accessible?

12) Are you buried in e-mails/faxes/telephone calls/meetings?

13) Do you have an open-door policy?

14) Do you eat well and exercise to ameliorate stress?

15) If I called your office at 10 a.m. on a weekday, could I find a way to talk to a live human being within one minute?

16) Do you deliver bad news in writing, in person, or on the phone?

17) Is your office a disorganized mess, an organized mess, or a perfect example of organizational efficiency?

18) Do you compile an annual report for your board of trustees?

19) Do you treat your employees with respect and dignity? Do you know the name of the person who cleans your office?

20) Do you feel appreciated for your contributions to your institution? Is it lonely at the top?

Give yourself a grade for each area, with an "A" being excellent and an "F" indicating a serious need for improvement!

SELF-GRADE: A   B   C   D   F

BOARD OF TRUSTEES: INSTITUTIONAL AUDIT QUESTIONNAIRE

Introduction

As a long-time theatre consultant, this "Institutional Audit Questionnaire" has proved invaluable as a communications and/or troubleshooting tool designed to assess the individual thoughts, concerns, attitudes, suggestions, objectives, and goals of board members who may be reticent about speaking up in board meetings (until the concerns have reached a fever pitch). Consider this questionnaire as a useful "crisis prevention" tool that could be administered by a trusted consultant or facilitator (in order to help ensure participation and to guarantee anonymity in the areas where confidentiality may be crucial). It is best used when the theatre's executive staff, board chair, and board agree on how this information will be gathered, analysed, used, and communicated prior to beginning the process.

Board-Staff Relations

Describe the three major strengths of the board of trustees at this time.

_____

_____

_____

_____

Describe the major issues facing the theatre and the board.

_____

_____

_____

_____

What advice do you have for the board of trustees?

_____

_____

_____

_____

_____

Describe the major strengths of the theatre's staff.

_____

_____

_____

_____

_____

Describe any weaknesses you perceive in the theatre's operations.

_____

_____

_____

_____

What specific advice do you have for the staff?

_____

_____

_____

_____

What suggestions do you have for the running of the theatre?

_____

_____

_____

_____

Budgeting, Finance and Season Planning

Do you have concerns with any aspect of the theatre's budgeting, financial reporting, or season planning process? Please explain.

_____

_____

_____

_____

What suggestions do you have for improving the following:

The budget _____

The budget process _____

Season planning _____

Deficit reduction _____

Fundraising _____

Do you feel you have a clear understanding of the current budget?

Please explain _____

_____

_____

_____

_____

Do you feel you understand the overall financial status of the theatre, including the "cash reserve, endowment, end-of-year status, etc.?"

_____

_____

_____

_____

Fundraising

Do you consider yourself a strong advocate of the theatre?

_____

_____

_____

_____

Do you contribute on an annual basis to the theatre? _____

Gift range over the past two years: _____

Are you actively involved in fundraising for the theatre? _____

Please explain _____

_____

_____

Are you aware of fundraising "prospects" that you feel the theatre hasn't approached or approached properly or completely?

_____

_____

_____

_____

Would you be willing to call on any of the above "prospects?"

Please explain _____

_____

_____

How long have you been on the theatre's board? _____

How long would you like to continue as a board member? _____

Please explain _____

_____

_____

Do you have suggestions for new board members who would be strong theatre advocates, contributors, and important partners in the fundraising process? What do you feel these individuals could bring to the board?

_____

_____

_____

_____

Marketing and General

Do you feel the theatre has a strong handle on the upcoming expansion?

_____

_____

_____

_____

What suggestions do you have for improving audiences or ticket income? Are there missed income opportunities for the theatre?

_____

_____

_____

_____

GRADE THE THEATRE (A=EXCELLENT, B=GOOD, C=FAIR, D=POOR)

Theatre productions:	A	B	C	D
Board-staff relations:	A	B	C	D
Fundraising efforts:	A	B	C	D
Staff support for fundraising efforts:	A	B	C	D
Theatre financial planning:	A	B	C	D
Theatre long-range planning:	A	B	C	D
Budget integrity:	A	B	C	D
Theatre audience development efforts (advertising, brochures, displays, and overall audience efforts):	A	B	C	D

Is there anything you would like to say confidentially to me as an independent consultant regarding institutional concerns?

_____

_____

_____

Is there anything you would like to say confidentially through this survey to the board chair? Anything written here will be typed and delivered without attribution to the board chair.

_____

_____

_____

Is there anything you would like to say confidentially through this survey to the artistic director? Anything written here will be typed and delivered without attribution to the artistic director and shared with the board chair.

_____

_____

_____

Is there anything you would like to say confidentially through this survey to the managing director? Anything written here will be typed and delivered without attribution to the managing director and shared with the board chair.

_____

_____

_____

Please return to this address by
[LIST SPECIFIC DATE WITHIN TEN DAYS]:

Dr. Jim Volz, President
Consultants for the Arts
Fullerton, California 92835

VOLUNTEERS: A PERSPECTIVE

Philosophically, all hierarchies for arts institutions should list volunteers at the very top! Non-profit institutions exist for the benefit of the public – and those individuals who cheerfully volunteer their time, happily donate their financial resources, gracefully support performance after performance through attendance and external advocacy, and willingly and unselfishly share their energies are indeed the best friends of every arts organization. We're not just talking about the board of trustees, but about all of the volunteers for the arts who may assist with everything from mass mailings to ushering to party planning to friendly subscription phone calls to fundraising.

There are many reasons to recruit and nurture a volunteer task force. Aside from helping to tackle obvious day-to-day needs of the theatre, volunteers can be instrumental in:

- Extending the theatre's outreach into the community;
- Creating new community partners;
- Broadening the theatre's base of "friend-raising;"
- Empowering audience members to deepen their involvement in the theatre;
- Developing "institutional ownership" that may quickly evolve into fundraising support;
- Engendering loyalty and commitment that might eventually result in a substantial "planned gift."

There are also a number of reasons *not* to recruit a volunteer task force:

- We need someone to do all the "junk work" the staff doesn't want to do;
- We don't want to pay a small fee for "mail-house services," so we'll have ten volunteers work eight hours per day attaching 10,000 labels to brochures;
- We need to get the work done but we don't have time to organize or supervise it.

That said, it seems important for every non-profit arts group to carefully outline its own volunteer needs, volunteer support plan, and volunteer strategy before plunging in. With that in mind, what follows are a sample "Manifesto" and sample guidelines for volunteer services and support.

A BRIEF VOLUNTEER MANIFESTO

Volunteers offering support to [THE THEATRE's] mission, goals, and objectives shall be:

Carefully recruited, structured, and organized;

Treated with respect, kindness, and appreciation; and,

Appropriately thanked for their service to [THE THEATRE].

Guidelines for the Recruitment and Nurturing of All Volunteers

- Don't even think of recruiting volunteers until you have outlined the appropriate objectives and tasks you have ready for them to accomplish. (The quickest way to frustrate volunteers is to tell them how much you need them and then fail to identify timely needs, projects, goals, and deadlines.)

- Someone on staff must be designated as the "Volunteer Coordinator" or "Volunteer Liaison," and this person must be ready to orient, train, nurture, and thank volunteers per the theatre's volunteer manifesto. It is naive and counterproductive to think that a new volunteer organization will run itself.

- A volunteer chairperson will most likely be able to outline and delegate tasks, recruit additional volunteers, and run a smoother operation than the paid staff liaison. However, the liaison will be crucial in providing structure, support, and timely communication to the volunteer chairperson.

- Rule of Thumb #1: If a staff member can accomplish all volunteer tasks in less time than it takes to recruit, orient, train, and thank volunteers, you might be better off without a volunteer task force!

- Rule of Thumb #2: If all you are offering volunteers is consistent "junk work" without any real interpersonal interaction or psychological benefits (such as satisfying a need to belong, to be part of a group, to be needed, and to accomplish something significant or worthwhile), you are doomed to long-range failure.

- Rule of Thumb #3: If the psychological benefits are on the meagre side, you might try real company benefits, such as the opportunity to see a show for each ushering assignment, a gift shop discount as a surprise "bonus," and a company appreciation party to say, "thank you!" to the volunteers.

- Rule of Thumb #4: The artistic director and managing director must offer their thanks and appreciation to the volunteers directly through notes, personal comments, and public recognition. The volunteer liaison is nice, but the volunteers want to hear from the top officials, including the board of trustees!

> "It's a rare person who wants to hear
> what he doesn't want to hear."
> *Dick Cavett*

CHAPTER 4

Strategic Planning for the Arts

> "Our plans miscarry because they have no aim.
> When a man does not know what harbour he is making for,
> no wind is the right wind."
> *Seneca*

STRATEGIC PLANNING FOR SUCCESSFUL THEATRE OPERATIONS

WHY DOES YOUR INSTITUTION NEED A "STRATEGIC PLAN?" A savvy non-profit strategic plan for the arts looks to the future, speaks to the institutional mission and vision, and provides long-range, intermediate, and short-range analysis, assessment, plans, goals, objectives, and action steps – with an appropriate timetable, financial plan, and identifiable leadership and personnel resources.

STRATEGIC PLANS ARE USEFUL FOR:

- Supporting the vision and providing focus for the mission;
- Recruiting and coordinating the board of trustees, employees, and volunteers;
- Defining organizational structure and priorities;
- Decision making and assessment planning and implementation; and,
- Shaping audience development and marketing plans.

STRATEGIC PLANS ARE ABSOLUTELY CRUCIAL FOR:

- Executive staff and board of trustees communications and planning;

- Most fundraising programs, but especially for individual large gift requests and planned giving; and,

- Many corporate, foundation, and government grant applications.

HOW DO YOU BEGIN?

Every smart strategic plan for the theatre begins with an analysis of the two basic components of performance: the *artist* and the *audience*. The institutional questions related to the *artist* are the obvious ones: "What can we do?" "What should we do?" "What do we want to do?" Or, in strategic planning jargon, "What is our institutional mission?" and "What are our strengths, weaknesses, opportunities, threats, and challenges?"

The institutional questions related to the *audience* may not be as obvious: "Who is our audience and who are our related customers, supporters, potential donors, and patrons?" "What do our audience members value, and why do they support the arts and our particular theatre?"

Finally, it's important to determine criteria for evaluating institutional success and the ongoing efforts to accomplish the institutional mission.

The ABCs of Strategic Planning

1) **Appoint a strategic-planning coordination team.**
   The "Coordination Team" should include:

   - The most active and forward-thinking members of the board of trustees (board chair, nominations committee chair, fundraising chair, strategic planning committee chair, etc.); and,

   - The theatre's executive staff (artistic director, managing director, director of development, director of marketing, director of finance); and,

   - Other individuals who might provide history or guidance that is valuable to the process (such as past board chairs and past fundraising chairs).

   The team is called the coordination team because it must be clear that all board and staff are important to planning and are invited to participate in the strategic-planning process, and that this group is simply "coordinating the process." This team will determine who needs to be involved in the strategic-planning process, who will write the strategic plan, what the timetable for strategic planning will be, what questions need to be asked, and how the answers will impact the mission, the plan, and the institution.

2) **Define or revisit the mission statement.**

First, define your mission (or revisit, revise, and/or rededicate yourself to your mission). Your mission statement should be a vibrant, concise statement that delineates *what* you do, *why* you do what you do, and your *unique* purpose for existing. It should be brief and, if you want support for your non-profit arts organization, it should inspire! A mission statement is also a legal requirement for incorporation and Internal Revenue Service tax exempt 501(c) (3) status.

3) **Outline strengths and opportunities.**

Why should audiences and donors support your institution? What makes you different from the thousands of other American theatres? Outline your institution's vision, artistic intent and integrity, the experience of your artists, and the value of the productions you plan to produce. Discuss your history of accomplishments, artistic success stories, and opportunities to be a leader in the field (regionally, nationally, or internationally).

4) **Face up to the challenges and potential threats.**

Whom might the public perceive to be "competition?" How might your community's demographics and/or history of artistic support challenge your institutional plans? How might the current funding environment threaten your financial planning and growth? Are there social or political hurdles that need to be considered as part of the overall strategic plan?

5) **Assess and evaluate.**

What are the standards that drive this institution that you lead? As both the IRS 501 (c) (3) and community liaison/representative, what does your board of trustees expect from you and your institution? How are you evaluated and how does the board and executive staff define results? Are standards and expectations outlined in board/executive staff contracts? Do your artists, craftspeople, and administrators understand the criteria by which they will be evaluated? Providing and/or utilizing assessment tools will promote productivity and identify areas that need to be improved, strengthened, replaced, or removed.

6) **Research current patrons and potential future customers.**

Who are your subscribers and why do they commit to a full season of plays? Who are your single-ticket buyers and why don't they commit to a full season of plays? Who are the donors who support your fundraising efforts, and are they also part of your faithful ticket-buying group? Why or why not? Who are the volunteers that commit time to your enterprise? Might they be converted to donors and ticket buyers? What motivates your customers to buy tickets? Is it price, seat selection, priority booking, special benefits, party invitations, or other incentives? How might your primary customers help recruit potential patrons?

Are there potential audience members who aren't being reached that are important to the theatre, in regard to either the theatre's mission statement or the institution's sense of social responsibility?

7) **Conduct an internal institutional analysis: analyze artistic and management personnel recruiting success, needs, and desires.**
The arts are obviously labor intensive, and the collaborative nature of theatre demands that actors, directors, choreographers, designers, craftspeople, and management staff excel as individuals and work together as a team. Therefore, conducting a company-wide institutional analysis that investigates the skills, interests, needs, expectations, and concerns of your collaborators and employees is central to strategic planning. If you can assess your current status, it's much easier to plan for where you need to be.

8) **Continue internal explorations: conduct a "zero-based" approach to artistic planning, budgeting, marketing, and fundraising.**
"Zero-based" means starting over. Usually applied to budgeting, the term implies that everyone starts with zero dollars and must request and justify every dollar that is allocated to them in the annual budget. This isn't recommended as an annual exercise, but applying this approach at least once during your three-to-five-year strategic planning cycle may prove to be educational, provocative, and worthwhile. Many institutions grow complacent, get "set in their ways," and even stagnate when the end result of years of financial, personnel, and program growth fails to match the dreams and excitement of either their original mission or the newfound dreams of a recently recruited artistic leader.

A clean approach to planning may be artistically and administratively instructive, can free up resources to fund new artistic initiatives, and, for the overall good of the institution, may lead to discoveries that remove deadwood and problem areas. A zero-based review of marketing, sales, and audience development strategies may lead to newer, technology-based improvements in communications; and a zero-based review of administrative areas could reveal opportunities for streamlining operations.

9) **Conduct external investigations.**
Set up staff teams, designate board representatives, or contract with consultants to conduct interviews and/or distribute questionnaires to your key constituencies. This would normally include season subscribers, single ticket buyers, volunteers, government funders, corporate sponsors, business

supporters, individual donors, select vendors, community leaders, and potential donors.

State and federal arts research and general census data may provide useful information on regional and national funding and demographics; and local research related to general economic indicators, non-profit capital campaigns, annual campaigns, population changes, and city and country politics may be available through nearby universities, community arts councils, or newspaper archives.

Finally, meetings with city, county, or state government officials and other key leaders in the community may be extremely useful.

10) Analyze the data and revisit the mission.

It is usually the staff's (or the hired consultant's) responsibility to process the internal and external data, work with appropriate personnel to analyze and interpret the data, and compile concise reports to communicate the data in preparation for strategic-planning coordination team meetings or reports to the entire board of trustees. The information should be disseminated at an appropriate time, allowing ample opportunity for the board to read and digest the edited, summarized, bulleted findings.

Once the board has had the opportunity to review the planning reports, a board retreat may be scheduled to gather key participants and involve the entire board of trustees in the strategic-planning process. At the board retreat, the strategic-planning coordination team can lead the board through the process of goal setting and mission exploration.

11) Set goals and tackle the mission.

Whereas the *mission* for professional theatres is generally set in stone as part of the original articles of incorporation, the board of trustees and company look to the artistic director to provide the vision for the institution. The vision offers a dream of the future. *The Random House Dictionary of the English Language* defines vision as "The act or power of anticipating that which will or may come to be," or "a scene, person, etc., of extraordinary beauty." Either may apply to the arts, and the institution's mission and the artist's vision should work hand-in-hand.

In order to tackle the mission and bring an artistic vision to life, there must be clear, inspirational, and attainable goals.

Long-time organizational management guru Peter F. Drucker explains it this way:

The most difficult challenge is to agree on the institution's goals – the fundamental long-range direction. Goals are overarching and should be few in number. If you have more than five goals, you have none. You're simply spreading yourself too thin. Goals make it absolutely clear where you will concentrate resources for results – the mark of an organization serious about success. Goals flow from the mission, aim the organization where it must go, build on strength, address opportunity, and, taken together, outline your desired future.

12) Develop specific objectives and delegate clear action steps.
Objectives are specific statements that indicate how the institution will achieve each goal. To be useful, the objectives should be able to be monitored and measured, and should be realistic and achievable. "Action steps" are simply a breakdown of the activities that need to be accomplished to successfully meet your objectives and goals. "*Who* will do *what* by *when*" is one way to articulate the various action steps.

For example, let's say that one of your institution's primary goals is to garner national attention for your production of new plays. An objective might be to successfully invite five out-of-town critics to visit your theatre and review your new plays. The statement that sums it all up might read, "South Coast Repertory Communications Director Cristofer Gross will convince five out-of-town theatre critics to review the world premiere of Richard Greenberg's *The Violet Hour* by opening night, November 5."

13) Write the report!
The final report should lead with the mission statement, a brief historical overview of the institution and planning process, and brief statements by the board chair, artistic director, and managing director. The plan should detail planned goals, objectives, action steps, and budgets; and discuss current strengths, opportunities, and challenges.

"The more you say, the less people remember.
The fewer the words, the greater the profit."
Fenelon

SWOT ANALYSIS

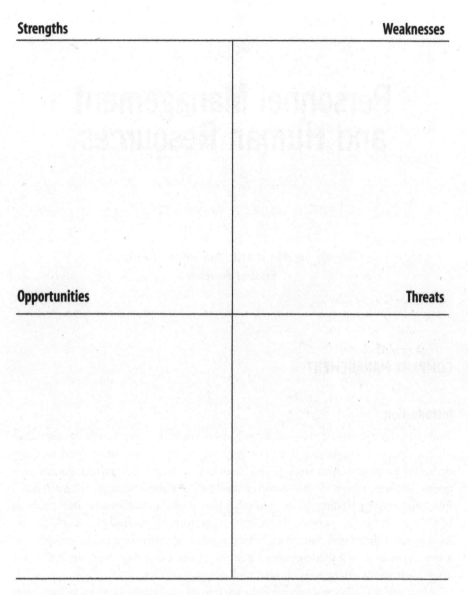

Strengths

Weaknesses

Opportunities

Threats

This SWOT worksheet (Strengths, Weaknesses, Opportunities, and Threats) is an excellent long-range planning and strategic-planning tool for board and staff working sessions. "Strengths" and "weaknesses" usually deal with internal evaluations, while "opportunities" and "threats" project outward in regard to the external environment.

CHAPTER 5

Personnel Management and Human Resources

"The only one who is wiser than anyone is everyone."
Napoleon Bonaparte

COMPANY MANAGEMENT

Introduction

Non-profit arts groups are generally notorious when it comes to taking advantage of, ignoring, or even abusing their number one resource: the creative, hard-working dedicated employees who work in the "trenches" to create, deliver, and sustain programs, services, and productions with a die-hard "the show must go on" mentality. Few corporations, businesses, or even other non-profit institutions commit the bulk of their financial and personnel resources to performing around-the-clock heroics for a product that, every four to eight weeks, must be ready for a public unveiling at a specific minute of a predetermined hour of an exact day. And then rip it all apart after a few weeks or one season to start all over again!

Although this labour-intensive industry centres on personnel, the arts have been slow to create personnel or human resource offices, or even to designate an individual as the "Head of Personnel." By default, various managers, directors, and heads of areas end up "dealing" with the complicated world of Human Resources. Artistic directors without the appropriate training end up consoling and counseling depressed actors; managing directors without the appropriate training wind up offering advice on everything from financial planning to bipolar personality disorders; and production managers without the appropriate training offer medical advice, relationship counselling, and their "take" on sexual harassment.

Important Advice

Proceed carefully in outlining your company management services, programs, and policies, and your carefully conceived institutional responses to personnel needs, interests, problems, and crises.

Key Personnel For Most Non-profit Theatres

Most non-profit theatres tend to rely on the following individuals, by the very nature of their positions, as the "Personnel Team:"

The Production Manager, who often supervises the largest number of hourly and seasonal employees (as well as the majority of independent contractors);

The Stage Manager, who is charged with assisting actors with their work-related concerns, and works closely with directors, designers, and production personnel to produce a quality product through the coordinated and cooperative efforts of the artistic/production staff;

The Company Manager, who is often the first to interact face-to-face on-site with artists, production personnel, and other company members while fulfilling transportation, housing, or contract responsibilities;

The General Manager/Business Manager, the individual or team that many employees go to for payroll, communication, personal problems affecting work, or work-related problem assistance;

The Artistic Director and Managing Director, the first point of contact for most artists and many company members; these are the individuals at the top who can cut through any perceived bureaucracy and/or are identified as the institutional leaders "with the answers."

The Company Handbook

Needless to say, it's important for an institution and its employees to understand their roles, their boundaries, and the proper referral sources for areas outside their areas of expertise and/or job descriptions. (See the section on stress reduction in Chapter 9.) But where are these roles, boundaries, and referrals identified in arts institutions?

The company handbook may be the best way to begin. Despite the misconceptions of many employees in America, a company handbook is usually written to protect the institution and is not provided to "safeguard" the employee. Still, the company handbook can serve many purposes. It can:

- Assist in the orientation of new employees;

- Communicate company policy;

- Provide essential information about the institution and the community;

- Serve as a boilerplate rider to the employment contract;

- Offer insights into the institution's mission and goals;

- Detail institutional benefits and services of interest to employees;

- Aid with crisis intervention/management by detailing common personnel problem areas.

Areas for Company Handbook Consideration

A review of various professional theatre company handbooks reveals many areas for consideration:

EMERGENCY INFORMATION: HEALTH, SAFETY, AND SECURITY

GENERAL INFORMATION AND OVERVIEWS
Institutional history, mission, and goals
Orientation and training procedures
Company structure or hierarchy (Who reports to whom?)
Referral lists for professional services (doctors, dentists, hospitals, insurance, etc.)
Pertinent community phone numbers
Key institutional phone numbers
Facilities descriptions, maps, and policies
Community relations
Typical schedules in each production area

EMPLOYMENT
Affirmative action
Equal opportunity statement
Employment forms
Insurance options, forms, and deadlines
Probationary periods
Personnel definitions
Work hours and overtime policy
Paycheck distribution
Personnel records
Evaluations and review
Grievance procedures
Disciplinary procedures
Termination procedures

Sexual harassment
Theft
Animals
Holidays/vacations
Leaves of absence
Parental leave
Bereavement leave
Sick leave
Injuries
Life-threatening illness
Jury duty
Health care and medical coverage
Workers' compensation
Life insurance
Retirement

PRODUCTION RELATED
Scheduling
Callboard notices
Performance calls
Valuables
Backstage tours
Photo calls
Complementary ticket policy
Pre-show speeches and announcements
Understudies
Reviews and press availability
Dressing rooms
Costume fittings
Union assistance
Costume and wig care
Program needs, biographies, and photographs
Emergency calls related to production

COMPANY EXPECTATIONS AND PLANNING
Company meetings
Staff meetings
Company calls
Company mail
Production meetings

Tech week planning
Equity meetings
Private facilities, equipment, and grounds use

FINANCIAL OVERVIEWS

Contracts
Payroll
Banking
Pay advances
Check cashing
Loans
Business office procedures
Purchasing
Supplies
Photocopying
Telephone use
Library use
Travel: in State
Travel: out of State
Travel: personal automobile use
Travel: company vehicle use

SECURITY AND SAFETY

General safety rules and requirements
Facilities use and safety procedures
Identification needs
Key procurement, use, and replacement
Complex security
Maintenance/janitorial considerations
Hazardous materials
Posting and communications
Visitor policies
Alcohol use and drinking-age information
Smoking: complex and grounds
Drug policies

"Your attitude, not your aptitude,
will determine your altitude."
Zig Ziglar

Managing People: a Day-to-Day Checklist

Managing a creative, ambitious, productive work force in the arts requires planning skills, patience, diligence, fortitude, perspective, and a sense of humor. If only we could all read a book chapter or two and master the world of people management. You will certainly develop your own style, create your own learning experiences, and benefit from your fair share of failures and triumphant success stories. The checklist detailed below is simply an attempt to help readers accelerate the learning curve and benefit from the experiences of other arts, corporate, and government managers without having to reinvent the wheel.

> "Intelligence and courtesy not always are combined;
> Often in a wooden house a golden room we find."
> Henry Wadsworth Longfellow

Supervisory Skills, Secrets amd Debatable Sins

- If you are a new employee or supervisor, consider keeping a low profile until you have had the opportunity to research the recent history of your institution and specific division, discover the strengths and weaknesses of your predecessor, determine whom you can trust, and start to get to know your colleagues, supervisors, and employees.

- Credibility is key. Be honest, trustworthy, and inspire your employees.

- Empathy can build bridges with employees. Excessive empathy may also lead to excuse-making, laziness, and the lowering of institutional standards.

- People skills, team building, and getting along are all admirable supervisory traits that can backfire if employee comfort levels replace productivity.

- Instilling employee pride in a job well done is considerably more important than heaping generic praise and affection.

- Managing conflict beats ignoring or avoiding conflict, and strategically planning to avert crisis is infinitely preferable to crisis intervention and management.

- Effective communication includes listening. Allow time to involve your team in key decision-making and strategic planning.

- Take responsibility and share credit. Don't complain to your peers. Admit your mistakes, offer solutions when outlining problems, set your ego aside, show initiative, and keep an open mind.

- Prove your reliability through action, facts, and work results. Avoid empty promises, grandstanding, and hogging credit for work developed as a team.

- Be a visible, supportive, productive employee. Your job satisfaction and longevity may be tied to your ability to garner the respect, trust, and good feelings of your co-workers and immediate supervisor.

- Playing favourites, abusing company perks, announcing dictatorial mandates, hiding from responsibility, refusing to communicate clear goals, and breaking employee confidences are among the most grievous of supervisory sins.

> "A committee is a group that keeps minutes and loses hours."
> *Milton Berle*

When Great Minds Gather: Running a Productive Meeting

- Running a great meeting involves a clear agenda, the appropriate personnel in attendance, specific objectives, and the involvement of those in attendance. Otherwise, send a memo, write an email, post the information online, write a letter, or put it on DVD.

- The meeting agenda must be specific so that participants can prepare for the meeting.

- Arrange the seating in the meeting for maximum effectiveness appropriate to the agenda. Generally speaking, seating should be arranged so that participants may face each other and contribute to the meeting agenda.

- Always start exactly on time, or know that you are reinforcing ongoing lateness and poor work habits.

- Encourage prompt attendance by closing the door when you start your meeting and placing important agenda items at the beginning of the meeting. Acknowledge, but don't embarrass, latecomers. Clarify your expectations following the meeting.

- Run meetings with high energy and a clear purpose. Let those in attendance know what your expectations are and what's in it for them to help facilitate a productive meeting.

- Encourage respect for each participant's time and ideas, and encourage professional rapport in meetings.

- Use appropriate gestures and visual aids to keep meetings interesting and on track.

- Realize that personnel pressures and tensions often influence meeting productivity, and seek to ease those tensions during your opening remarks.

- Encourage employees to talk with, not at, meeting participants.

- Allow time for questions and clarifications – but never repeat information provided earlier in a meeting to latecomers (thereby wasting the time of the individuals who were on time)! Delegate this "catch-up task" after you have had your "be on time" talk with the offending latecomer.

- Get your meeting participants involved in the agenda at the earliest possible time.

- Use humor, be approachable, be brief.

- End meetings with all participants crystal clear as to what is expected of them. All action items should be emphasized in meeting minutes or, if minutes aren't taken, each participant must know "who is going to do what by when!"

> **"Cleverness is not wisdom."**
> *Euripides*

Communication Basics: Memos, E-Mails and Letters

- Keep written documents short and to the point – and proofread, proofread, proofread.

- Know your reader and shape your correspondence accordingly.

- In today's highly political, seemingly-endless-lawsuit-oriented workplace, consider the fallout if your correspondence ends up being read and analyzed in a court of law (or, perhaps, worse yet, on the front page of your hometown newspaper)! Correspond accordingly.

- Use correspondence to document policy and procedures, confirm appointments and assignments, and congratulate personnel for their outstanding performance.

- Don't waste your reader's time! If you want a book mailed to you, perhaps you should include your address in your e-mail! If you request a phone interview, leaving your phone number in your e-mail or letter would be wise.

- It's best to deliver sad, bad, or troubling news in person. Your delivery may be crucial to the interpretation of the news, and it's almost always better to discuss grievances or concerns face-to-face.

- Gossip, accusations, off-colour remarks, rude jokes, and overly personal observations are just a few of the many items that should never appear in company correspondence or on institutional computers.

- Unless the main point of your correspondence is confusing, get to it quickly and avoid extraneous or long-winded explanations or historical overviews.

- Even e-mails can be well written, carefully organized, and visually appealing. Use a salutation and sign your name to your e-mails. Take care to read your quickly worded e-mails before hitting the "send" button!

- Consider waiting twenty-four hours before sending correspondence dealing with difficult negotiations, irritating employees, temperamental board members, or angry customers. It's okay to write the correspondence – but feel free to burn it after a twenty-four-hour cooling-off period!

> "Loyal and efficient work in a great cause,
> even though it may not be immediately
> recognized, ultimately bears fruit."
> *Jawaharlal Nehru*

Building Character and Careers: Theatre Personnel Development

INTRODUCTION: Savvy arts executives seek, recruit, and hire quality employees; and nurture, develop, and take full advantage of their skills and experiences to further the mission and objectives of their institution.

As a smart employee with an eye on the future, you can contribute to the institution in many ways, and there are myriad opportunities to prove your worth to your company. Here are just a few:

1) **Take this job and love it!**
   Take care of your day-to-day assignments, but work above and beyond your daily to-do list and assignments. Prepare a detailed list of everything your supervisor has assigned you and everything else that you think needs to be done to support this work, expand on this work, and prepare for the next set

of objectives. Review this at an appropriate time with your supervisor, add it to your "Job Description Manual," and include it in your "Friendly Quarterly Job Summary."

For example: if you are a casting assistant and are assigned to stuff resumes into a file and call a dozen acting candidates for an audition, volunteer to work late (or faster or smarter) to organize a comprehensive filing system that can be used forever; book the audition space; prepare files for the auditions; arrange for coffee and donuts for the bleary-eyed artistic director and out-of-town guest directors; and meet the candidates and casting team as they arrive.

2) What's a "Job Description Manual?"

How many times have you interviewed for a position (as either the employer or the candidate) without a clear and comprehensive job description? Help your institution prepare for the future and better understand your position by creating and updating a job description manual. This will help in future orientation and training, clear the way for you to move up in the organization, and, perhaps, pave the way for a clearer understanding regarding your work load and the skills necessary to survive in your position.

3) What's a "Friendly Quarterly Job Summary?"

This easy-to-read, carefully (but casually) written report is a general document that you compile, listing your assignments, special efforts, outside (and maybe unseen) work-related activities, and major successes over the preceding three months. "Casual" means that it is typed in friendly memo form and delivered to your supervisor without ceremony or expectation of a response. These reports may form the basis for your ongoing evaluations and future salary reviews.

For example:

Dear Mr. Johnson, Just a short note to report on my general work activities over the past few months to make sure I'm on the right track and that I understand your priorities. No need to respond unless I'm missing something you feel is important. Thanks for the opportunity to be a part of [NAME OF INSTITUTION].
Sincerely, [NAME]

4) Look to the future!

Establish clear objectives and think strategically. What does the institution need for you to accomplish on a given day or in a week's time? Looking to the future, how can you help improve your area of the institution's work and make a long-term contribution to your company?

5) **First impressions.**
"The body is the shell of the soul, and dress the husk of that shell; but the husk often tells what the kernel is," explains an old, anonymous expert on the fretful realities of first impressions. Arts representatives tend to interact with the community at large, and dress, manners, and an upbeat personality are often the key to making your first impression a good impression.

6) **Be there or beware!**
Personal respect, professional civility, and long-term business relationships customarily begin with all parties arriving on time and prepared for meetings, luncheons, performances, and related activities.

7) **Your attention, please!**
In a ridiculous world seemingly ruled by cell phones, Twitter and Facebook, make sure that you offer your undivided attention to individuals or groups who have committed to meeting with you in person. It shouldn't be surprising that answering cell phones and allowing beepers to interrupt professional meetings is just as rude and obnoxious as barging unexpectedly into personal conversations or private meetings used to be in the twentieth century! The message is still the same: "This person who is interrupting our work is more important to me than you are!"

8) **Stay out of the ditch!**
Matthew 15:14 says, "If the blind lead the blind, both shall fall into the ditch." Don't be afraid to ask questions and let your employer know when you are over your head or out of your league. Ask for assistance, clarification, or time to research the project in question.

9) **Practice the sounds of silence.**
William Hazlitt used to say that "silence is one great art of conversation," and sometimes it is important to simply listen, take notes, learn, and move on with your work. Perhaps it's soothing to know that not every debate, argument, political controversy, or tidbit of gossip demands your participation.

10) **Get (others) involved!**
Prove that you have sophisticated leadership skills and desirable facilitation skills by nurturing collaboration, expressing empathy, encouraging others to speak up, building rapport among the ranks, and generally creating a climate of support. When every conversation begins with "I," "I," and "I," your colleagues will soon be screaming, "*Ayaiiiiiiiiieeeeee!*"

"Make sure you're right, then go ahead."
Davy Crockett

HUMAN RESOURCES: THE GOOD, THE BAD AND THE UGLY

Hiring, orientation, training, resolving disputes, and firing are often considered unpleasant, crisis-oriented tasks within arts organizations. This is understandable, as such time-consuming jobs generally pull many employees' focus away from their day-to-day work, and these processes are generally outside the realm of most professional artists' training, education, experience, and comfort level.

Although hiring, orienting, and training new employees may be an exciting growth experience for employees and the institution, resolving disputes, moving individuals out of the organization, and retraining employees can be frustrating, demoralizing, and angst-producing.

What follows are pointers for various human resource processes culled from arts organizations throughout the nation.

Hiring

- Consider using a lawyer to review your company handbook and hiring/firing policies, employment contracts, and other key human resource documents. Oftentimes, non-profit arts groups use lawyers serving on the board of trustees for pro bono assistance. The board of trustees should sign off on crucial non-profit organization practices and policies.

- Create a comprehensive position description based on both day-to-day tasks and long-range expectations. Ensure that the language is non-discriminatory. (Take care with references to sex, gender, age, etc.)

- Make sure that the job title matches the position realities.

- Stress intangibles of the position such as career development opportunities, family-friendly environments, artistic prestige, and national/international networking potential.

- Don't be afraid to hire "overqualified people." Many CEOs pledge to "only hire key employees who are smarter than they are."

- Distinguish between the hiring team that is interviewing and recommending candidates, and the many people whom you'd like to have meet and visit with an incoming candidate. Too many cooks . . .

- When considering candidates of equal strength, experience, and ability, lean toward the individual who is most enthusiastic about the position and the company.

- Avoid all references to long-term employment and future promotion promises. Probationary, part-time, and permanent employee labels can backfire when individuals who believe "permanent" was a contractual agreement for lifelong employment file lawsuits.

- In a competitive market, maximum wages and benefits may be appropriate.

- Never lower your standards in terms of checking references, analysing an employee's work history, or accepting someone who doesn't meet the minimum requirements of the position.

- Conduct a detailed preliminary job interview by telephone before committing to an interview on site.

- Do check references. Checking references after you have offered a position could lead to lawsuits if you don't follow through on the offer.

- *U.S. News & World Report* notes that 80% of all employers are reluctant to give bad references, and 47% are leery of doing so even when they have proof of employee wrongdoing. Keep this in mind when weighing hiring decisions.

- Be honest and straightforward about working conditions and future company opportunities.

Sample Interview Questions

INTRODUCTION:

From a legal standpoint, it is generally considered important to ask the same questions of all interview prospects applying for the same position, and to treat all prospective employees applying for the same job in a similar manner. Aside from all of the obvious questions related to the specific job, here is a list of the more interesting and probing questions that have surfaced in recent interview situations:

- What work habits and personality traits do you most admire in your current colleagues?

- How would your current boss describe your contributions to the company?

- Are there recent books that you have read that you would recommend to me or a colleague or friend? Why?

- Obviously, not every individual is valued by every other individual in an organization. What would the people who didn't particularly care for you in your last position say about you?

- Tell me about your community service activities over the years.

- How would you handle an angry customer?

- Of all the bosses you have had, which one did you like the best? Least?

- Tell me about your dream job.

- Review a time when your work on the job didn't go so well.

- How is your experience particularly well suited to this position?

- What is it about our institution that is particularly interesting to you?

- What are your long-term goals in this field?

Orientation and Training

- Provide new employees with a welcome letter, mission statement, organizational manuals, to-do lists, a company handbook, a company telephone directory, and appropriate e-mail lists of important contacts. Make sure their computer and software is ready to conduct company business.

- Organize a priority listing of immediate needs.

- Introduce co-workers and key contacts to the new employee.

- Review all financial processes and expectations with new employees so they are aware of their budget limitations, responsibilities, travel reimbursements, and company-wide expectations.

- Set goals for your employees and establish ongoing evaluation procedures.

- Make sure that the proper tools, office supplies, equipment, and files are available to the new employee on his/her first day of work.

- Consider assigning a "buddy employee" or mentor to assist the new employee in the first few weeks on the job.

- Review job specifics, but also explain the general "non-profit culture" of your company.

Promotion & Retention

- Be specific in praise and appreciation for a job well done. Cite particular details of your employees' accomplishment(s) and let them know how they helped the institution.

- Acknowledge significant contributions in written employee evaluations.

- Offer advancement opportunities to your most productive employees.

- Reward merit with salary raises and benefit options.

- Banish all unfair promotion practices, like rewarding the "squeaky wheel," and offering inappropriate attention to complaining, obnoxious, or threatening employees.

- Promote people who show respect for you, the institution, and their colleagues.

- Encourage employees who whine, fail to meet crucial deadlines, and are always making excuses to find other employment. If they don't improve (or find other employment in a timely manner), terminate them.

- Ask employees to assess their own performance during ongoing position appraisals, and consider their statements when reviewing their supervisor's assessment and your own assessment of their performance.

- Everyone wants to jump on a winning bandwagon. Hire winners. Encourage winners. Promote winners.

- Set up win-win objectives, goals, and performance perks for your employees.

- Understand that positive reinforcement has a tendency to lead to improved job performance and goal achievement.

- Productive behaviour that is ignored or undervalued leads to demoralized employees and decreased performance.

- Recognize improved performance and be consistent in your treatment of all employees.

- Employee rewards should mirror employee contributions. Don't offer the same salary increases and other perks to fabulous employees, mediocre employees, and poorly performing employees.

- Insist on high standards in all areas of your organization's productions, communications, and internal and external contacts. Reward high standards and do not tolerate poor work.

- Constructively criticize behaviours, not the individual. Personnel matters should be handled with the utmost discretion.

- Consider rewards other than salary increases for your most valued employees: a Friday afternoon off, more autonomy, tuition assistance for special programs, health club dues, a contribution to an IRA, extra vacation time, or comp tickets to a special community event, area resort, or World Series game.

Termination

- The institution's company handbook should carefully outline grievance and termination procedures, and the company's employee policies related to "cause for dismissal." That said, perhaps the best way to terminate an individual is to let him or her resign.

- Follow the orientation and training procedures mentioned above and ensure that performance reviews are conducted in writing and in a timely manner, and that all reviews are signed by the employee and the employee's supervisor. Note that the performance reviews should document and validate the decision to terminate an employee.

- Be fair, thorough, honest, and specific in all evaluations. Be consistent in your evaluations and disciplinary procedures for all employees.

- Handle the termination meeting as a serious business meeting with a specific agenda, prepared statements from at least two company representatives, a detailed separation plan, and a respectful, dignified approach to the employee. Keep the meeting short, be prepared for defensiveness or anger, avoid rehashing past concerns and evaluations, and don't make promises that the institution isn't prepared to honor. Having two company representatives present thwarts allegations that may surface from one-on-one meetings.

- Delineate the details of a separation package for each terminated employee. Be sure to include the termination date, salary, and insurance details; and rules for how company files, computer files, and Rolodex files will be maintained and/or protected.

- A study reported in *Management World* indicates that the top reasons employees lose their jobs are (in order) incompetence, inability to get along with others, dishonesty, negative attitude, and lack of motivation.

- An exit interview should be considered for the purposes of collecting keys, computer equipment, and other company property, settling any outstanding financial accounts, reviewing the separation package, and evaluating the perceived strengths, weaknesses, and opportunities related to the employee's department.

- Again, an experienced lawyer who may also be on the institution's board of trustees may be consulted to assist with difficult cases. Firing an employee could subject the institution to huge liability payments for the intentional infliction of emotional distress or for other alleged misconduct.

- Consider discussions with and reassuring the fired employee's colleagues: let them know that the terminated employee was treated fairly and in line with the grievance and termination procedures outlined in the company handbook.

- Although many arts leaders fear that terminations hurt morale, my experience and a report in *Psychology Today* indicate that terminations actually enhance morale and increase productivity, because "bosses are relieved of the frustration caused by having to work with poor performers and no one needs to plan work around under-performers." Terminating such employees rids the company of the sense that some aren't pulling their weight. This, in turn, results in smoother operations, greater enthusiasm, and enhanced productivity.

> "Always be prepared to negotiate,
> but never negotiate without being prepared . . .
> Never lose faith. In a just cause, faith can move mountains.
> Without faith strength is futile,
> but strength without faith is sterile."
> Richard Nixon, The Real War

NEGOTIATING TIPS FOR ARTS MANAGERS

Introduction

Successful win-win contract negotiations should be taught as part of every arts management curriculum. Agents negotiate with producers, actors negotiate with agents, designers negotiate with directors, directors negotiate with artistic directors, and arts managers generally negotiate with everybody, every day, in myriad ways. Negotiating in the non-profit world can be very different than corporate negotiations. Oftentimes, there are specific values, personal needs, and competitive realities that motivate arts employees in ways that would be foreign to many for-profit employers. For example, how many employers are hiring in an atmosphere in which, historically, there has been 80–90% unemployment (actors), or in which an employee is thrilled with the salary and company but turns down the position because he doesn't like his specific "role?"

I once consulted with the treasurer of the board of directors of a non-profit theatre that was experiencing labor concerns due to low, non-competitive salaries; morale problems; and leadership concerns. His solution to the problem was summed up in his opening statement: "If they aren't happy in their jobs, just fire them and hire new people – that's what I do in my factory!" However, the reality in this rather isolated professional theatre was that the workers were highly skilled as costume-shop cutters, theatrical welders, scene painters, and props designers. Replacing them in a timely fashion would involve more than twice the resources and result in either a delayed theatre opening or an inferior product. Everyone would lose. The arts *are* a different beast and there is a reason why Hollywood producers, film agents, theatre casting directors, personal managers, and savvy arts negotiators are among the highest-paid professionals in America.

This isn't to say that arts professionals can't learn from the negotiating skills of corporate "sharks," or that the basics of an effective negotiation aren't similar in the for-profit and non-profit arenas. In every instance, it is crucial to know your prospective employee's wants, needs, and desires, and to plan out a negotiating strategy that either meets or shapes his or her expectations.

Whether you are negotiating a million-dollar Broadway contract or soft drink pouring privileges for your outdoor drama, it's important to understand what motivates the parties with whom you are negotiating. What do they want, what do you want, and what are your mutual objectives? What are the key priorities on both sides, and what are the negotiable and non-negotiable issues?

Motivational Points to Consider

- **A Sense of Belonging**
  Many prospective arts employees crave an artistic home, a creative family, and an institutional base, especially in the early stages of their careers. Never underestimate the power and attractiveness of inviting someone to be a member of your very exclusive, creative, exciting arts institution. Establishing rapport in a negotiation can set the stage for productive proposals and agreements.

- **Artistic Challenge**
  Why do "stars" choose to do Don Quixote, Hamlet, a brilliant new play, or Lady Macbeth for free (or union scale), when they could be making millions of dollars by pursuing television and film projects? The answers center on the performer's desires for artistic challenges, creative yearnings, and once-in-a-lifetime opportunities. The right project for the right artist at the right time may be worth much more than the most competitive salary you could ever offer.

- **Fair Compensation**
  In big business it's fairly easy to determine the identities of your best sales-people and reward them accordingly. In non-profit environments that stress collaboration (music/dance/theatre, etc.), it is not only difficult, but potentially crude to attempt to pay orchestra members, dancers, or theatre cast members

on the basis of their individual contributions to the project. Granted, additional compensation often goes to individuals who bring name recognition, years of experience, or rare skills to a performance. Generally speaking, however, most arts employees simply want to be treated and compensated fairly and honestly.

- **Being Needed**
  Communicating the institution's need for the unique skills of potential employees while instilling in them a sense of importance and prominence may help motivate non-profit employees who want to be wanted. Too often, brilliant artists, craftspeople, and managers are put off by recruiters who blatantly use a "take it or leave it," "there's plenty more where you came from," or "you're lucky just to have the opportunity to work for us" sales pitch.

- **Career Advancement**
  A liberal arts college in Colorado was straightforward in its recruiting assertion that "we pay our employees with mountains vs. money." The college knew that the glorious weather, awe-inspiring vistas, and snow-covered mountain peaks were worth thousands of dollars as recruitment lures. In other words, use your every advantage to full advantage. Many professional orchestras, museums, and Tony Award-winning theatres use their reputations in the field to recruit free interns, low-cost entry-level employees, and ambitious middle-managers. These institutions know that their prestigious names on an employee's resume have the potential to translate into future dollars, benefits, and positions; and they use this clout for bargaining purposes. What do you have to offer?

The Bottom Line and Golden Rules

Although it's true that considering the "whole individual" (including the needs, wants, desires, and expectations of an employee) is a great way to research negotiations, a strong negotiator certainly understands the power of money, benefits, and related compensation. "Fair Compensation" is certainly a debatable topic, and researching industry standards while applying regional differences and cost-of-living indexes usually leads to market standards for the non-profit field. It's the job of the employers, agents, personal managers, and prospective employees to know what these market standards are and how they may impact the negotiation. Understanding how to research, prepare, and conduct a negotiation should also be part of every arts manager's job description.

GOLDEN RULES FOR NEGOTIATION PREPARATIONS

1) Nothing is set in stone until everything is set in stone;

2) Bargaining is a mutual proposition ("if you give me this, I'll give you that");

3) Never give up anything without receiving something in return;

4) Never offer what you can't deliver;

5) Don't bluff unless you can afford to lose;

6) The strategy of "splitting the difference" can work for and against you;

7) What goes around, comes around (don't resort to stretching the truth, half truths, dirty tricks, or unsavory deal-making unless you want your long-term reputation sullied and your future effectiveness compromised).

The Negotiation Tip Sheet

1) **Select the right negotiator!**
   Once your institution has conducted the proper research (resume analysis, interviews, auditions, etc.), matching the perfect recruiter and negotiator with the prospective employee is often the next step. One theatre company utilized a frustrating, mind-numbing actor-hiring process that often proved useless for all involved. The artistic director would play the "good guy," call actors personally, and dangle fabulous theatre roles for their consideration. A few days later, a business office negotiator would call with the "bad news" that the actors would be expected to take significant pay cuts and work at low "favored nations" rates if they wanted to work for the company and play these "great roles." Although some actors complied, they usually reported to work feeling bamboozled and were forever suspicious of the company leaders. Many actors and agents simply refused the contract, devastated that they were built up for a financial letdown. Learning from its mistakes, the company eventually found one negotiator who would outline the financial constraints of the offer (and the institution) and proceed with the great news of significant roles and the company's strong desire to work with the talented, unique, much-needed actor. The results were phenomenal – two entirely different outcomes utilizing the same institutional resources.

2) **Match the skills to the negotiation.**
   Knowing how to do the job is not the same as knowing how to negotiate. Often, arts professionals delegate crucial negotiations to an area head who is brilliant at his or her core position. Unfortunately, this is most likely *not* the best person to conduct high-level, difficult negotiations. An expert welder is not necessarily the best person to negotiate the best deal for thousands of

dollars' worth of welding equipment, or to hire a fellow welder. A technical director who is adept at motivating young workers may not be the best person to negotiate lumber purchases, or to close a deal with a senior scenic, lighting, or costume designer.

3) **Yipes! My pots are overflowing!**

This is a running joke in my negotiating classes and serves as a reminder to "negotiate only when you are prepared to negotiate" and to "do your homework." Actors, directors, designers, and other arts personnel who do most of their negotiations over the telephone often receive a surprise call out of the blue following a series of large, "cattle-call" auditions or interviews. The point is to make an excuse, *any plausible excuse*, to get off the phone, find your notes, research the negotiator and the negotiation, and find a mutually agreeable time to reschedule the phone call. While "My pots are overflowing on the stove," may be a bit melodramatic, something like, "I'm surrounded by a dozen dinner guests," or, "I'm driving my friend to work and we're just heading out the door," or "I'm on my way to an audition; may I call you back?" are certainly plausible reasons to postpone a contract discussion by an hour (or more) to allow you time to prepare, research, rehearse, and succeed.

4) **Be a problem solver, not a prima donna.**

Keep ego, past history, irritation, and anger out of the negotiation. Focus on the goal, do your homework, listen carefully to what is being requested, and respond accordingly. Provide a range of solutions rather than blanket rejections or ultimatums. Again, how can the negotiation turn into a win-win situation?

5) **There's a reason actors have agents!**

It's best not to negotiate for yourself as an individual, and to have someone at least a step removed from the CEO negotiating for the institution. This allows healthy psychological distance on both sides, and it separates the key leaders from the actual discussion (including potential angst, emotional outbursts, and personal attacks that could be deal-breaking confrontations). Perhaps more importantly, this also provides backup and a place for the negotiation to move on to if the original negotiation bogs down. Unfortunately, due to their small size, organizational structure, or personnel composition, some non-profit arts groups use their theatre's artistic director, symphony conductor, museum director, or lead choreographer to negotiate artist contracts. Difficult negotiations during the day followed by creative, artistic collaboration in evening rehearsals is a risky proposition.

6) **You start ... no, you start ... no, you first ...**
    If you sense that an offer may be near or substantially higher than your
    expectations, it's often a smart idea to simply listen and take notes when
    someone is approaching you with the offer. This allows you to benefit from the
    information the negotiator is providing and build it into your response and
    subsequent request. However, this can backfire. If you sense that the initial
    offer is going to be substantially lower than your expectations, it may pay to
    outline your expectations first and start much closer to those expectations. It
    may be more difficult to negotiate a "steep uphill climb" from a lowball offer
    than to clarify your range of expectations up front. Classic pitfalls of "being the
    person who speaks first" is that the potential is there to undercut your position,
    show your hand too soon, or inadvertently put up a barrier to the negotiation
    and final contract with demands that the negotiator isn't prepared to meet.

7) **Sometimes, silence is mandatory.**
    Charles de Gaulle said it best: "Silence is the ultimate weapon of power."
    Once you have prepared and presented your offer, wait for a response before
    weakening your position with modifications, excuses, or additional informa-
    tion. It literally pays to be patient. "Silence is one of the hardest arguments
    to refute," explains Josh Billings.

8) **Anything is possible!**
    Understand that "company rules," "mandatory salary levels," "basic benefits,"
    and "consistent employment packages" were all created by men and women
    who have the power to change, rearrange, reinterpret, or move around the
    rules if so inspired. Don't let these standardized excuses inhibit your negoti-
    ating progress. Strategize clear scenarios for moving beyond the objections to
    the world of "yes."

9) **Question strategically.**
    During negotiations, questions may be used to stall, to redirect arguments, to
    lighten up a difficult discussion, or to secure actual information. Know when
    an appropriate question may help in the negotiation process.

10) **Keep the door open and your fingers to yourself!**
    Stay focused on the final result and avoid such deal-breaking phrases as
    "that's impossible," "this is non-negotiable," "take it or leave it," "this is my
    final offer," "I can't do that," or "over my dead body!" Don't make it personal.
    Avoid personal judgments such as "this isn't fair," "you're being
    unreasonable," and "you're a jerk." Keep veiled threats (and actual threats)
    out of the negotiation. "I wasn't born with enough middle fingers," laments
    Marilyn Manson. However much you empathize with that – don't act out.

11) **It's not enough to be tough.**

A humanistic, friendly approach to a negotiation has the potential to be much more effective than a tyrannical, dictatorial set of directives and demands.

12) **A sweet beginning.**

Prepare the way for a happy resolution to a contract negotiation by focusing first on issues that may be easily set in stone. This provides a starting point and a feeling of progress before heading into more difficult areas.

13) **Show acceptance.**

In psychology classes, we all learned the importance of acknowledging other people's feelings. In a negotiation, paying attention and restating someone's position is a technique that buys you time while allowing you to shape your counterpart's feelings into a mutually agreeable solution. For example: "I hear you saying that you are having trouble making ends meet, but we're locked into specific salaries due to prior salary parity agreements. If we could assist you with your housing expenses by negotiating a better interest rate or rental payment, would this make it possible to complete this contract?"

14) **Negotiate with a "who cares" bag of perks.**

Arts marketing and fundraising professionals do this every day. "If you sub-scribe (or make a donation), here are all the benefits you will enjoy!" And most of the purported benefits (10% gift shop discounts, $2-off parking, the first opportunity to subscribe again next year, etc.) are either free to the institution or actual money-makers for the institution. Whether you are negotiating personnel contracts or airline flights, this strategy can work for you. Find contract elements and perks that may be important to the person with whom you are negotiating, and substitute items that aren't costly to the company but may be very meaningful to your partner in negotiation. A better position title, a designated parking space, more substantial responsibilities, and professional development opportunities are just a few of the many perks that may endear and excite an employee. As a theatre executive in negotiations with Delta Airlines, I found that offering access to mailing lists, ad space in play programs, and lobby space for dazzling travel displays served a dual purpose: the association with Delta Airlines enhanced the image of the arts institution while saving tens of thousands of dollars in cold cash for artist transportation.

15) **Seal the deal: follow up quickly in writing!**

Immediately following an oral negotiation and agreement, put the details into an e-mail or letter and send it to the party with whom you are negotiating to ensure that you have agreed to the same key points. Too often, negotiators *believe* they have reached agreement, only to encounter shocking differences in hearing or perception when reviewing the final contract.

ETHICS AND THE ARTS: MAKING A COMMITMENT TO HUMAN DIGNITY

Introduction

In my coast-co-coast travels as a theatre consultant, questions of ethics surface on a daily basis. So often, the honorable women and men who guide arts organizations do so with impeccable grace, unquestionable scruples, and undeniable skill. Unfortunately, driven by financial pressures, ego, and mounting pressures to achieve results, there is another breed of theatre professionals who choose to ignore crucial personnel issues (and ethical concerns) and pursue their own agendas at all costs.

Stories of casting couches, unethical advertising, and sexual harassment certainly run rampant in the American theatre and film industries. Hollywood's old theatre publication, *Drama-Logue*, used to run the telephone numbers of both the "Bunco Squad" and the Los Angeles "Vice Squad" on a weekly basis as a service to its readers.

In the best-managed enterprises, legitimate ethical questions surface as the black-and-white of right and wrong inevitably blends into difficult grey areas in the ever-evolving work place. In America's best-run cultural institutions, it is at these times that careful consideration and considerable soul-searching goes into debating the issues and tackling tough problems. Unfortunately, in many of the cultural institutions and support agencies, questions of ethics and human dignity are seldom discussed and rarely addressed. Perhaps there are lessons to be learned from others around the nation.

This compendium of policies and position statements is an attempt to assist those who have not yet developed institutional guidelines intended to protect the dignity of the individual and commit to "fair play" in the treatment of all employees. The information contained in this article focuses on general "Code of Ethics" needs and sexual harassment issues, and was provided by sources in arts and education during six months of surveys, phone calls, and personal interviews.

Too Busy for Ethics?

Surprisingly, many theatre leaders surveyed cited a lack of time and the absence of any semblance of a company handbook as the main reason they don't commit to a formal code of ethics, or clear-cut policies on sexual harassment, or a host of other ethical issues. Board of trustee insensitivity or bias, legal concerns, public opinion, and fear of media scrutiny were also reported as key reasons for not addressing these important issues.

Perhaps even more surprising was many theatres' complete lack of response to a call for information-sharing on this subject. When pressed during follow-up phone calls, many theatre leaders acknowledged their companies' lack of formal or informal guidelines on virtually any ethical issue (and on many other personnel issues and concerns). It's worrisome to note how many theatre companies haven't committed to *any* company guidelines or policies in a published company handbook.

Ethics and the arts is obviously a hot topic in arts and education. The National Education Association (NEA) addressed various issues through a series of resolutions; the National Association of Schools of Dance (NASD) devoted an entire day of an annual meeting to "Ethics in Professional Dance Education and Training;" the Association for Theatre in Higher Education (ATHE) created a "Visionary Task Force" to consider timely policy formation; and professional theatres and the Shakespeare Theatre Association of America (STAA) have made it a topic of discussion for the better part of the last decade.

Many individual theatres are scrambling for information, and in many cases, the arts leaders I interviewed requested copies of other institutional policies, hoping that they wouldn't have to "reinvent the wheel," or that, if they could share the sensible language of similar organizations, they might be able to convince their boards of trustees to step up to the plate. These requests inspired the following compilation, and every attempt has been made to credit the institution that made the submission.

Taking a Stance: Codes of Ethics, Human Dignity and Sexual Harassment in Arts and Education Associations

In its resolution, the National Education Association acknowledged that "sexual harassment is a form of sex discrimination or abuse. The Association believes that classroom teachers, faculty, staff, and students should be protected from sexual harassment. The Association encourages its affiliates to work with local school districts and institutions of higher education to:

A) Establish strong policies defining and prohibiting sexual harassment;

B) Develop educational programs designed to help people recognize, understand, prevent, combat, and eliminate sexual harassment;

C) Develop and publicize a grievance procedure that encourages the reporting of incidents of sexual harassment, resolves complaints promptly, and protects the rights of all parties."

The United States Institute for Theatre Technology (USITT) "Code of Ethical Practice" offers a broader blanket of generic language that may be more palatable to arts leaders who fear the wrath of "political correctness" referees. An excerpt from the preamble, adopted in 1984, reads as follows:

"Entertainment professionals employed in the fields of Theatre, Television, Film and their allied entertainment forms are obliged by the society at large of which they are a part, as well as by their working relationships with colleagues and the public, to conduct themselves responsibly as artists, as craftsmen, and as members of the team or group effort with which they are associated . . . they are also expected to adhere to the highest standards of responsible ethical conduct in their relations to their employees, their colleagues, and the public."

A subsequent USITT "Canon" excerpt maintains that "since the entertainment industry cannot exist in a vacuum, professionals must consider the consequences of their work and the societal issues pertinent to it, and shall seek to extend public understanding of their role in these areas . . . professional decisions shall be made and actions taken without bias because of race, religion, sex, age, national origin or physical handicap."

An excerpt from the "Code of Ethics" of the National Association of Schools of Theatre (NAST) simply charges the membership to "impress upon its faculty the importance of personal and professional integrity," to be "responsible for attempting to safeguard the health and safety of their students to the fullest extent of their ability," and to "recognize their responsibility to respect the legal rights and human dignity of all individuals."

The New York City-based University/Resident Theatre Association (U/RTA) mirrors both the USITT and NAST documents, calling for each institution to "impress upon its faculty, staff, and students the importance of personal and professional integrity" and "their responsibility to respect the legal rights and human dignity of all individuals." The U/RTA "Code of Ethics" concludes with a call for member institutions to be "responsible for attempting to safeguard the health and safety of students, staff, and audience."

Individual Theatre Policies

Fortunately, more specific language related to ethical issues is available from individual professional theatres (such as the Guthrie Theatre, the Oregon Shakespeare Festival, The Cleveland Play House, and the California Shakespeare Festival) and university theatres (including the University of Michigan, the University of Houston, and The University of North Carolina at Chapel Hill).

For example, following boilerplate statements on "Equal Opportunity" and "Affirmative Action," the Guthrie Theatre clearly defines its policy on sexual harassment: "The Guthrie strives to maintain a work environment free of any form of sexual harassment. Unwelcome sexual advances, requests for sexual favors, and other verbal or physical conduct of a sexual nature is harassment when: (1) submission to such conduct is made as a condition of employment, or (2) submission to or rejection of such conduct is used as the basis for employment decisions, or (3) such conduct interferes with work performance or creates an intimidating, hostile or offensive work environment. If you feel you are a victim of sexual harassment, contact the Administrative Director who will investigate your complaint. Employees who file complaints in good faith will experience no retaliation for doing so."

The Houston Shakespeare Festival and the University of Houston Department of Theatre abide by forcefully written interim university policies that detail more than thirty pages of sexual harassment and sexual assault policies, definitions, university actions, statutory references, advising, formal complaint procedures, board and hearing procedures, sanctions, appeals, and records retention and confidentiality.

The policy includes a commitment to "providing a professional working and learning environment free from sexual harassment . . . sexual harassment is a form of sex discrimination and is illegal." By definition, the University of Houston describes sexual harassment "as consisting of: (1) unwelcome sexual advances, (2) requests for sexual favors, (3) verbal and written requests of a sexual nature, (4) and/or physical conduct of a sexual nature; when such conduct: (a) is made, either explicitly or implicitly, a term or condition of instruction, employment or participation in a university activity; or (b) is used to be a basis for evaluation in making academic or personnel decisions affecting an individual; or (c) has the effect of creating an intimidating, hostile, or offensive university environment; or has the purpose or effect of substantially interfering with an individual's employment or learning."

In relation to the foregoing statements that were part of the University of Houston interim policy, "sexual harassing behavior may include, but is not limited to the following:

- Unwelcome sexual flirtations, advances, propositions, or leering;

- Favoritism based on a sexual relationship (or adverse impact on other members of a group);

- Verbal remarks of a sexual nature whether directed to an individual or group, or in the guise of humor, including sexually explicit derogatory remarks, suggestive comments, demands or jokes found to be offensive or objectionable to the recipient;

- Use of sexually oriented photos, posters, cartoons, materials, or themes unrelated to instruction and/or the pursuit of knowledge;

- Graphic or degrading verbal, written, or electronic comments of a sexual nature about an individual or the individual's appearance;

- Any suggestive or unwelcome physical contact, any aggressiveness such as touching, pinching, or patting; or actual or threatened physical assault . . . "

The company handbook for the Oregon Shakespeare Festival (OSF) also offers very specific language regarding sexual harassment: "We are committed to providing a work environment that is free of all forms of discrimination and harassment . . . we will not tolerate sexual harassment of our employees by anyone – supervisors, co-workers, patrons or vendors. Sexual harassment consists of unwelcome sexual advances, requests for sexual favors, and other verbal or physical conduct of a sexual nature if:

- Submission to the conduct is in any way made a term or condition of employment; or

- Submission to (or rejection of) the conduct is used as the basis for any employment oriented decisions; or

- The conduct has the purpose or effect of unreasonably interfering with an individual's work performance or creating an intimidating, hostile, or offensive work environment."

The OSF urges individuals who feel they are being sexually harassed to *"contact the Personnel Manager or General Manager immediately. Please bring a friend with you if that would make you feel more comfortable."*

In a statement on "Other Harassment," the OSF policy continues, "We want to maintain a working environment free from all forms of discrimination and harassment, whether based on race, color, religion, ancestry, national origin, age, marital status, veteran status, physical and mental disabilities, sexual orientation, on-the-job injuries or gender."

The California Shakespeare Theatre (CSF) reviews many of the policies already reviewed in the Oregon handbook, with the strong proviso that "any employee who violates this policy will be subject to disciplinary action up to and including termination." The definition of sexual harassment varies only slightly: "Sexual harassment is a form of employee misconduct that is demeaning to another person and undermines the integrity of the employment relationship . . . behavior that may be considered offensive to another employee, and therefore should not occur, includes: unwanted physical contact; foul language; lewd or sexually suggestive remarks; jokes, comments or obscene gestures; the display of sexually explicit pictures, photographs, cartoons, objects or other materials; sexually oriented propositions, whether explicit or implicit; any sexual touching; or making any sexual favors of any kind whatsoever a condition for any job or benefit."

Many universities have expanded their sexual harassment policies to include policies on "amorous relationships." A letter from the chancellor of The University of North Carolina at Chapel Hill describes the prohibition of "amorous relationships between students . . . and faculty or instructional staff who evaluate or supervise them in teaching, research, or administrative contexts." The rationale for the policy is described as follows: " . . . such relationships present serious ethical concerns, in that they are fraught with potential conflict of interest and risk of misunderstanding, exploitation, or intimidation in the learning environment . . . it serves as an appropriate complement to the University's Sexual Harassment Policy and reflects the ethical values of this educational community."

The University of Michigan Department of Theatre and Dance has established an "Affirmative Action Advisor," a "Sexual Harassment/Discrimination Committee," and a detailed "Harassment/Discrimination Resolution Procedure."

Finally, one of America's oldest professional theatres summarizes its position in one short paragraph: "It is the policy of The Cleveland Play House to prohibit sexual harassment of one employee by another employee, supervisor or patron. Sexual harassment of any kind will not be tolerated and any incident of harassment should be reported immediately to the Artistic Director, Managing Director, or Director of Finance. All complaints involving sexual harassment will be immediately investigated and dealt with accordingly."

Summary

The above just scratches the surface of the available information regarding the "hot" topics of ethics and sexual harassment. Where human dignity and individual livelihoods are concerned, there's little reason to hide behind excuses of time, the insensitivity of various colleagues, legal concerns, media scrutiny, and public opinion. There's also no need to reinvent the wheel. As demonstrated above, many courageous companies and associations have spent countless hours and dollars on legal counsel establishing words that work. In addition, the National Organization for Women, the Alliance Against Sexual Harassment, Working Women United Institute, and the Project on the Status and Education of Women all offer additional information. Company handbook policies should reflect the institutional mission and character of those involved in carrying it out. As theatres come to terms with twenty-first-century expectations, prudent management should involve the careful consideration of policies and guidelines that impact all crucial areas of the operation. Would this not include a basic code of ethics and sexual harassment policy?

"The first step in the evolution of ethics is a sense of solidarity with other human beings."
Albert Schweitzer

CHAPTER 6

Fundraising for the Arts: Basic Strategies For the 21st Century

"Never think you need to apologize for asking someone to give to a worthy project . . . "
John D. Rockefeller

INTRODUCTION TO FUNDRAISING

Fundraising Can Be *Fun*

Remember, you are offering individuals, businesses, corporations, granting institutions, and foundations the opportunity to touch souls, change lives, inspire creativity, and open doors to the joyous youth, boisterous baby-boomers, and sensational seniors of America!

Fundraising Can Be *Poignant*

As an arts representative, you are offering donors a rare and remarkable chance to be a significant part of a rare and noble enterprise that has the potential to reap the myriad educational rewards, economic development benefits, and cultural awakenings that the arts bring to audiences and communities night after night, performance after performance!

Fundraising Keeps Institutions *Alive*

Americans give over $200 billion to charities annually and, according to a survey by the American Association of Fundraising Counsel, individuals accounted for 82% of all giving, while foundations (13%), and corporations (5%) added to the total. As arts institutions plan for the future, it's important to recognize national trends and to plan accordingly. Most people give money because they believe in a project and they want to be of help. It makes them feel good. Give them that opportunity to believe in your institution and feel the great thrill of supporting the arts!

Fundraising *By Any Other Name* . . .

It used to be that you just asked for money, donations, or contributions. Then the term "Fundraising" was invented, and volunteers everywhere were collecting funds for non-profit programs to meet their annual operating or capital expense needs. Eventually, the word "Development" was applied in fundraising terms to indicate the broader, savvier, more complex modes of gathering funding, including foundation, corporate, public assistance, planned giving, individual giving programs, membership options, and simply fundraising – on a grander scale with more planning! Finally, the terms "Institutional Development" and "Institutional Advancement" came into play to acknowledge the highly sophisticated research, strategic planning, and communications programs that go beyond "simple fundraising" into the realm of overall strategies and programs that "advance" the entire institution vs. simply putting unearned income in the bank.

Marketing-Based Fundraising Is *Here To Stay*

During the early 1990s, perhaps as a response to falling corporate profits and dwindling foundation funds, many corporations seemed to partially abandon the idea of charitable altruism and true philanthropy to move toward "partnerships," corporate "sponsorships," and what's often been referred to as "marketing-based fundraising." In today's non-profit world, a great deal of the funding that's available is based in corporate marketing departments, and series of trade-offs, benefits, or marketing deals are replacing no-strings-attached donations. Many donors are now actively articulating their interest in "more bang for the buck," "value for contributions," and "partnerships of mutual interest."

In this environment, "contributions" or "investments" include contractual agreements for advertising space, mailing-list access, media acknowledgement, prime box seats, endorsements, merchandising rights, and a whole range of other marketable assets that the non-profit arts institution might be able to deliver. For example, Delta Airlines offers free seats in exchange for mailing list access; Coca-Cola trades contributions for pouring rights and logo displays; Toyota donates cars for raffles in exchange for prime car display access outside a theatre's front doors; and Del Taco, Pepsi, and Evian water spend sponsorship money for food-service access outside concert halls. The corporate sponsorship and marketing-based fundraising approach seems to be the wave of the future.

Start *In Your Own Backyard*

Although it's easier to sit in staff meetings and board meetings and debate the giving power of international corporations and nationally recognized foundations, it's usually not nearly as productive as searching in your own backyard for individuals who have the influence, affluence, and potential interest in helping your institution.

Certainly, recruiting your board of trustees and other volunteer groups is a great way to start. Using the care, clout, and connections of your board and volunteer groups will help you target influential peer-to-peer fundraising prospects, and, if properly nurtured, these groups should form the foundation of your strategic fundraising plan.

Whatever you do, don't forget that board of trustee recruitment is of major importance to future fundraising efforts, and choose carefully!

HOW TO RECRUIT A BOARD OF TRUSTEES THAT UNDERSTANDS FUNDRAISING RESPONSIBILITIES

Introduction

Fundraising is a major priority for non-profit board members in the arts, and many institutions depend on fundraising for 40–100% of their annual budgets. A few non-profit arts institutions (such as summer musical theatre operations and tourist-oriented Shakespeare festivals) earn a significant amount of their budgets through box office and ticket income, while others (museums, free Shakespeare in the parks, etc.) fundraise the majority of their budgets. In every case, the key to balancing the budget and planning for the future is a strategic fundraising plan and a motivated, organized, creative, and productive board of trustees. (See Chapter 2 for additional board of trustees and fundraising information.)

So, how does one recruit a great fundraising board? First, and foremost, be honest when recruiting and orienting new board members. Fundraising responsibilities are too often left out of the initial board recruitment discussions. The concepts of "friend-raising and fundraising" and "giving and getting" need to be introduced right from the beginning.

Fundraising expectations should be spelled out in a board recruitment brochure, and individual and corporate giving expectations should also be discussed. See Chapter 2 for samples. Although some arts institutions set a specific amount that board members must give on an annual basis, I generally resist this mandate for two major reasons:

It may limit giving. If someone has the capability of giving $20,000 to your institution, but the mandated board level is set at $2,000, the individual may feel that giving more than the limit would be grandstanding (or may be relieved to be let off the hook for the larger amount);

It may preclude some board members who may be marvellous fundraisers, but whose personal situations don't allow the mandated contribution. If someone can organize an auction that raises $50,000 for your institution, but can't afford a $2,000 annual contribution, do you really want to exclude that individual?

Still, most arts leaders and board members agree: board giving must be a part of board responsibilities, and 100% of the board must participate in annual contributions. It is difficult, if not impossible, to solicit outside individuals, local businesses, major corporations, and regional foundations, or to attain grants, if the board of trustees is not fully engaged and committed to the project. Many arts institutions use these kinds of words in their board recruitment materials:

"Board members are expected to contribute annually to the best of their abilities. In addition, all board members are involved in assisting in the identification of prospective patrons, requesting contributions from individuals, businesses, corporations, and/or foundations as needed, and participating in at least one annual fundraising event."

"It is expected that each board member will annually contribute an amount that is personally significant and meaningful and in line with their commitment to the institution. Board members will also work closely with the development office to identify prospects, request contributions, and assist in the successful development of fundraising events."

KEY CONCEPTS RELATED TO FUNDRAISING LEADERSHIP

Creating Enthusiasm

Ditch the dreary board meetings and embrace the unique, capable group of community leaders and professionals that you have selected for your board of trustees. Use your "Fundraising Coordination Committee" to handle the donor list development, "ratings" of prospects (how much to ask for), and overall organizational fundraising plan. Use a portion of board meetings for the board fundraising coordination committee leaders to cheerlead, challenge, and invigorate the board!

Establishing a Sense of Urgency

Set specific, realistic, and rational fundraising goals and deadlines. Outline institutional needs, prepare cash-flow statements, and make the case for an absolute beginning, middle, and end to the annual fundraising campaign. Use the board and community leaders to research other community campaigns and to coordinate the timing of your institution's campaign.

Defining Your Mission

Your institutional mission defines who you are and what you do. Make sure your strategic fundraising plan lines up with your mission!

Establishing a Case Statement

Build a persuasive set of criteria, or reasons why your institution deserves support, and delineate exactly what needs to be done and how your institution is going to meet this need. Why should an individual, or a corporate or foundation head, contribute to your organization?

Determining Feasibility

Community research, donor research, board knowledge, community leader advice, and cultivation discussions with prospective patrons should all be considered in determining the feasibility of a strategic fundraising plan. How have donors responded to similar arts campaigns in the community? What is their giving history with your organization? How have they responded to various cultivation efforts (lunch meetings, attendance at events, fundraiser invitations, arts centre tours, meetings with key artists, or one-on-one discussions with current board members)? Oftentimes, an outside consultant can be an objective source of information if invited to interview major donors as part of a feasibility study.

Clear Public Communications

It's difficult to raise money in a void or in a negative atmosphere. Strategic fundraising includes a coordinated and positive marketing, public relations, media, and overall communications plan that takes advantage of the artistic achievements of the company, the track records of the artistic and management team, the success stories of the artists, and the commitment and involvement of a volunteer board of trustees that believes in the institution.

Setting Goals

Setting goals for a strategic fundraising plan includes defining objectives, evaluating the overall fundraising prospect list, matching fundraising vehicles to prospects, preparing staff management support, maximizing the volunteer pool, and coordinating the timetable of fundraising events. Fundraising vehicles include, but are not limited to, one-on-one personal visits, group solicitations, telephone calls, direct mail, grant applications, foundation proposals, challenge gifts, special fundraiser events, media advertising, etc.

Timing

"The secret of success in life, is for a man to be ready for his opportunity when it comes," asserts Benjamin Disraeli. Many of the largest contributions in corporate history were solicited during the high-flying technology times of the late 1990s that boosted the NASDAQ to amazing heights. By March 2000, billions of dollars had disappeared and opportunities had dissolved. A similar stock market tumble and worldwide loss of wealth in 2008 contributed to the current economic climate. Proper research and asking the right questions of the right individuals at the right time will smooth the path to fundraising success.

Staff Support

Your board of trustee members' time is precious. Don't waste it on time-consuming administrative tasks that may be accomplished by other staff or volunteers. Basic prospect research, setting appointments, preparing informational packets, drafting letters and follow-up thank-you notes, and other crucial fundraising support should be coordinated so that the board members' time is spent on high-level consultations and one-on-one solicitations with peers.

Budget

In institutional theatres, you have to spend money to raise money. Your skimping on research, support materials, personnel, and planning will frustrate fundraisers, offend potential donors, and threaten goals. On the other hand, extravagance in fundraising may also offend donors and cause them to question your true needs and values. Integrity is paramount in all non-profit budgeting and fundraising projects.

Orienting Fundraisers

Never allow your fundraisers to flounder! Make sure you prepare answers to the "most-asked questions" about your institution and divulge all appropriate aspects of the fundraising campaign to your fundraisers. Orient your board and fundraising volunteers so that they follow a coordinated plan of "asking for contributions," "dealing with objections in a positive manner," and "reporting on contributions and fundraising results."

Developing Prospects and Suspects

Who are those individuals who are of prime potential in your fundraising campaign (prospects), and how can you identify individuals who might be interested in your institution (suspects)? Past donors, satisfied subscribers, delighted vendors, and corporate partners should all be prime prospects. Donors to similar community arts enterprises, general audience members, friends of friends, corporations interested in bolstering their community image, and businesses that profit from your existence may all be worthwhile suspects. Researching, brainstorming, compiling, analyzing, narrowing, and determining priority lists is a central task in strategic fundraising.

Solidifying the Prospective Donor List

Using historically successful community fundraising leaders to evaluate your priority lists of prospects can save time, money, and wear-and-tear on your staff and volunteers. Often, key volunteers with the United Way, symphony, museum, library, or hospital campaigns can be of assistance.

Matching Fundraisers to Prospective Donors

Peer-to-peer fundraising is usually the key to successful arts fundraising, but don't underestimate the power of asking family members to approach other family members, middle managers to make the case to corporate executives or foundation directors, or presidents of companies to request support from the rank-and-file. Oftentimes, finding the right person to "make the ask" is the most important decision to be made in the fundraising process.

Cultivating Potential Donors

In preparing for solicitation of large gifts, it's generally important to cultivate, nurture, and involve the prospect in some aspect of the organization. Inviting potential donors to performances, asking for professional advice related to the institution, involving prospects on board committees, introducing them to key artists or executives, or responding to their interests and community projects are all ways to cultivate a prospect. No one likes to be blindsided, embarrassed, or taken by surprise, and the more a prospect understands the artistic product, needs, and goals of the institution, the more likely the individual will be to contribute.

The Ask and Follow-Up

Finding the right person to ask for a contribution is important, but how the prospect is approached for a gift may be equally important. Again, well-trained fundraisers who understand the breadth of the campaign, the mission of the institution, and the interests of the prospect are the key to success. Often, a board member and a staff member will work together, with the board member providing the peer-to-peer relationship and "ask," and the staff member along to provide information and history about the institution. Each prospect for a major gift should be evaluated in regard to ability to give, interest in your organization, and past professional, philanthropic, and/or community activities.

CONSIDER THIS APPROACH THAT A BOARD MEMBER INITIATES:

Introductions. "Good morning, Bob, and thanks for seeing us today. This is the Magic Theatre's managing director, John Smith, and he's assisting me with my part in the Magic Theatre's fundraising campaign. This campaign is crucial to the theatre's future, and I'm on the board of trustees and one of many volunteers who are committed to helping this theatre succeed. I've contributed significant amounts of time and money to the theatre, and I'm happy to say that we have 100% board participation as contributors. We really value your opinion, and your opinion carries a lot of weight in the San Francisco community. I'd like to tell you about this campaign, what we hope to accomplish, and why I feel it is so important for our community."

[At this point, offer a brief background on the campaign, the theatre, and importance of the theatre to the community.]

Finally, the ask! To quote John D. Rockefeller, "I like for the solicitor to suggest how much it is hoped I will give. I do not like to have anyone tell me what it is my duty to give. There is just one man who is going to decide that question and that is myself. But, I do like for a man to say to me, 'We are trying to raise $4,000,000 and are hoping you may be desirous of giving blank dollars. If you can see your way clear to do so, it will be an enormous help and encouragement. You may have it in your mind to give more, if so, we will be glad. On the other hand, you may feel you cannot give as much, in view of other responsibilities. If that is the case, we shall understand. Whatever you give after thinking the matter over carefully in light of the need, your other obligations, and your desire to do your full share as a citizen, will be gratefully received and deeply appreciated.'"

Anticipate objections and approach them positively and enthusiastically. Mirror the strategies of the best telemarketers. Prepare a script of the most common objections and review them prior to fundraising calls. ("We've already committed all of our donations this year . . . We don't contribute to the arts . . . We only give to education," etc.)

Ask again for a commitment or pledge for the future. A pledge card may be produced and filled out at this point. If you leave with the pledge card, follow up the next day with a thank-you note on behalf of the board and institution. If you don't obtain the pledge card at the meeting, call within seventy-two hours to ascertain the status of the request.

Ongoing Cultivation

Make sure that the next time you visit or contact your donor is not a year later when you are asking for a contribution renewal. In the meantime, each donor should have received a thank-you note, perhaps a personal phone call to say thanks, a season brochure, a priority invitation to a fun party or fundraiser or two, an annual report, an invitation to tour the theatre, a discount pass to the gift shop or special events, a company newsletter, and the warm smiles and appreciation of your fellow fundraisers.

Renewing Contributions

It's all pretty easy if you've accomplished what you promised, followed the advice under "ongoing cultivation," and if the donor's financial circumstances haven't changed significantly. The key is to take nothing for granted, use Rockefeller's approach to attempt to "upgrade the contribution," clarify how last year's contribution assisted the company, and make the ask personally.

BASIC FUNDRAISING VEHICLES

Annual Campaign

Annual campaigns provide the "unearned income" or fundraising dollars that most non-profits use to balance their annual budgets. Annual campaigns may include small gifts, medium-sized gifts, or large gifts. Generally the large gifts are solicited through personal contacts and the base of smaller gifts is secured through direct-mail campaigns and telemarketing (or "friendly phone call") campaigns. Fundraising from community foundations, corporate foundations, family foundations, corporations, businesses, and individuals may all be part of the institution's annual campaign.

Planned Giving

Planned-giving campaigns take advantage of tax-favored giving arrangements that are available to an individual to control taxable income through wills and charitable bequests. These gifts may be gifts of cash, appreciated property, tangible personal property, stocks, life insurance, etc. A planned-giving specialist or a lawyer familiar with tax laws and planned-giving options should be retained to assist in setting up a planned-giving program for non-profit arts organizations. Planned giving is usually associated with major gifts and estate planning.

Capital Campaigns

Capital campaigns are usually conducted by non-profit arts organizations for the purpose of buying land, building new spaces, renovating old spaces, or purchasing major equipment. The campaigns are often billed as "one-time" contributions. The fundraising campaign tends to target large gifts for the majority of the goal, and to create special programs (seat naming, space naming, memorial walls, etc.) to involve the larger community in medium to smaller gifts.

Endowment Campaigns

Endowment campaigns provide a core fund that protects the principal of every contribution while using the majority of the annual interest to supplement the annual budget or special projects. A portion of the annual interest may be used to replenish the principal to ensure that the original dollar value remains stable and accounts for annual inflation. Endowment campaigns tend to target larger gifts, and planned giving is often a major component of endowment campaigns.

To avoid any concerns over "conflicts of interests" in managing endowment funds, many non-profits create a separate board to manage the endowment. Appropriate representation from the institution's board of trustees is usually included on the endowment board.

Fundraisers

In the arts world, the term "fundraisers" applies to people who raise money, as well as to special events (dinners, parties, auctions, etc.). Fundraising events can be an important and potent "friend-raising" and fundraising component of an overall development campaign. Fundraisers are considered extremely labor intensive and must be carefully budgeted and planned. The expenses involved in planning and producing special events can be significant, and there may be a risk of losing money although the intent is to raise money. Some organizations will "invest" money in fundraisers in hopes of nurturing future donors and/or creating new friends, subscribers, or supporters for the organization. In-kind, or donated, services often play a major role in keeping costs down and the community involved in fundraising events.

FUNDRAISING THEORIES

Introduction

At a national gathering of Shakespeare festival leaders assembled at the Tony Award-winning Utah Shakespearean Festival, fundraising consultant Scott W. Hansen of Utah's Clement & Associates offered the following theories of fundraising:

- People give to people.
- Theory of Needs: people give when the benefits are greatest for themselves or those they care about.
- Theory of Wealth: donors make large gifts when circumstances and resources are conducive.
- Theory of Influence: people give when they have experienced the influence of the charity – either personally or by association.
- Theory of Involvement: interest grows as people become involved as active participants in a project.
- Psychology of Giving: giving is an emotional and rational process.
- Law of the Harvest: the best donor is a past donor.

"A theory is something usually murdered by the facts."
Anon

FUNDRAISING MYTHS

A fundraising article in *Contributions* detailed the following fundraising myths:

1) Fundraising is becoming so competitive that the wells of philanthropy will soon run dry.

2) Professional fundraisers are as effective at asking for money as volunteers.

3) A worthy cause will sell itself.

4) Tax deductibility is a prime motivation for giving.

5) You can't raise money in a down economy.

6) All fundraising is altruistically motivated.

7) People who don't like to raise money, won't.

8) Our organization isn't well positioned for a capital campaign because we don't have wealthy board members.

9) In direct mail, you should solicit only one gift a year from donors.

10) Short letters work best; long letters work best.

11) We don't need a feasibility study done by an outsider. We can do it ourselves.

COMMON FUNDRAISING MISTAKES

1) Plunging into a special fundraising event and suffering a double loss: the loss of the original investment to produce the event, and the loss of the budgeted income attributed to the failed "fundraiser."

2) Short-changing the institution by asking for a gift that is too small.

3) Irritating a potential donor by asking for a gift that is too large.

4) Failing to conduct proper research and involve your board of trustees.

5) Declining to set fundraising deadlines, or establishing a timetable that conflicts with other community campaigns.

6) Forgetting to properly orient and train new board members.

7) Operating without the full support and involvement of the board, artistic director, managing director, and key support staff.

8) Establishing a weak case statement or failing to make a strong case.

9) Using volunteers poorly.

10) Beginning without a clear budget, budget controls, and timely reporting mechanisms.

11) Budgeting unrealistic fundraising goals.

A SAMPLE EXECUTIVE OUTLINE OF A STRATEGIC FUNDRAISING PLAN

A. STATEMENT OF FUNDRAISING MISSION, RESOURCES, AND PRIORITIES
For educational, cultural, and historical reasons, [YOUR ORGANIZATION] is firmly committed to [FILL IN YOUR MISSION STATEMENT].
To make this possible and to keep ticket prices reasonable, the board and volunteers will engage in an active fundraising campaign to attract:

> 1) Corporate sponsors;
>
> 2) Business partners;
>
> 3) Foundation support;
>
> 4) Individual patrons and members;
>
> 5) Grants;
>
> 6) Special-events participants;
>
> 7) In-kind services.

Through ongoing personal visits, direct mail, special events, grants efforts, and volunteerism, [YOUR ORGANIZATION] will endeavor to raise [CAMPAIGN AMOUNT] for [SPECIFIC, COMPELLING PROJECTS/ NEEDS/ PROGRAMS]. Community funding will make this possible.

B. STRATEGIC FUNDRAISING PLANNING: RESOURCES AND TOOLS

> 1) Fundraising personnel and advisors
> > a) Your board of trustees
> > b) Your staff
> > c) Your consultants and volunteers
>
> 2) Related fundraising personnel
> > a) Team members that your team captains recruit
> > b) Committed educational partners

    c)   Interested area professionals
    d)   Your company members

3) Volunteers/grass roots sources
    a)   Community volunteers
    b)   Press
    c)   Service clubs
    d)   Arts council friends
    e)   State tourism professionals
    f)   Chamber of Commerce officials
    g)   Business contributors
    h)   The neighborhood
    i)   Friends of all of the above

4) Consultants (volunteer/paid/service)
    a)   Ad agencies
    b)   Professional colleagues
    c)   Professional development agents and agencies
    d)   National arts groups (the Institute of Outdoor
           Drama, Theatre Communications Group, etc.)

5) Linkage-connections of all of the above

6) Institutional tools and resources
    a)   Comprehensive mailing lists, e-mail lists, social
           networking sites
    b)   Testimonials
    c)   Statistics
    d)   Files
    e)   Budget
    f)   Publications (Your own publications and the research that
           can be obtained from names, gift history, and gift ranges
           in other non-profit publications that list donors
           (Symphony/Museum/Dance programs, etc.)
    g)   Photos
    h)   Historical data
    i)   Library
    j)   Display materials

C. FUNDRAISING PERSONNEL AND RESOURCE PRIORITIES

1) Corporate and foundation sponsorships:
Attractive, mutually beneficial opportunities will be presented for "marketing-based fundraising." Through board member and volunteer visits and proposals, ten corporations will have the opportunity to be listed and enjoy the privileges of "Corporate Sponsors."

2) Business partnerships:
In efforts to subsidize student attendance and the multiple educational outreach opportunities, ten businesses will have the opportunity to be listed and receive the perks of "Business Partners."

3) Individual patrons:
Through one-on-one visits and myriad personal outreach efforts (speeches, tours, meetings, presentations), a broad array of residents will be called on to contribute to our programs, outreach, and performance efforts as "Patrons."

4) Special events:
Through a series of informal lunches and special promotions, community patrons will be invited to join us as "Founding Patrons" and "Premiere Supporters."

5) Direct mail:
A timely direct-mail membership campaign will be conducted six months prior to the opening, to offer membership opportunities to as many people as possible.

6) E-mail blasts:
Strong, well-designed e-mail solicitations offer full-color support and easy web-supported donation options. This is a follow-up to direct mail or even a replacement for direct mail for institutions who are concerned with printing and mailing costs and opt for the visual impact of an "e-mail blast."

7) In-kind services:
Every effort will be made to secure pertinent donations of services, materials, housing, advertising, and production resources on an in-kind basis.

8) Press and publication support:
To support the above efforts, appropriate publications, news releases, and public service announcements will be developed to promote community interest and entice broad-based financial support.

9) Friendly phone calls:

With volunteer help, a comprehensive telemarketing follow-up of the above efforts will touch base with the community on an "as appropriate" basis.

D. POSITIONING STATEMENT

[*An exciting statement of where you fit into the community and what makes you unique and worthy of support . . . a mini-case statement that everyone can remember and articulate quickly.*]

FUNDRAISING OBJECTIVES, TARGETS AND GOALS

A. MAJOR FUNDRAISING OBJECTIVES & GOALS

1) Objective:

Design a grass-roots campaign to fundraise for [YOUR ORGANIZATION] using key resources from area data banks and tools from other professional performance venues that have produced results.

Prime targets:
a) Arts and education supporters;
b) Area corporations and businesses with a community conscience;
c) Foundations and businesses desiring to raise their community profiles or improve their images;
d) Individuals interested in investing in the future of the community's youth and quality of life;
e) Cities, societies, organizations, and groups interested in promoting tourism and economic development prospects.

2) Objective:

Create and retain positive local attention for [YOUR ORGANIZATION] while making major efforts to develop a regional reputation that will expand the overall support base for the development of [YOUR ORGANIZATION]'s major performance and "off-season" educational, cultural, and subsidiary events.

3) Sample goal: $200,000

a) Goal: Corporate/foundation sponsorships	$100,000
b) Goal: City/county/government sources	$25,000
c) Goal: Business/corporate partnerships	$25,000
d) Goal: Individual patrons and members	$50,000
e) Goal: Special event "Friend-raisers"	Break even
f) Goal: In-kind service	Already built in as budget subsidy
TOTAL	$200,000

B. SAMPLE FUNDRAISING OVERVIEW

Over the past year, the board of trustees has attended numerous board development and fundraising sessions and has used a national consultant for planning purposes. The board is dedicated to the artistic, cultural, and educational nature of the project, and is committed to producing a production with fiscal integrity. The production budget is skeletal for a professional production, and many volunteer services and donated items will make the professional production possible. In addition, the entire volunteer board has been meeting weekly for several years to plan, organize, secure non-profit status, meet with the community, hire a creative team, reach out to other artistic professionals in the community, seek the counsel of area artistic and tourism personnel, and interview community leaders. All of the board's time has been volunteered, and many in-kind donations and services have been offered and secured by the board, including legal services, marketing services, publications assistance, meeting rooms, and food services.

The board fundraising coordination committee and a professional consultant have thoroughly discussed a fundraising plan and have outlined the plan in the fundraising executive summary. The board has also delineated an overall fundraising process, set fundraising guidelines, and produced fundraising literature for the committee's consideration and approval. The board understands that fundraising is everyone's responsibility and is a crucial aspect of budget fulfilment and season/vision fulfilment on an institutional level. The board embraces the view that non-profit fundraising is challenging, exciting, and worthwhile when the project for which you are fundraising benefits the greater good of the community.

To ensure confidentiality and the appropriate timing, solicitor, and amount of individual fundraising requests, the board has established a prospect list, ratings sheets, fundraising research sheets, and fundraising ledgers. These confidential lists include the prospect name, address, telephone number, and name of person to be contacted; the rating (amount to be requested); and research information that includes any past contributions, advertising history, arts-and-education support history, and any other information that would be pertinent to the solicitation. This list is carefully and confidentially prepared, monitored, coordinated, and used.

Ratings are accomplished by having key board members with a history of area giving trends review the list together and agree on appropriate amounts, the key person to solicit, and any suggestions for solicitors. After prospects are rated, they are divided up among the fundraising team in a fair and equitable manner with clear deadlines, timetables, and reporting requirements. Reporting is bi-monthly to ensure progress is being made and to alert the overall fundraising coordinator to any concerns. The board understands that a set time frame for each aspect of the fundraising campaign is very important.

Regarding corporate sponsorships, foundation grants, and other large gifts, either a development director or the board and volunteers will organize, research, and prepare support materials while soliciting volunteers for team fundraising. The committee chair or development director will organize the forces, arrange the meetings, and, oftentimes, will lead the "ask." The board understands that it is helpful if a team of two board members and a development director meets with the larger givers.

Volunteers will also be prepared to provide any necessary correspondence (letters confirming meetings, thank-you notes following meetings, reports, pledge cards, etc.). Either the fundraising committee chair or a development director will be the "overall point person" in regard to prospects, meetings, etc., to avoid calendar mishaps, duplications of efforts, and prospects "slipping through the cracks."

Raising and giving money to support the vision and mission of this exciting artistic, educational, cultural, historical project should be considered a joint responsibility. Fundraising is also friend-raising, and an opportunity to "tell our story" and "provide the opportunity" for the involvement of as many community members as possible.

> **"Nature is a revelation of God;**
> **Art is a revelation of man."**
> *Henry Wadsworth Longfellow*

CHAPTER 7

Marketing the Arts in the 21st Century

"Everybody gets so much information all day long
that they lose their common sense."
Gertrude Stein

Introduction

Artistic visionaries, brilliant artists, solid management, an able board of trustees, and inspired fundraising are the dream of every institutional planner. Still, without a loyal, committed audience, only half of the performance equation exists. Artists and audiences are the only truly necessary ingredients for performance, and an entire industry has surfaced to chase every leisure-time dollar that the American consumer has available. Can the arts compete with surfing the internet, 300-plus around-the-clock television channels, movies-on-demand at home and in theatre megaplexes, sports, family commitments, and the joy of a quiet novel? You bet! And the tools to compete are now more readily available than ever. The Worldwide Web and your local bookstores are filled with marketing plan profiles, audience-development tools, media advice, market research and case studies that you can apply to your institution.

While an actor and an audience are all it really takes to make a theatre performance, it's your responsibility to rally the troops. In this chapter, I've included some basic tools and a few more hard-learned lessons that you may find helpful.

Overview

This chapter will review:

1) Basic arts marketing terms;

2) Press and media;

3) Job descriptions;

4) Image-building and strategic-planning notes;

5) Nuts-and-bolts staff communications and relations tips;

6) Income and image strategy basics;

7) Marketing on a limited budget;

8) Social networking opportunities and resources;

9) Sample: strategic-marketing planning guide.

Entrepreneur Michael Levine offers an explanation that ties many of these crucial areas together: "People in public relations sometimes use this analogy to explain their craft: When the circus comes to town and you paint a sign about it, that's advertising. Put the sign on the back of an elephant and march him through Beverly Hills, and that's promotion. If the elephant walks through the mayor's flowerbed, that's publicity. And if you can get the mayor to laugh or comment about it, that's public relations."

BASIC ARTS MARKETING TERMS

1) **Marketing**

In the non-profit arts world, the term "marketing" is generally applied to every area of the arts that has to do with "sales;" "earned income;" and building relationships between the institution, ticket sales, and both real and potential customers. This would include all direct and indirect efforts to generate ticket sales, concession sales, parking fees, costume and scenery rentals, building rentals, tour bookings, and a successful market for a host of other earned-income activities.

2) **Audience Development**

Audience development is the process of researching, creating, nurturing, developing, and expanding the base of subscribers and single-ticket buyers for the arts.

3) **Targeting**

Every arts institution would love to "hit the bull's-eye" with each new marketing or audience-development initiative. Targeting is simply the process of directing marketing and audience-development initiatives to specific customers (as opposed to the "shotgun approach" of scattering initiatives over a broad and undefined market base).

4) **Positioning/Branding**

Positioning is the establishment of a unique identity for your institution and artistic product that is instantly recognizable and associated with success, and with an extraordinary or peerless product. In recent years, the term "branding" has become synonymous with positioning.

5) **Packaging**

Packaging is adding pizzazz, opportunities, or value to your overall product by "dressing it up" with desirable options at an exceptional price. For example, a touring production of *The Producers* may be packaged with a luxury suite downtown, dinner for two at a nearby restaurant, and late-night cocktails (all for the price of what the suite would normally cost).

6) **Segmenting**

In arts marketing terminology, segmenting involves dividing your potential audience base into categories based on shared characteristics, interests, or history for the purpose of "tailoring and targeting specific initiatives to specific groups." For example, a marketing plan to boost ticket sales for *West Side Story* might include different direct-mail strategies to approach high school English teachers, university theatre students, Shakespeare enthusiasts, Stephen Sondheim fans, school guidance counsellors, martial arts classes, dance studios, and musical theatre followers.

7) **Publicity**

Informing the public regarding the who, what, where, when, why, and how of productions, educational programs, subscription options, etc., is the main function of a strong arts publicity program. For maximum impact, publicity should have potential news value and be absolutely clear, accurate, and easy to read. Publicity usually implies communications and initiatives that don't involve direct payment, including direct mail, posters, flyers, community speech-making and outreach, special community event displays, etc.

8) **Advertising**

Advertising in the arts usually implies paid announcements in print or electronic media. Free "public service announcements" on television and radio are often available to non-profit organizations, and "sponsored media advertising" involving "free ads" through marketing deals that benefit the co-sponsor are very popular. But most advertising is paid. Advertising vehicles include billboards, banners, magazine ads, Yellow Pages ads, newspaper ads, website ads, radio and television time, movie trailers, store windows, "branded" merchandise giveaways or placement, and the display of logos or production information in virtually any arena.

9) Promotions

Clever, creative, sexy, or sassy promotions often result in a lot of public attention at low-cost or no-cost prices. Special events or happenings can be an important part of an overall public relations and publicity campaign, and don't necessarily require a newsworthy set of circumstances. For example, free radio giveaways, film star visits to the theatre, and the monstrous Audrey II from *Little Shop of Horrors* set up in city hall are all promotional gimmicks that have been successfully used to garner attention for productions or institutions.

10) Public Relations/Social Networking

By combining publicity, advertising, promotion, and many other marketing tools, a strong public relations campaign builds awareness and relationships in the long term and contributes to audience development and sales in more subtle and strategic ways. Social networking through Facebook, Myspace, Linkedin and other websites offer myriad opportunities as reviewed later in this chapter. Also, being a visible community booster, a savvy and truthful media interviewee, a Chamber of Commerce committee member, a supporter of fellow non-profits, an articulate spokesperson for the life-changing power of the arts, or a willing corporate liaison who helps with industrial recruitment by touting the benefits of the community to new recruits and their families – these may all be part of your institutional public relations strategy.

PRESS AND MEDIA

Relationships with newspapers, magazines, television stations, radio stations, websites, and the whole host of print and electronic media now available to arts institutions must be carefully developed, nurtured, and based on honest, credible, objective information. Again, the five Ws (who, what, where, when, and why) are the essential ingredients (especially if you add the one "H" for "how"). Press releases are typed, double-spaced, carefully proofread documents that are tailored to meet the needs of the intended receiver. Include the name and telephone number of the press representative somewhere on the letterhead for easy access. Savvy writers number their pages, write sparkling headlines, leave ample margins, condense information to one to two pages, and end the release with "###," "-30-," or "end."

It's important to understand that the media is *not obliged* to provide space and kind comments to support your artistic events. A professional, assertive, and friendly approach almost always beats commands and demands. Understanding the difference between hard news or a "straight" news story vs. feature articles, editorials, and reviews will help in your communications with the media. Press releases or tip sheets should be objectively written with "just the facts." You can "pitch" subjective articles to feature writers, and your credibility is based on your knowing the difference between objective and subjective information.

Helpful Media Hints

1) Make personal contact. Get up from behind your desk and visit your local newsroom to meet the key players. Develop a friendly, professional relationship.

2) Write follow-up notes thanking the media for their attention . . . good or bad.

3) Call with timely, breaking news and offer your key media a scoop when something really important happens. If you ignore them on stories that interest them, they'll ignore you on stories that are important to you.

4) Research each medium's timetable and submit stories that meet its deadlines, not your standard mailing date.

5) Offer complete calendar listings in the format used for each medium's vehicle. Many writers won't work to dig out your events, dates, ticket prices, and phone number from a long press release or brochure. They'll simply move on to the next very needy non-profit listing.

6) Structure your news releases in "pyramid form," with the most important and all-essential information at the top of the pyramid. If your last paragraph is simply deleted to make the story fit, will your phone number, address, email contacts, and the dates of your event be cut?

7) A picture is truly worth a thousand words when promoting the arts, and your photos should be exciting, riveting, or at least interesting. They should be well lit, offer clear contrast, and look natural (vs. posed). "Cutlines" or captions (who is in the photo and where they are placed, left to right; name of show; name of producing organization; dates of show; telephone number or web address for follow-up; name of photographer) must be included!

8) Don't "sell" the same feature idea to two competing newspapers or send competitors exactly the same photographs.

9) Use electronic means to send press materials, photographs or graphics, and identify your photos with captions and detail all the basic information that should be included.

> "Newspapers have degenerated.
> They may now be absolutely relied upon."
> *Oscar Wilde*

JOB DESCRIPTIONS

Director of Marketing

The individual in charge of all earned-income initiatives. Directs market research; creates marketing plans; hires all marketing-related staff; recommends income goals; supervises key staff; collaborates with development/fundraising efforts in communications, publications, website development/maintenance, and image building; and is responsible for meeting budgeted goals. Reports to the managing director.

Director of Audience Development

The individual responsible for earned-income initiatives related to subscription sales, single-ticket sales, group sales, and all other efforts to maximize the customer base for productions and special events. Reports to the director of marketing.

Director of Publications

The individual in charge of all sales brochures, show programs, fundraising brochures, annual reports, and informational brochures. Oftentimes, this person also supervises the institution's website and photography. Reports to the director of marketing and works closely with all senior staff to facilitate accuracy.

Director of Press and Public Relations

This individual plans, initiates and coordinates the media plan and the communication of press releases, public-service announcements, media relations and photography needs. He or she is often the designated institutional representative who responds to media inquiries, conducting or coordinating media interviews with company members. They often assist with writing assignments related to advertising, publications and web-communications. Reports to the director of marketing.

Sales Manager

This ambitious go-getter directs specific earned-income initiatives related to audience development and marketing as needed. Depending on the organization's product and the marketing timetable, the sales manager may focus on web-based social networking initiatives, telemarketing, group sales, class tuition/fees, gift shop merchandising, subscription promotions, or a number of other projects. Reports to the director of marketing or the director of audience development as needed.

Group Sales Manager

This persuasive self-starter matches specific community groups (religious, educational, cultural, recreational, etc.) with specific productions and programs, and aims for sales of entire performances or large groups of customers. The group sales manager often uses the promise of lower ticket prices, good seats, educational materials, teacher training, and personalized visits and tours to close the sale. Reports to the director of audience development.

Telemarketing Manager

This employee-training specialist is charged with successfully implementing a high-powered program involving teams of paid professionals and/or volunteers who make "friendly phone calls" to customers and potential customers in hopes of converting single-ticket buyers into subscribers, creating new attendees, and, in what is usually a separate campaign, transforming audience members into donors as part of the fundraising campaign. Reports to the director of audience development for seat sales and to the director of development for contribution solicitations.

Box Office Manager

The box office manager recruits, orients, and trains the box office staff involved in daily communications, public relations, marketing, financial transactions, and accounting of all ticket sales. In many non-profit arts organizations, this individual reports to the director of finance, as a significant portion of the institution's budgeted income flows through the box office. Although it's crucial for the box office to have absolute financial integrity, organization, and supervision (provided by the director of finance), because the box office is crucial as a centre of front-line customer service, the director of marketing or the director of audience development should have a firm hand in the training, organization, evaluation, and day-to-day supervision of the box office.

Director of Education

The director of education usually has split responsibilities on the artistic and management side of the theatre. Artistically, the director of education needs to make sure that all educational initiatives are in line with the artistic mission and goals of the theatre, and that the artistic director is involved in and/or signs off on all artistic decisions. On the management side, the director of education assists in attracting new audiences, nurturing all audiences, and adding to the bottom line of earned income development. Reports to the artistic director and the managing director/ director of audience development.

SOCIAL NETWORKING AND THE ARTS

Introduction

Economic realities and internet opportunities have revolutionized longstanding audience development and marketing planning, publications, processes, staffing and budgets. With the rising costs of postage and paper, season brochure and single ticket mailings are often replaced by e-mail "blasts," electronic newsletters, Facebook reminders, and postings on various social networking sites. With Facebook more than halfway to a *billion* members, many theatres are finally recognizing that social networking sites are a marketing force that cannot be ignored.

In the not so recent past, company members were asked to share their address books and friend, relative and colleague business cards with theatres in order to develop a "mailing list." Today, friends of the theatre are asked to share their Twitter accounts, Facebook space, MySpace network, LinkedIn contacts and other social networks in hopes of exponentially compounding the number of "personal" appeals and stretching the reach of theatres who couldn't hope to make contact with so many potential patrons through "old-fashioned traditional tools" of the theatre trade. In a recent e-mail column, *Noises and Tweets, American Theatre*'s Rob Weinert-Kendt, notes that "some minds were blown by Devon V. Smith's timely and practical breakout session" at a Theatre Communications Group (TCG) conference. He reports that eleven TCG member theatres have more than 2,000 followers on Twitter, and four TCG theatres have more than 10,000 fans on Facebook. "The excuse that, 'Well, my audience members aren't on Facebook,' doesn't work anymore," cajoles Smith. "These aren't college students...both of my parents are on Facebook."

With the ability to reach so many people through electronic communications, it's important to remind ourselves that matching the right audience to the right plays and developing audience of "substance" is strategically more important than simply developing audience of "size." We sometimes forget that season subscriptions were originally developed for artistic reasons – to encourage, challenge and develop audiences for less "marketable" productions and spread audiences out over an entire season.

It's easy to churn out slick, mind-numbing "PR" that puts a positive, oftentimes misrepresentative spin on both new plays and classic theatre. However, the glow of the larger-than-usual opening night audience is quickly dimmed by dissatisfied, disappointed theatre patrons who feel that they didn't "get what they paid for" and were misled by the theatre's sales materials. Restaurant owners often talk about how a satisfied diner will tell two or three of their friends about their great meal while an unhappy diner will "tell the world." The same is true of theatre patrons.

Many of these concerns and initiatives are discussed and debated by professionals on the internet, and the technological boundaries of these audience development and marketing opportunities are shifting so rapidly that it seems best to share websites that blend "cutting edge" solutions, practical tips and entrepreneurial thinking that will keep you appraised of the latest in arts marketing strategies.

Tips on creating website trust and traffic, generating brand buzz, creating links, and developing customer loyalty may be found on the following ten websites.

www.artsmarketing.org

This marvelous website of the National Arts Marketing Project, provides information, tools, and practical ideas to design high-quality, cost-effective marketing programs and strengthen arts organizations. The National Arts Marketing Project also hosts an annual conference, organizes regional training programs, and provides on-site workshops on a range of arts marketing topics. ArtsMarketing.org and the National Arts Marketing Project are managed by the Arts & Business Council of Americans for the Arts, and were developed with support from American Express Company.

http://arts-marketing.blogspot.com

This arts marketing blog features savvy, strategic discussions on wide-ranging arts marketing issues and processes with some of the best marketing minds of the non-profit theatre world weighing in.

ww.artsjournal.com/diacritical/2009/05/power-in-numbers-there-ought.html

Read Douglas McLennan's blog on the *ArtsJournal* site referenced above for *10 Ways to Think About Social Networking And The Arts* and you'll be all the wiser on the how to get started and make true connections. He talks about the reach, power, investment, rewards, fickleness and consistent work that needs to be accomplished to develop, maintain and build an online community.

www.nytimes.com/allbusiness/AB11702023_primary.html?ref=smallbusiness

This "How to Use Social Networking Sites for Marketing and PR" is a nice primer for planners and is an ongoing reminder of how useful *The New York Times* Business Sections can be for arts planning.

www.labforculture.org

In its own words, LabforCulture works "with and for artists, arts and culture organizations and networks, cultural professionals and audiences in the 50 countries of Europe, as well as providing a platform for cultural cooperation between Europe and the rest of the world."

www.technologyinthearts.org

Worthwhile articles on "Building Audience Diversity Through Social Networking" and much more may be found courtesy of Carnegie Mellon University on this *Technology in the Arts* website that explores the intersection of arts management and online technology through blogs, podcasts and workshops.

www.websitemarketingplan.com/online/socialnetworking.htm

Bobette Kyle has a straightforward, down-to-earth website with at least two marvelously clear and instructive overviews on social networking.

www.artsconsulting.com

President Bruce D. Thibodeau and the team at the Arts Consulting Group graciously e-mail timely "Arts Insights" articles and post the historical articles on their website to share with companies and boards of trustees. Topics include everything from branding and social networking to research, trends and strategic planning in the arts.

http://hootsuite.com

HootSuite offers a social media dashboard "for teams using Twitter, Facebook and LinkedIn" and is designed to "save your time and save your sanity" by managing "multiple social networks through one client."

www.openforum.com/idea-hub/topics/technology/article/how-to-get-the-most-out-of-social-media-using-hootsuite-zachary-sniderman

Finally, Zachary Sniderman's article on the American Express Small Business website provides a number of useful links related to Twitter, Facebook, WordPress, LinkedIn, HootSuite, Foursquare, TweetDeck, SocialTalk, Radian6, Seesmic, CoTweet and other social networking tools that may prove useful.

IMAGE BUILDING AND STRATEGIC PLANNING NOTES

1) Work to improve all publications to reflect the desired professional quality and image of the "new and improved" operation.

2) Consider your institution's professional image regarding:

> Hiring;
>
> Personal grooming;
>
> Signage;
>
> All contact with the public (phones, e-mail, correspondence, front-of-house operations, community meetings, etc.).

3) Maintain professional conduct and upkeep regarding:

> Office organization;
>
> Company housing;
>
> Support spaces;

Vehicle use and maintenance;

Parking lots;

Entryways;

Restrooms;

All areas used by public.

4) Evaluate the design, printing (or web-based electronic initiatives), and dissemination of all publications, websites, blogs, e-mail blasts, press releases, and other positive statements about your institution regarding potential audience and public relations targets outside of the originally intended market.

5) Create opportunities for public relations and long-range marketing, and discuss them with the marketing director and director of public relations to ascertain feasibility and overall impact.

6) Develop guidelines within your own area that will help you communicate and relate your institution's overall objectives to employees, interns, and volunteers who work within the area you supervise.

7) Proofread all correspondence to ensure professional quality of all letters, grants, reports, websites, etc. Have a co-worker do a final quality review of all work that goes outside the office or is posted anywhere electronically.

NUTS-AND-BOLTS STAFF COMMUNICATIONS AND RELATIONS TIPS

1) Copy and distribute, post, or otherwise circulate data, correspondence, or other internal or external information that relates to staff members in other areas. This may also be communicated appropriately in staff meetings or via e-mail, website postings, electronic bulletin boards, etc.

2) Know the difference between cc's and bc's in correspondence, and use appropriately. Always consider "carbon-copying" someone whose name you use in a correspondence or report. Consider ethical, legal, and personnel guidelines.

3) Support administrative decisions, policy, and personnel both publicly and privately within the organization. Support is essential. Staff meetings or individual sessions with your supervisor, or, when appropriate, with executive staff, are the two channels for expressing concerns or qualms about institutional policy and decision-making.

4) Grievances within individual areas should be handled in the following manner:

a) The individual with the grievance discusses the concern with the person with whom he or she has the grievance;

b) If the grievance remains unresolved, the area head is asked to mediate with both parties present. If the grievance involves the area head, the matter is referred to the appropriate supervisor (usually the managing director) for mediation.

5) Organize materials and prepare for staff meetings and individual meetings with personnel in efforts to make the best use of fellow staff members' time and energy. Advance notice of meetings with clear agendas is strongly encouraged.

6) Restrict personal business, phone calls, emails, social networking, office visits, and noise to allow for the efficient use of office time for all employees. Advance notice of large "in-house" meetings involving outside parties (volunteer work sessions, etc.) is strongly encouraged.

7) Keep personal belongings and professional work within your work area. Temporary projects involving additional workspace should be coordinated with your supervisor.

8) Consider registering with your supervisor time spent out of the office during normal working hours. State departure time (rather than appointment time), destination, number where you may be reached, and approximate time you will return to the office.

9) Date all correspondence and keep carefully organized files for your area.

10) Prepare a "Handbook for Your Area" for emergency purposes. This handbook would include:

   a)   Long-range strategies;
   b)   Day-to-day working processes;
   c)   Telephone, address, and e-mail directory of key contacts;
   d)   Working budget and ledger samples;
   e)   Sample correspondence;
   f)   A guide to your computer files;
   g)   An index of your working paper files;
   h)   Anything else that would help your replacement.

> "*Before* you criticize someone, walk a mile in their shoes.
> That way, when you criticize them, you're a mile away,
> and you have their shoes."
> Ann Brashares

INCOME AND IMAGE STRATEGY BASICS

1) Develop and maintain accurate files and mailing lists (electronic and postal) for use within the organization. Mailing lists are the heart of income development.

2) Clearly articulate and separate marketing and development responsibilities and efforts, and carefully coordinate the areas and tasks that obviously link both areas.

3) Encourage and request public relations assistance, communication, and support internally and externally. Ask the board, actors, staff, and crafts-people for their help. Ask vendors, tourism officials, city personnel, educators, and others for their specific assistance.

4) Coordinate efforts with all public institutions and work as a clearinghouse for your institution's contact with the public.

5) Develop audiences and contributors who will assist your institution in meeting its artistic and administrative goals and objectives.

6) Clearly report (through planning notes, samples, evaluations, etc.) in a manner that may be easily integrated into staff and board correspondence.

7) In a timely manner, track down and circulate to the executive staff pertinent stories about your institution (news stories, reviews, features, editorials, etc.).

8) Distribute copies of all of your institution's news releases to the artistic director and managing director (as appropriate) prior to release.

MARKETING ON A LIMITED BUDGET

Every long-time CEO, managing director, marketing director, and publicity manager has a long list of favorite "low-cost, no-cost" tricks for publicizing events. Here are ten proven tips that have been worth their weight in gold for non-profit marketers:

1) With direct-mail costs skyrocketing, let someone else pay the postage for you! Negotiate with your gas company, electric company, water company, phone provider, cellular providers, and mortgage companies to include your season in their newsletters and on their websites or to simply pop in a brochure with their bills;

2) Buy inexpensive poster frames from the mall, Target, or K-Mart, and ask local businesses with a lot of public traffic to hang your posters in their waiting areas;

3) Disguise theatre coupons as bookmarks and distribute in area libraries, bookstores, and schools;

4) Distribute great color and black-and-white photos to area corporations, government agencies and businesses, and encourage them to use your action shots on the covers of their annual reports, telephone books, employee handbooks, etc.;

5) Ask your local banks to put your coupons on their drive-through teller envelopes or on their websites and in their mailings;

6) Negotiate with your regional soft drink bottling companies to put your season and/or coupons on their liter bottle labels and twelve-pack cartons;

7) Buy cheap brochure racks at Staples or Wal-Mart and ask area hotels, realtors, and restaurants to display the racks in their public areas;

8) Provide fluorescent orange directional maps to your theatre to all area gas stations and convenience stores, for patrons searching for your theatre;

9) Visit with your local Kiwanis, Rotary, Sertoma, YMCA, and other service clubs, and encourage them to book an annual theatre party in your theatre;

10) Use the internet to market your theatre and to target specific audiences without the high cost of direct mail and telemarketing.

TWO AUDIENCE DEVELOPMENT TOOLS FOR STRATEGIC PLANNING AND GOAL SETTING

It is crucial for arts institutions to have an ongoing, always-ready-to-update "Audience Development Strategic Plan" and "Annual Marketing Plan" in place to maximize board resources; to guide staff activities; to document the institution's planning integrity for donors, sponsors, and grant officers; and to use as a base of ongoing evaluation.

The "Outline for Strategic Planning and Nuts-and-Bolts Marketing" offers a process for conducting an analysis of your institution's resources and priorities, and the executive summary of a "Sample Marketing Plan" provides a check-off sheet that demonstrates how the strategic planning process might translate into specific goals, objectives, and sales initiatives.

OUTLINE FOR STRATEGIC PLANNING AND NUTS-AND-BOLTS MARKETING

A. OVERVIEW

Your institutional mission statement goes here.

B. POSITIONING/BRANDING STATEMENT

A clear, substantive statement clarifying your unique position in the community and the impact you have on your community.

C. STATEMENT OF AUDIENCE DEVELOPMENT MISSION AND PHILOSOPHY

Based on the overall institutional mission, this statement articulates your audience-development and outreach philosophy, how you perceive your audience, and how you plan to introduce, retain, or "capture" it for your institution.

D. GENERAL AUDIENCE DEVELOPMENT OBJECTIVES SAMPLE

1) Establish [YOUR INSTITUTION] as an enjoyable, exciting, annual, not-to-be-missed entertainment event or series of programs;

2) Establish art/music/theatre/dance as an important cultural entertainment option in the lives of [YOUR INSTITUTION'S AREA] students and adult residents;

3) Encourage travellers to spend twenty-four to seventy-two hours in your city by packaging attractions and accommodations;

4) Capitalize on the appeal of your city and other area attractions by [?];

5) Clearly communicate *all* of [YOUR INSTITUTION'S] activities to the public, including public service, economic impact, artistic, educational, cultural, historical testimonials, etc.;

6) Recognize and capitalize on opportunities for local, regional, and national exposure.

E. STRATEGIC AUDIENCE-DEVELOPMENT PLANNING: RESOURCES AND TOOLS

1) Your board of directors

2) Related organizations
    a) Tourism professionals
    b) Resorts, convention/visitors' bureau
    c) Other non-profit organizations
    d) Service clubs (Rotary, Kiwanis, etc.)
    e) State tourism professionals
    f) Chamber of Commerce officials
    g) Colleges/universities/high schools, etc.
    h) Military organizations
    i) Area arts professionals

3) Media: newspapers, radio, television, internet, etc.

4) Consultants (volunteer/paid/service)
   a)   Management consultants
   b)   Ad agencies
   c)   Professional colleagues
   d)   Professional development agents and agencies
   e)   National arts groups (Institute of Outdoor Drama, Theatre Communications Group, etc.)

5) Tools and resources
   a)   Comprehensive, segmented mailing lists of subscribers, single ticket buyers and others;
   b)   Social networking sites
   c)   E-mail blasts
   d)   Publications
   e)   Testimonials
   f)   Historical documents
   g)   Photos/videos
   h)   Statistics
   i)   Library
   j)   Display materials

F.   AUDIENCE-DEVELOPMENT PERSONNEL, FINANCIAL, AND RESOURCE PRIORITIES

1)   Personal outreach: speeches, tours, visitations, meetings, presentations, dinners, parties, and special promotions;

2)   Educational and cultural outreach: ongoing programs that are accessible to the public and broaden the enrichment value of [YOUR INSTITUTION'S] performance experience;

3)   Publications, news releases, public service announcements, and direct-mail solicitations;

4)   Telemarketing follow-up on the above;

5)   Networking with area hotels, attractions, Chambers of Commerce, tourism and travel agencies, travel councils, and city officials throughout your community;

6)   Media development: reviews, features, special promotions;

7)   Advertising;

8)   Special promotions during major events: local school events, area school meetings, cultural events, arts festivals, etc.

SAMPLE MARKETING PLAN

I. Major Marketing Objectives and Goals

A. Design a grass-roots campaign to market [YOUR INSTITUTION'S] services, programs, and productions using statistical and demographic data from past audience research, and/or key resources from area data banks, and tools from other professional performance venues that have produced results.

1) Sample goal: 3,000 subscriptions and 10,000 single tickets;

2) Prime target areas:
    a) 10-mile radius of [YOUR INSTITUTION];
    b) Past patrons.

B. Retain positive local attention for [YOUR INSTITUTION] while making major efforts to develop a regional reputation that will help in expanding the overall support base for the development of [YOUR INSTITUTION'S] major performances and "off-season" educational, cultural, and historical events.

1) Goal: 60 news stories or prominent social networking space placements in the next fiscal year;

2) Goal: 20 photographs in local/regional media and 20 prominent web-based photograph placements in the next fiscal year;

3) Goal: One regional speaking engagement per month in the next fiscal year;

4) Goal: 25 appearances at high school, college, area arts or community meetings in the next fiscal year;

5) Goal: 12 community service contacts by company members for worthwhile local causes in the next fiscal year;

6) Goal: 15 written testimonials from community, regional, or national leaders in the next fiscal year.

II. Marketing Plans

A. TICKET SALES

1) Single-ticket drive

a) Direct-mail campaign all available lists
   • Past audience and contributor lists

- Mass mailer from all captured lists
- Hotel, motel, welcome center mailer
- Phone bills/gas bills/water bills/city mailings

b) Telemarketing campaign

c) Mass media campaign
- Print
- Radio
- Television
- Social networking sites/e-mail blasts

d) Grass-roots campaign
- Board of directors
- Volunteer groups
- Staff and artists

e) Special promotions
- Banks/fast food/hotel/retailer tie-ins
- Historical parties/fundraisers/events

2) Group and corporate sales

a) Mail campaign and volunteer visitations
- Letter
- Brochure/e-mail/website initiatives
- Volunteer visitation follow-ups

b) Speaking engagements
- Clubs and organizations
- Area arts groups
- Area high schools, junior high schools, colleges, universities

c) Networking campaign
- Area arts councils and city committees
- Chambers of Commerce
- City/county tourism and historical societies
- State tourism and travel agencies

3) Student ticket programs

a) City proclamations of support
b) Corporate subsidy support
c) Special teacher incentives
d) Student study packets

B. LOCAL, STATEWIDE, AND NATIONAL ATTENTION

1) Actor and scholar outreach programs in the schools

2) Guest artists and speakers program

3) National organizations and publications
    a) Participation and membership
    b) As host

4) Special promotions
    a) Fundraisers
    b) Speaking engagements
    c) Travelling displays
    d) Opening festivities with honored guests
    e) Hand distributions
    f) Taped testimonials

5) Solicit testimonials of support

6) Volunteer your support for worthwhile community activities and encourage board members to volunteer their time and special skills in the name of [YOUR INSTITUTION].

TIMELY THEATRE ETIQUETTE TIDBITS

Robert Redford notes that "A lot of what acting is is paying attention," and the same is true for actors, directors, craftspeople, administrators and all theatre folks attending rehearsals and performances. Audience members at a live theatre and dance event are also expected to show common courtesy and respect for their fellow audience members who have invested time, energy (and usually a significant amount of money) to attend the production.

On a recent trip to Boston (that included meetings with artistic directors, marketing directors and production directors), innovative approaches to allowing cell phone calls and text-messaging in theatres "so people can call their friends during the production and tell them how great it is" were discussed and debated! "It's the wave of the future if we want young people in the theatre," cajoled one participant. "Who wants them in the theatre if they disturb the production?" countered a concerned producer. "They can be A PART OF the production experience," offered a third attendee. "I don't want them to be a part of my Chekhov, Ibsen or Tony Kushner production," grumbled an unhappy director.

Be that as it may, be ready for these discussions in the future and know that, as an audience member, you really can influence a show. In the meantime, be a brilliant and attentive audience member and you will often find that actors, dancers and other performers will reward you with their very best performance. Here are Twelve Timely Etiquette Tips to modify and/or pass on to your friends, audience members, or school groups as you deem appropriate:

CHECK YOUR TICKETS WHEN YOU PURCHASE THEM! First of all, purchase tickets well in advance, as many performances sell out! Make sure you know exactly when the show starts, where you are going to park, which theatre the production is in, and the date printed on your ticket before you leave the box office window so that you will always . . .

BE ON TIME FOR EVERY PRODUCTION. Many theatres will not seat latecomers until intermission, as they disrupt the live theatre production, perturb patrons who arrived on time, and threaten the overall artistic product and the audience experience. Allow ample time for parking, traffic, picking up tickets, etc.

RETURN TO THE STONE AGE BEFORE YOU STEP INTO THE THEATRE. Turn off all beepers, cell phones, watch chimes, CD/MP3 players, iPods, laptops, Gameboys and any other electronic gadgets in your possession, and unwrap candy in noisy wrappers before you enter the theatre! Don't even think about shaking out tic-tacs, texting, sneaking in Happy Meals, eating and drinking, or digging into your backpack or shopping bags during a performance!

STOW YOUR KEYS, PROGRAMS, COATS, HATS, PURSES, BOOKS AND OTHER PERSONAL ITEMS BEFORE THE LIGHTS DIM FOR THE PRODUCTION! These items belong under your seat or in the coatroom where they won't be stepped on or tripped over by patrons exiting during the intermission. (One exception: It's ok to slide these items out to trip latecomers who are climbing over you during a pivotal dramatic scene!)

QUIET PLEASE (UNLESS YOU ARE LAUGHING, REACTING, OR CLAPPING IN AN APPROPRIATE MANNER FOR THE ACTORS). This means waiting until intermission to explain the plot or missed lines to your companion and keeping the humming and song lyrics in your head (no matter HOW MUCH you loooove that song)!

NO CAMERAS, TAPE RECORDERS AND CAMCORDERS. These are dangerous and distracting for actors and dancers on stage. Oh, yes, it also drives audience members crazy! Finally, copyright laws absolutely forbid recording or taking photos of most plays and productions.

WE LOVE CHILDREN BUT UNLESS THEY ARE QUIETLY ENGAGED IN THE PRODUCTION, THEY SHOULD NOT BE IN THE THEATRE. Wiggling, giggling, and even sleeping children are a distraction to other theatregoers. If they are engaged, happy patrons who behave appropriately – we love them (and you) for creating future audiences!

NOW IS THE TIME TO MAKE SOME NOISE! At a musical or opera, it is customary for audiences to acknowledge the entrance of the conductor with applause. Oftentimes, this custom also carries over into applause for the curtain rising to reveal brilliant scenery, costumes or a "star performer" in a play or production.

TURN OFF YOUR FLASHLIGHT! WATCH NOW, TAKE NOTES LATER. We understand you want to do a good job on that school report or critical review but scribble down your notes during the intermission and after the play. Even the smallest penlights are distracting to fellow theatregoers and actors on stage. Go to the library and check out the script if you need to write down actual dialogue – no one wants a "blow by blow" description of the play's minutiae while you are missing the crucial themes, overall plot, and major character moments because you are staring at your lap (or laptop)!

NO MISCELLANEOUS CRAZINESS! Of course, it should go without saying that it's important to stay off the stage. Never put anything on the stage; keep your feet off all the seats; and keep your hands off of other people's seats. Be gentle with perfume and cologne – many patrons are allergic. Smoking is not permitted inside or anywhere near many theatres or state buildings.

IT'S ALMOST OVER! Please stay in your seat until the curtain call is over, as a show of courtesy to the actors and respect for your fellow theatregoers. They deserve to show their appreciation without being trampled and/or distracted by rude people who can't wait an average of 180 seconds for the house lights to rise and signal that it's now appropriate to leave the theatre.

IT AIN'T OVER TIL WE SAY IT'S OVER! Most theatres reserve the right to refuse admission or remove individuals who disrupt the audience's enjoyment of productions that they have worked so hard to prepare for the cultural, social, and entertainment value of their many kind patrons who honor the theatre with their presence. I was recently escorted from a Broadway theatre for having the audacity to bring my next day's breakfast (a croissant) in a small bag into the theatre and refusing to discard it in the trash. Theatre etiquette certainly works both ways and a good dose of mutual respect always goes a long way!

> *"Never confuse motion with action."*
> Ernest Hemingway

CHAPTER 8

Budgeting and Financial Management

"Long-range planning does not deal with future decisions,
but with the future of present decisions."
Peter F. Drucker

BUDGET BASICS: A TO Z

1) Protect your institution and live up to the confidence that the city, county, state, and federal governments; patrons; contributors; and board members place in your arts institution.

2) When in doubt about budgetary decisions, personnel decisions, and other crucial choices, ask, "What is in the best interest of my institution as a whole?" vs. "What's in my personal best interest?" or "What is in my specific area's best interest?" If in doubt, bring it to your board, lawyer, or other trusted colleague.

3) Spend your institution's money with the same care as if it were coming from your personal savings account. Consider the budget as a roadmap that guides you from day to day. Consult it, follow it, and revise it as necessary.

4) Project your expenses based on realistic research and planning aimed at creating the best possible product with the available resources. Project your income based on careful estimates of past fundraising, ticket sales, and other income sources. Involve the experts in budgeting! This would include front-lines staff and the individuals who lead each area year to year.

5) Conduct annual financial analyses of other similar theatre budgets to determine feasibility, competitiveness, and financial trends.

6) In many arts institutions, once annual budgets are set "the button is pushed," and it is extremely difficult to trim budgets and react to expense overruns or income problems within that fiscal year. This is especially true given the labor intensive nature of the arts, the fact that most expenses are incurred early in the season, and that income is based on delivery of the artistic product. Therefore, careful analysis of the initial budget is crucial.

7) Take calculated risks to maximize artistic product and services based on the best available research, information, planning, and board-staff consensus.

8) Endeavor never to spend money before you have earned it. For example, don't spend *next year's* season-ticket income on *this year's* season expenses, and don't spend all of the contributions intended as long-term pledges in the year they are pledged, etc.

9) Always maintain professional integrity, but defer paying expenses as long as possible to protect working capital and a positive cash flow.

10) Never "borrow" from the expense accounts of future shows to cover overrun production expenses from earlier shows.

11) Don't budget, spend, or trim the same dollar twice. Give yourself plenty of time to research and prepare the budget!

12) Every budget line should be reviewed and scrutinized to ensure maximum productivity each year. Plan for problems and allocate money for contingencies.

13) An employee handbook detailing policy, employment guidelines, expectations, and procedures should be developed by the current administration and issued as a rider to every employee's contract.

14) Keep aware of all collective-bargaining agreements that impact your organisation, such as those of Actors' Equity Association, the Stage Directors and Choreographers Society, and United Scenic Artists. Generally, collective bargaining agreements lock your institution into specific minimum wages and relatively high benefit packages that may include housing, transportation, per diem, pension, welfare, and/or other conditions.

15) The artistic director and the managing director are typically directly responsible to the board of directors for maintaining the integrity of the budget. In reality, in larger organizations, the general manager assumes general responsibility for the day-to-day control of the expense budget, while the managing director monitors the overall budget and plans with the upper-level staff through monthly reports and variance analyses. In many arts organizations, only the managing director and the general manager are

permitted by the board of directors to authorize purchases, sign checks, or commit the institution to contracts. The managing director and the general manager often co-sign all checks over $2,500 as an additional safeguard. A board's exception to this general policy may be checks written between accounts (e.g., transferring money from a bank savings account into a bank payroll account to pay weekly salaries).

16) It is recommended that stock contributions generally be traded immediately except in cases where the arts institution endeavors to follow the instructions of the donor.

17) An independent auditing team should examine the institution's balance sheets and related statements of activity, entity capital, and changes in financial position, annually. The examinations must be made in accordance with generally accepted auditing standards.

18) The board of directors, executive staff, and upper-level staff are involved in budget planning and approval. The staff recommends to the finance committee, which recommends to the board of directors. Upper-level staff members should seek input from their teams or company members. Salaries for the executive staff (artistic director and managing director) are set by the board or by an ad hoc committee usually composed of the chairman of the board and a key member of the finance committee. All other salaries are set by the managing director and artistic director in consultation with the appropriate staff members. The board approves the overall package, and has access to all salaries on request.

19) Endeavor to hire quality personnel at competitive salaries in an effort to retain experienced employees for longer periods of time.

20) Personnel contracts are often negotiated on a show-by-show, seasonal, or annual basis by either the managing director or an upper-level staff member as appropriate. Due care is always exercised in regard to maintaining and protecting the ongoing efficiency of the operation without tying the institution to long-term contracts that could prove disastrous in difficult financial times.

21) Subsidiary areas of the budget relate to events or projects that are organized and approved individually *after* the overall budget has been approved.

22) Entry into the specific subsidiary project is often determined by a firm consensus of the executive staff, after the project has been carefully organized by the individual(s) proposing the project, and after the income and expense budget has been reviewed and accepted by the key financial personnel involved.

23) As a general rule, subsidiary projects are designed to either make money or break even.

24) Subsidiary projects must not endanger the core work, mission, goals, and responsibilities of the arts institution or its staff. In the end, the final income and expenses of each project are reviewed, and the project is evaluated.

25) Related financial/personnel documents to consider include:
   a) The company personnel handbook;
   b) All contracts and letters of agreement;
   c) All benefit packages and commitments.

26) Be conservative in estimating income, exercise a "worst case scenario" attitude when budgeting expenses, and plan for contingencies.

SUMMARY OF STANDARD THEATRE FINANCIAL TERMINOLOGY AND PROCESSES

Introduction

Hundreds of financial guidebooks and computer programs are available to help your institution organize your financial accounting, business management, budgeting processes, and overall reporting systems. It's also a good idea to include at least one accountant, business manager, lawyer, benefit specialist, and/or overall financial expert on your board of trustees to assist with pro bono guidance as needed.

This book won't attempt to replace these tools and people, but this section will provide some of the basic terminology and standard practices of theatre business offices.

Terminology: A To Z

Accounts Receivable: The amount due from customers – subscribers, ticket buyers, gift shop sales, etc.

Accounts Payable: The amount owed by the institution to individuals, vendors, creditors, etc.

Accrual Basis Accounting: Realizes income when it is earned vs. when it is received, and expenses when they are incurred vs. when they are discharged.

Cash Basis Accounting: Realizes income when it is received and expenses when they are paid.

Balanced Budget: A budget projection with an exact match of income and expenses. Also used loosely to indicate past budgets or financial reports where income exceeds expenses.

Balance Sheet: The report detailing the assets, liabilities, and fund balances of the institution as it stands on one particular day (e.g., the end of the fiscal year).

Capital Budget: Generally involves one-time expenses for "bricks-and-mortar" building expenses, purchases of property, or major equipment.

Cash Flow: Availability of cash and the balance of income and expense on a month-to-month basis.

Comparative Budget Analysis: A financial tool that involves analyzing budgets by comparing them to historical budgets in your own institution, similar budgets of other non-profit organizations, and/or line-by-line expense audits based on actual market-based prices prior to approving the budget. This procedure should also be used to periodically compare the budget to actual expenses during the fiscal year.

Current Assets: Cash and any assets (marketable securities, accounts receivable, etc.) which could be turned into cash within a reasonable period of time (e.g., within a year).

Deficit Spending: Spending funds in excess of income.

Earned Income: Income earned as a result of specific programs, goods, or services, such as single-ticket sales, subscription sales, concession sales, class tuition, parking, coat checks, program sales, ad revenues, and costume rentals. Earned income is the opposite of unearned or contributed income.

Incremental Budgeting: Begins with the past year's budget, projecting overall income estimates, and providing adjustments to the expense and income budget based on these estimates (usually allowing for percentage-based inflationary increases).

Invoice: An itemized, dated bill detailing goods purchased or services provided and the charges and terms of the billing.

Notes Payable: Money owed by the institution to lenders, including banks, individuals, and corporations.

Operating Budget: Ongoing estimated expenses and revenues for a fiscal year or another specifically defined period of time.

Pro Bono: Latin phrase, "for good," usually meaning a service provided without charge as a contribution to the public good or welfare.

Purchase Order: A budget-control form used to approve the purchase of goods or services.

Requisition: A written request, order, or form for specific goods or services. Usually a requirement for budget-control systems in the arts.

Unearned Income: Contributions, grants, endowments, etc., given to the institution as a gift or as support with philanthropic intent, including annual campaign gifts, corporate donations, government grants, foundation grants, planned gifts, and endowment funds, as well as fundraiser/special event donations (minus the cost of any goods or services provided at the event).

Working Capital: The difference between total current assets and total current liabilities.

Zero-based Budgeting: Start-from-scratch budgeting! History may be taken into consideration, but every dollar must be justified for each budget period.

SAMPLE BUSINESS OFFICE PROCEDURES

Purchase Orders

[THE THEATRE] uses a "Purchase Order" (P.O.) system to monitor cash flow and expenditures. Purchase orders are generated by the various departments and must be signed by the supervising staff member in control of the budget line before they are submitted to the business office. All purchase orders must be approved by the managing director or general manager before a purchase is made or items are ordered. Purchase orders are marked as to terms of payment (i.e., check or invoice); two copies are retained by the business office and all other copies are returned to the department head.

Cash Receipts

All revenues received by [THE THEATRE] are turned in to the business office, where they are to be received and deposited. No cash should be held overnight and all receipts must be deposited within two days. [THE THEATRE] maintains a separate account for payroll, and deposits are made to cover payroll checks and taxes out of this account. Periodically, transfers are made from the general checking account into a money market account to take advantage of higher interest rates.

Cash Disbursements

[THE THEATRE] will only write checks supported by invoices that have been purchase ordered unless approval is granted by the managing director. A paid receipt or other documentation is required if a check is hand-delivered to a vendor. Ongoing overhead expenses (telephone, electricity, gas, insurance, etc.) may be paid without a purchase order after the bill is approved by the managing director or general manager before the check is written. Account numbers are assigned to each disbursement by the various departments and are approved by the managing director or general manager. Two signatures are required on any check for more than $2,500 except for those checks simply transferring money from one account to another.

Bookkeeping

[THE THEATRE] records all transactions and balances the books on a monthly basis. All bookkeeping records are computerized and journal entries are approved by the managing director or general manager. By the twenty-second of each month, the business manager produces an "Income/Expense" statement and budget comparison of activity during the previous month. The business office makes all [THE THEATRE] deposits and makes all required federal and state tax deposits in a timely manner.

Annual Audit

[THE THEATRE] uses an independent accounting firm to conduct a complete audit of all records and transactions each fiscal year. During this time, all accounts receivable and payable are verified, all records are checked for accuracy, payroll records and files are examined, and changes in procedure are recommended as appropriate. A copy of the completed audit is distributed to the board of trustees, artistic director, and managing director as soon as it is complete.

Business Office Flow Chart

A purchase order is generated by a staff member.
The purchase order is approved by the department head.
The purchase order is approved by the managing director or general manager.
The purchase order is forwarded to the business office for processing.
Copies of the purchase order are returned to the originating department.
Merchandise is ordered by the department.
A check is generated by the business office (if advance payment is required).
The merchandise is received by the department.
Acknowledgement of receipt is sent to the business office.
Upon receipt of the invoice, a check is written for payment.
The check is signed by the managing director or general manager.
The check is mailed by the business office.

AT THE END OF EACH MONTH:

Cash receipts are posted.
Cash disbursements are posted.
Bank statements are reconciled.
A trial balance is run.
The business manager reviews the trial balance for accuracy.
The final books are run for the month.
Budget comparisons are analyzed.

A FINANCIAL WORKSHEET FOR THEATRE BUDGET PLANNING

Salaries & Overall Expenses Worksheet

SALARIES

ARTISTIC COMPANY (Select List)

Artistic Director   _____

Directors   _____

Scene Designers   _____

Costume Designers   _____

Lighting Designers   _____

Sound Designers   _____

Composers   _____

Musical Directors   _____

Actors   _____

Stage Managers   _____

Dramaturge   _____

Production Assistants   _____

Choreographer   _____

Fight Choreographer   _____

Musicians   _____

Contract Services/Hourly/
Overtime Employees   _____

SUBTOTAL ARTISTIC SALARIES: _____

ADMINISTRATIVE STAFF (Select List)

Managing Director   _____

General Manager   _____

Marketing/Audience Development Staff   _____

Development/Fundraising Staff   _____

Financial/Business Staff   _____

Box Office Staff   _____

Company Management Staff   _____

House Management Staff   _____

General Administration   _____

(Assistants/Secretarial)   _____

Hourly & Overtime Employees   _____

Contract Services   _____

SUBTOTAL STAFF SALARIES: _____

PRODUCTION STAFF (Select List)

Production Manager _____

Technical Director _____

Scenery Staff _____

Costume Staff _____

Electrics Staff _____

Sound Staff _____

Stage Operations Staff _____

Wardrobe Staff _____

Hourly & Overtime Employees _____

Contract Services _____

SUBTOTAL PRODUCTION STAFF
SALARIES: _____

FACILITIES STAFF (Select List)

Facilities & Maintenance Staff _____

Security Staff _____

Night Receptionists _____

Janitors/Housekeeping _____

Hourly & Overtime Employees _____

Contract Services _____

SUBTOTAL FACILITIES STAFF
SALARIES: _____

OVERHEAD

Telephone _____

Utilities _____

Insurance _____

Taxes & Users' Fees _____

Vehicles Equipment _____

Maintenance _____

Janitorial _____

Building Supplies _____

Bank Charges & Licenses _____

SUBTOTAL OVERHEAD EXPENSES: _____

ADMINISTRATION

Mailing Costs _____

Printing _____

Out-of-state Transport _____

In-state Transportation _____

Equipment _____

Supplies _____

Accounting _____

Management Consultants _____

Publications _____

Special Projects _____

SUBTOTAL ADMINISTRATION EXPENSES: _____

MARKETING

Printing & Publications _____

Photography/Media _____

Mailing Costs _____

Supplies _____

Advertising _____

Public Relations _____

Educational Services _____

Telemarketing Commissions _____

Telemarketing Expenses _____

Groups/Buses/Tourism _____

Special Projects _____

SUBTOTAL MARKETING EXPENSES: _____

FUNDRAISING/DEVELOPMENT

Publications & Printing _____

Fundraisers/Special Events _____

Supplies _____

Travel & VIP Work _____

General Assistance _____

Postage _____

Board of Trustee Meetings/Work _____

Research and Development _____

Contract Services (Grants, etc.) _____

SUBTOTAL FUNDRAISING EXPENSES: _____

PRODUCTION ARTISTIC

Actors' Equity Transport   _____

Casting & Hiring   _____

Scripts   _____

Royalties   _____

SUBTOTAL PRODUCTION ARTISTIC EXPENSES: _____

PRODUCTION TECHNICAL

Scenery   _____

Properties   _____

Costumes   _____

Wigs   _____

Shoes   _____

Makeup   _____

Lights   _____

Sound   _____

Video   _____

Production Maintenance   _____

Stage Operations   _____

Designer/Director Costs   _____

Storage   _____

Rental   _____

Shop Equipment   _____

SUBTOTAL PRODUCTION TECHNICAL EXPENSES: _____

PRODUCTION ADMINISTRATIVE

    Concessions (Food)   _____

    Concessions (Non-alcoholic Drinks)   _____

    Concessions (Alcoholic Drinks)   _____

    Gift Shop Expense   _____

    Box Office/Computers   _____

    Box Office/Supplies   _____

    Special Projects & Mileage   _____

SUBTOTAL PRODUCTION ADMINISTRATIVE EXPENSES: _____

SUBSIDIARY BUDGET

    Special Projects/Rentals/ etc.   _____

SUBTOTAL SUBSIDIARY BUDGET EXPENSES: _____

PAYROLL TAXES & BENEFITS

    Payroll Taxes   _____

    Company Benefits (Non-union)   _____

    Contractual Union Benefits   _____

SUBTOTAL PAYROLL TAXES & BENEFITS EXPENSES: _____

GRAND TOTAL EXPENSES: _____

OVERALL INCOME CHECKLIST

EARNED INCOME

Subscription Ticket Sales _____

Single Ticket Sales _____

Group Ticket Sales _____

Touring and Outreach Fees _____

Educational Programs, Services & Tuition _____

Advertising _____

Food Concessions _____

Drink Concessions _____

Gift Shop Sales _____

Rentals: Properties, Costumes, Scenery, Equipment _____

Rentals: Building and Grounds _____

Subsidiary Programs/Special Projects _____

Handling Fees/Charges _____

Bank Interest _____

Miscellaneous _____

SUBTOTAL EARNED INCOME: _____

UNEARNED INCOME

Individuals/Memberships   _____

Business/Corporate Donations   _____

Foundation   _____

Grants   _____

City Grants   _____

County Grants   _____

State Grants   _____

Federal Grants   _____

Arts Council Grants   _____

Miscellaneous Fundraisers   _____

SUBTOTAL UNEARNED INCOME: _____

EARNED & UNEARNED INCOME TOTAL: _____

GRAND TOTAL EXPENSES: _____

GRAND TOTAL INCOME: _____

IMPORTANT NOTES

1) ONE person should be in charge of each budget line! (Continue to break down the budget into categories to make sure this happens!)

2) "Subsidiary" indicates projects initiated after the initial budget process with the guarantee that budgeted income will exceed budgeted expenses.

3) Taxes and Benefits are based on total payroll, union agreements, and contractual obligations.

4) This checklist isn't intended as an exhaustive list. Each theatre will have unique categories.

5) Each organization should determine how it will account for and audit "In-kind Contributions," non-cash donations of materials, services, etc.

6) The Grand Total Expense and Income Projections for non-profit theatres should balance.

A BUDGET EXERCISE

Page 1: TITLE PAGE:
NAME OF THEATRE, BUDGET YEAR PROJECTED,
YOUR NAME & DATE

Page 2: BUDGET REFERENCE SHEET

Page 3–4: INCOME SUMMARY & EXPENSE SUMMARY OVERVIEW

This budget exercise is designed to offer students and personnel without a great deal of financial experience, a boilerplate approach to developing a balanced non-profit theatre budget.

Use the financial guidelines and inventories included in this chapter and involve your personnel in any other expenses or income opportunities that may be unique to your organization.

1) Budget every area of your theatre and fill in the summary categories below.

2) Only budget one "Projected Year" (just one column of numbers under expenses and income). Comparisons to past years would be the next step!

3) Make sure your Income and Expenses Totals are an exact match. Who gives to theatres projecting annual surpluses? Who wants to give to theatres with projected deficits?

4) Make sure your Earned Income is higher than your Unearned Income. (60%/40% ratio is a common non-profit theatre starting point) . . .

5) Under Expenses budget 20% of total budget for Marketing; 10% of total budget for Fundraising; and 40% of the Salary Budget for "Taxes/Benefits." The rest is up to you, based on your theatre's needs and plans.

6) If you budget your income first, this will dictate your expense budget and make your calculations easier for this budget exercise. However, some theatres choose to budget their necessary expenses and then figure out how to raise and earn the income to support the annual needs.

7) Remember, this is an exercise and you are simply estimating costs based on "common sense" and research.

8) Under EXPENSES, breakout (or subtotal) Salaries and Expenses.

9) Under INCOME, breakout (or subtotal) Earned and Unearned Income.

10) In estimating ticket income, multiply the number of shows (6 for example) x the number of available seats [size of house x # of weeks of performance x number of performances per week (8 for example)] x the average ticket price ($20 for example) x the anticipated minimum audience capacity (60% for example) = ESTIMATED ANNUAL TICKET INCOME.

11) If you are hiring professional actors, budget appropriate salaries ($500 per week for example); if you are working with volunteer or non-professionals, budget "at will" but consider Federal Labor Laws (minimum wage standards) . . .

Provide the following on a "BUDGET REFERENCE SHEET" that follows the cover sheet and is in front of the actual budget:

1) "The season is (fill in the blank)_____ shows;"

2) " There are _____ available seats;"

3) "Each production will run for _____ weeks with _____ performances per week."

4) "The average ticket price is $_____;"

5) "Ticket income is anticipated to be 60% of capacity or $_____." Show the math so that your Staff & Board can follow your assumptions.

6) "The season includes ... " (Add the names/playwrights of the shows to support or help clarify your income projections.)

7) Add these lines: "Fundraising, fundraiser and government funding levels must equal the amounts in the budget in order to balance this budget. Board of Director support is required."

NAME OF YOUR THEATRE

Earned Income

Ticket Income
Education/Outreach Programs
Concessions
Advertising

Other? (Fill in the blank _____)

Earned Income Subtotal

UNEARNED INCOME

Fundraising Events
Contributions from Individuals
Contributions from Businesses
Contributions from Corporations
Government Grants

Unearned Income Total

TOTAL INCOME

SUMMARY OF EXPENSES

Salaries

Artistic Salaries
Production Salaries
Administrative Salaries
Facility Salaries

Total Salaries

EXPENSES (Non-Salary)

Overhead
Production
Administrative
Marketing
Fundraising
Payroll Taxes & Benefits

Total Expenses (Non-salary)

GRAND TOTAL EXPENSES

A SAMPLE COMPARATIVE BUDGET ANALYSIS
OF EXPENSES IN EXECUTIVE SUMMARY

As a tool for monthly or bi-monthly budget comparisons and analysis, this summary should be extended to every budget line on the expense and income side of the budget and used to chart progress, report to the board, control expenditures, track income, and monitor cash flow.

SUMMARY OF EXPENSES	LAST YEAR ACTUAL	THIS YEAR PROJECTED	VARIANCE	PERCENT CHANGE
SALARIES				
ARTISTIC	$1,048,000	$1,351,000	$303,000	28.91%
PRODUCTION	$462,500	$556,000	$93,500	20.22%
ADMINISTRATIVE	$562,500	$642,460	$79,960	14.22%
FACILITIES	$209,000	$221,540	$12,540	6.00%
TOTAL SALARIES	$2,282,000	$2,771,000	$489,000	21.43%
OVERHEAD	$537,000	$650,000	$113,000	21.04%
ADMINISTRATIVE	$181,000	$197,000	$16,000	8.84%
MARKETING	$307,000	$346,000	$39,000	12.70%
PRODUCTION ARTISTIC	$80,000	$129,500	$49,500	61.88%
PRODUCTION TECH.	$212,000	$284,000	$72,000	33.96%
PRODUCTION ADMIN.	$139,000	$161,000	$22,000	15.83%
FUNDRAISING	$69,000	$90,000	$21,000	30.43%
TAXES & BENEFITS	$545,000	$677,500	$132,500	24.31%
SUBSIDIARY	$239,000	$239,000		0.00%
IN-KIND	$187,000	$187,000		0.00%
ARTISTIC RESERVE	$195,000	$0	($195,000)	-100.00%
TOTAL EXPENSES	$2,691,000	$2,961,000	$270,000	10.03%
GRAND TOTAL EXPENSES	$4,973,000	$5,732,000	$759,000	15.26%
GRAND TOTAL INCOME	Actual Income $4,999,000	Projected Income $5,732,000	$733,000	14.66%

"In action, be primitive, in foresight, a strategist."
René Char

CHAPTER 9

Surviving in a Competitive Field

"It usually takes more than three weeks to prepare a good impromptu speech."
Mark Twain

TRIPPINGLY ON THE TONGUE: A GUIDE TO SPEAKING THE SPEECH (OR PUBLIC SPEAKING)

If You Are In The Theatre You Are Expected To Know How To Speak

One thing most theatre students learn from their studies of Greek and Roman theatre history is that in those times, public speaking was considered an art form in itself. In ancient Greek and Roman classrooms, rhetoric students were taught that reading masterful writing and observing brilliant speeches helped improve their own speaking or writing. This also helped students to polish their listening skills and develop debate strategies and speech techniques that they could imitate.

Simply put, one of the basic tenets of speechmaking is that *how* one says something may be as important as *what* one says. The "how" is the form and the "what" is the content.

Content and Form

In Aristotle's *Poetics*, he describes the essence of great tragedy as related to the plot, character, theme, diction, music, and spectacle of the play. Most great speeches also pay close attention to *content* (plots, characters, themes) and rely heavily on form (diction/language, music/rhythm, and spectacle) to provide vocal fireworks, punch, and pizzazz to the speech.

Speaking-the-Speech Tips

1) **No last-minute performances, please!**
   The three keys to an excellent speech are preparation, practice, and more practice. (Oh, yes – having something that is worthwhile to say is also important!) As Ralph Waldo Emerson so eloquently put it, "Speech is power: speech is to persuade, to convert, to compel."

2) **Exactly why are we here?**
   Research your audience, walk the space where the speech will occur, check acoustics and equipment in advance, control the design of the space to maximize your speaking effectiveness, and investigate what your audience was doing just prior to the speech and what its objectives and expectations are for attending your speech.

3) **See me, hear me, touch me.**
   Establish eye contact with your audience and speak with vocal energy. Consider shaking hands with audience members as they enter the room. Endeavor to rally support, team-build, and find common bonds prior to your speech.

4) **Howdy!**
   Greet your audience with sincerity. ("Hi," "Hello," "Good Morning!") Avoid overused opening lines. ("It's such a privilege . . . ," "I'm so happy to be here . . . ," "Have you heard this bad joke?")

5) **What am I talking about/where are my notes?**
   At the very least, endeavor to memorize the first few sentences and your conclusion.

6) **MKDPSKDIODLLLLLXXXXWY? Got it?**
   Speak clearly (appropriate volume and enunciation, please).

7) **This isn't the time to count your change!**
   Control nervous physical habits (no hands in pockets, wiggling or twisting fingers). Use appropriate gestures or simply hold still.

8) **My kids taught me these bad habits!**
   Eliminate "uh," "um," and "like" from your speaking vocabulary.

9) **Organization helps delivery!**
   Consider a clear five-point outline for your speeches:

- Introduction
- First major point
- Second major point
- Third major point
- Conclusion

10) **Humor and the 3Bs.**
Of course everyone knows that a sense of humor helps keep people tuned in and alert, and that the goal of every speech is simply to "be brief, be brilliant, and be seated!"

11) **In conclusion . . . thanks . . . and, um . . . goodbye!**
End your speech with strength and power.

> "Half the world is composed of people
> who have something to say and can't, and the other half
> have nothing to say and keep on saying it."
> *Robert Frost*

TIPS FOR STRESS REDUCTION: STAYING FIT FOR LIFE

Introduction

Every opening night is a serious, strenuous, soul-searching series of deadlines if you work in the arts. In the non-profit arena, artistic directors work to break new ground and satisfy, sway, or soothe guest directors, actors, designers, board members, and critics with each new production. Marketing directors have sky-high sales goals, development directors are on the line to meet wildly optimistic fundraising goals, and production managers coordinate the complex creation of hopefully dazzling scenery, costumes, lights, and sound with a generally unrealistic budget that would make most for-profit producers gasp (or laugh . . . or cry)! Add the realities and frailties of a personal life to a highly charged, competitive work place, throw in high rates of unemployment, overwork, and low pay, and the arts are often a prime breeding ground for stress.

Unfortunately, few non-profit arts organizations employ a human resources staff, or even a specific individual who handles personnel matters. Most professional theatres have a company manager who is burdened with housing, transportation, scheduling, and contract assistance, with little time to tend to the morale of the company. Artistic directors, managing directors, and business managers oftentimes "handle" or "deal" with tense contract concerns or unhappy employees. Stage managers usually do their best to keep actors on track, and individual supervisors tend to bear the brunt of the personnel load. This is not an ideal situation, and there's a reason that most businesses and corporations have a personnel office or a human resources division. It's important that employees work within their realms of training and experience, and few arts employees are hired, first and foremost, for their personal counselling skills, medical diagnostic training, or first-aid experience.

With this in mind, it's crucial for arts managers to know and communicate their expectations and the boundaries and referral sources and options when it comes to "handling personnel matters" vs. "personal counselling" or "offering advice."

> "Try not to become a man of success
> but rather try to become a man of value."
> *Albert Einstein*

Stress Reduction Tip Sheet

1) **Understand your limitations!**

    As an individual, work to clarify the source of your stress and determine if the problem is within your control. Agonizing over concerns that are impossible for you to influence is most likely an exercise in futility. Are the sources of your stress related to fear, anger, anxiety, depression, low self-esteem, passivity, conflicts with friends, or control issues at work? Or are they related to world events, ethical concerns, family frustrations, or current or recent crises?

    For employers, it's certainly appropriate to be helpful, provide a listening ear, and assist your friends, colleagues and employees within your level of experience, training, and comfort. However, whether you are a supervisor, employee, friend or colleague, make sure you understand your limits as a counsellor and as an individual. If you are an employer, devise a company referral list of professional services for your staff to use when an employee's stress levels stray "beyond the norm."

2) **Pay attention to number one!**

    If you are in poor mental or physical health, it's difficult for you to be of help to anyone else. See your doctor for a complete physical and make sure you are healthy, eating appropriately, and meeting your sleep needs.

3) **Work out!**

Physical activity and exercise help break up the day and may help you sort out myriad problems, achieve perspective, and relieve a host of psychological and physical challenges. If you've dedicated your life to the arts, you've certainly been taught that the mind and body work together in wonderful and mysterious ways. A consistent workout regimen may also assist with weight control, lowering cholesterol, and sound eating and sleeping habits. A brisk walk, fifty-minute racquetball game, or biking to work could make all the difference in the world.

4) **A little research goes a long way!**

Every Borders, Barnes and Noble, and downtown bookstore has a plethora of volumes on self-help and stress-reducing techniques. Many of them may work for you. In addition, many community centres and nearby universities offer stress-reduction seminars, and the more progressive healthcare providers are scheduling ongoing stress-reduction programs as part of their proactive health screening services.

5) **Accept reality . . . or change your realities!**

Don't waste time fighting institutional policies, horrid employers, or world events that you can't control. Sometimes it's best to simply cut your losses and move on. Working with unethical, rude, or wildly obnoxious colleagues or employers can impact your day-to-day attitude, self-image, and long-term health. If you can make a difference and create change and a positive work environment, more power to you! If your work environment is getting the best of you and adversely influencing your health and psyche, it's time to step back and evaluate your values, goals, and strategic plans.

6) **Hunt for a mentor and develop a support group!**

Sometimes just having someone or a group of people you respect with whom discuss issues, try out ideas, explore the corporate culture, share concerns, or help with priorities will make all the difference. Ask for help.

7) **Use those acting exercises!**

Many arts professionals started as actors, dancers, or theatre students. Remember those deep-breathing exercises, muscle-tension release improvisations, and sensory-awareness seminars that seemed so silly in Acting 101 or Beginning Dance? Now is the time to revisit these great stress-reducing techniques that can lighten up your day and add a sense of balance to a tense moment.

8) **Look out for burnout – consider a time-out!**

Often, just hiding away, finding quiet time, vacationing, and regaining per-spective can work wonders for the battered soul. Monitor sudden weight loss, rise in blood pressure, emotional swings, withdrawal, self-destructive thoughts or actions, feelings of desperation, or physical symptoms (ulcers, teeth grinding, nail biting, back pain, colds, flu, rashes, neck pains, headaches, lowered sexual interest, fatigue, reliance on alcohol or drugs, shaking, unusual sweating, or facial tension).

9) **Choose your battles!**
I once had a colleague who would consistently pick fights with subordinates in the morning, drive to McDonald's and argue about cold French fries and long lines with serving staff at lunch, return to work to irritate his direct supervisor, and leave at 5 p.m. every day to complain to his wife about her housework. His extreme competitiveness; charged, accusatory speech patterns; relentless impatience; and body tension reflected his hyper-stress-filled existence. When he finally mellowed and decided to more carefully select his battles, he was a much happier individual. (And do I need to mention the relief of everyone around him?)

10) **Stress lists typically include these "events:"**
Death or illness of a family member, marriage, separation, divorce, personal illness or injury, being fired at work, going back to school, pregnancy, supervisor troubles, quitting smoking, change in residence, sexual concerns, financial difficulties, arguments with spouse, work changes, burnout/overwork, sleeping-habit changes, eating-habit changes, major holidays, large purchases, family concerns, and legal problems.

11) **Don't play doctor.**
Avoid self-medication and self-prescribed over-the-counter drugs to temporarily avoid the main problem (which is whatever is causing the stress in the first place). See a doctor. Don't procrastinate!

12) **A mini-list of stress relievers:**
Play soothing music, get a massage, learn to prioritize, limit the hours you work, take a walk in the woods, read adventurous fiction, take a coffee break, go to an upbeat movie, read a little Norman Vincent Peale, think optimistically, question negative thoughts that haunt you, write down everything that's going right in a journal (and review it often), and, finally, believe that your personal best is just around the corner.

> "Wisdom is oft-times nearer
> when we stoop than when we soar."
> William Wordsworth

FIVE TIPS FOR STARTING A NEW JOB

First impressions are essential in every field, but often take on even greater significance in a creative field where jobs are won and lost based on one-minute auditions, quick perusals of scene design and costume design portfolios, and fast, furious, and fleeting onstage moments. Here are five proven suggestions for making a strong first impression (and a powerful ongoing impression) when you are starting a new job:

1) When you start a new job, shake the hand of your boss or board members, look them in the eye, and make it clear that you are excited about your work; that you are loyal, trustworthy, hardworking, and really happy to be working with them on *their* agenda. Employers need to know that they can count on you.

2) Always arrive at work *at least* a half-hour to an hour early every day the first six months, and be the last person to leave the office! Be there on a weekend or a holiday if you can contribute in some significant (and hopefully visible) way. Be productive. Results count more than effort.

3) Leave a paper trail – document your successes and failures. Let your successes be known with great subtlety. Own up to your failures and take responsibility . . . but don't dwell on them!

4) Asking for advice is a way of creating mentors, allies, and potential partners in your success. Be humble, quiet, and easygoing in your approach, and generous with your thank-you's.

5) Inspire, cultivate relationships and strive to understand your boss and co-workers. What motivates *them*? What are their interests and career plans? Look at the big picture: *their* lives and *your* career!

TEN TIPS FOR LOSING YOUR CURRENT JOB

Introduction

Perhaps you are new at this whole "work thing," are naive about how businesses operate or somehow feel entitled to "stretch the truth" when it comes to padding your resume or expense accounts, charging international phone calls to your office phone or lying about your inaccessibility for crucial work sessions. Watching the hilarious reruns of George Costanza's work habits on *Seinfeld* or episodes of *The Office* will tell you all you need to know about self-slaughter in the job market. It all seems so obvious, but many of us observe horrific behaviors and recalcitrant attitudes in places where we do business virtually every day. Here are ten tips for making yourself instantly dispensable:

1. Tweet, blog or e-mail rude, obnoxious or otherwise inappropriate thoughts about your employer, co-workers or productions. While you're at it, post drunken, half-naked photos of yourself on your Facebook and "Tag/Identify" someone in your office so that they are sure to spread word of your indiscretions to the rest of your workplace.

2. Embarrass your direct supervisors or anyone above your direct supervisors in the institutional hierarchy by the way you talk, dress, or address them in business or social situations.

3. Arrive at work late, be the first to run out at 5 p.m. (or whenever the institutional work day ends) and bother or harass co-workers who are trying to get their work done.

4. Stick to a "this is the way we have always done business" motto, refuse to stay current on common business, marketing or fundraising practices.

5. Take credit for other people's ideas and talk behind a colleague's back with other co-workers.

6. Just say NO! Say no to new company initiatives, loyal patrons, generous donors and eager volunteers.

7. Never venture beyond the boundaries of your basic position description. Hide away when volunteers are being recruited to help with the weekend fundraising event, sneak out to lunch when a crucial mailing needs to make it to the Post Office by 2 p.m., and walk by the beer bottles, cigar stubs or hamburger wrappers that are trashing the front of your theatre when you arrive in the morning. Not my job!

8. Be your company's naysayer historian! "We tried that once before and it didn't work," is your major contribution to strategic planning, audience development and company management discussions.

9. Answer your cell phone or office phone and conduct personal business on company time while you are in meetings, serving customers or engaged in one-on-one meetings with your co-workers or boss.

10. Play video games, e-mail your friends, check your stock portfolio, log on to inappropriate websites, engage in long Facebook/MySpace conversations and search for a "better" job on your company computer, ignoring the fact that many businesses legally audit and/or actively monitor their employees' web traffic and/or e-mail correspondence.

FOURTEEN ARTISTIC NETWORKING SURVIVAL SKILLS FOR THEATRE PROFESSIONALS YOUNG AND OLD

Introduction

Most directors, choreographers, designers, artistic directors, general managers, and other arts executives rise up through the ranks. Many remember the lessons learned on the way up the ladder, but it never hurts to hear from the front lines. "He that won't be counselled can't be helped," observed Ben Franklin. When a group of Equity and non-Equity actors gathered in Southern California, in the spirit of "counselling and sharing," they traded tips on surviving the highly competitive and financially perilous profession of theatre. This generally wise and sometimes wacky list of fourteen tips comprises:

1) **Believe in instant karma.**
   What goes around *will* come around. Treat others exactly as you would like to be treated. Be kind and courteous. The tech person you step on today could be your producer or director tomorrow.

2) **Avoid people who suck energy.**
   These people only give you permission to procrastinate. You are not the person who is losing if you miss a few social gatherings in order to work.

3) **To read or not to read?**
   That is the question. The only answer? Read as many plays as possible. Be familiar with all types of writing. The more familiar you are with a play, the better your audition will be.

4) **Leave your worries at the door!**
   Remember, the people you work with are not your therapists. Don't be so wrapped up in your personal problems that you let your frustrations impact your work.

5) **Who died and made you king?**
   Nobody likes to hear a scolding "shhh!" from another actor. Let admonishing the parties involved be handled by the stage manager or director. If they aren't present, remember that you catch more flies with honey, and be diplomatic.

6) **Who died and made you Elia Kazan?**
   Never, ever, ever, ever, ever direct another actor in your show.

7) **Respect the clock.**
Be on time. Punctuality shows that you respect and value a person's time. Being late is rude. Show up ready to work.

8) **Include time for yourself every day.**
Treat yourself to a walk, a trip to the local nursery or a hot bath – experience one of those International Coffee moments that can change your life.

9) **"We'll always have Utah."**
Falling for someone you work with intimately and for such a long time may be inevitable, especially in the veil of drama and "make believe." But rarely do these romances go beyond the run of the show.

10) **Be kind to your dressers.**
Actors need to worship costume designers, staff, and dressers. They make or break how you look every day on stage.

11) **Make Makita a part of your method.**
Offer to help with strike. Be a good sport. You will be remembered for being the kind of person you are to work with, not for the believability of your page twenty-six speech on Thursday night.

12) **Know thyself.**
Avoid making life-changing decisions under stress, pressure, or on the spot. Make *your* decisions on *your* own time. Be clear in your own mind about what you want and what you are willing to do to get it – before you go in!

13) **Prepare for the worst, hope for the best.**
Go beyond basic preparation of the required or expected workload. Anticipate possible negative outcomes and have contingency plans.

14) **Build support . . . six degrees of separation.**
You can never know too many people. You can never be nice enough to people. You may be surprised at the small world of professional theatre.

(Special thanks to: Krystal Allan, Brooke Aston, Evelyn Carol Case, Noelle Forestal, Kathy Hardoy, Amber Howard, James Hunt, Michelle Martinez, Melissa Maxwell, Erin McReynolds, Aleia Melville, Josh Miller, Justin Milley, Caitlin Volz, Nicholas Volz and Pamela Woo.)

AN ABBREVIATED DIRECTORY OF THEATRE-RELATED LABOR UNIONS, GUILDS, CONTRACTS & ASSOCIATIONS
(State/Phone/Website)

ACTORS' EQUITY ASSOCIATION (AEA)
New York: (212) 869 – 8530

www.actorsequity.org

ALLIANCE FOR INCLUSION IN THE ARTS
New York: (212) 730 – 4750

www.inclusioninthearts.org

AMERICAN ALLIANCE FOR THEATRE & EDUCATION
Maryland: (301) 951 – 7977

www.aate.com

AMERICAN ARTS ALLIANCE (AAA)
Washington, DC: (202) 207 – 3850

www.americanartsalliance.org

AMERICAN FEDERATION OF TELEVISION AND RADIO ARTISTS (AFTRA)
New York: (212) 532 – 0800

www.aftra.org

AMERICANS FOR THE ARTS
Washington, DC: (202) 371 – 2830

www.artsusa.org

AMERICAN GUILD OF MUSICAL ARTISTS (AGMA)
New York: (212) 265 – 3687

www.musicalartists.org

AMERICAN GUILD OF VARIETY ARTISTS (AGVA)
New York: (212) 675 – 1003

www.agvausa.com

AMERICAN THEATRE CRITICS ASSOCIATION (ATCA)
New Mexico: (505) 856 – 2101

www.americantheatrecritics.org

ARTS CONSULTING GROUP (ACG)
Los Angeles: (323) 936 – 0626

www.artsconsulting.com/artsinsights/index.html

ASSOCIATION OF FUNDRAISING PROFESSIONALS (AFP)
Virginia: (703) 684 – 0410

www.afpnet.org

ASSOCIATION OF THEATRE IN HIGHER EDUCATION (ATHE)
Colorado: (303) 530 – 2167

www.athe.org

ASSOCIATION OF PERFORMING ARTS PRESENTERS (APAP)
Washington, D.C.: (202) 833 – 2787

www.apap365.org

ASSOCIATION OF THEATRICAL PRESS AGENTS AND MANAGERS (ATPAM)
New York: (212) 719 – 3666

www.atpam.com

BOARDNETUSA
New York

www.boardnetusa.org

BUSINESS COMMITTEE FOR THE ARTS (BCA)
Washington, D.C.: (202) 371 – 2830

www.americansforthearts.org

THE DRAMATISTS GUILD OF AMERICA (DGA)
New York: (212) 398 – 9366

www.dramatistsguild.com

THE FOUNDATION CENTER
New York: (212) 620 – 4230

www.foundationcenter.org

FREE MANAGEMENT LIBRARY
Minneapolis: (800) 971 – 2250

www.managementhelp.org

GUIDESTAR CHARITY CHECK
Williamsburg: (800) 421 – 8656

www2.guidestar.org

INSTITUTE OF OUTDOOR DRAMA (IOD)
North Carolina: (252) 328 – 5363

http://outdoordrama.unc.edu

INTERNATIONAL ALLIANCE OF THEATRICAL STAGE EMPLOYEES (IATSE)
New York: (212) 730 – 7809

www.iatse-intl.org

INTERNATIONAL THEATRE INSTITUTE (ITI)
www.tcg.org/international/iti/itiworld.cfm

LEAGUE OF HISTORIC AMERICAN THEATRES (LHAT)
Baltimore: (410) 659 – 9533

www.lhat.org

LEAGUE OF RESIDENT THEATRES (LORT)
New York: (212) 944 – 1501

www.lort.org

NATIONAL ALLIANCE FOR MUSICAL THEATRE (NAMT)
New York: (212) 265 – 5376

www.namt.org

NATIONAL ASSEMBLY OF STATE ARTS AGENCIES (NASAA)
Washington, D.C.: (202) 347 – 6352

www.nasaa – arts.org

NATIONAL ASSOCIATION OF PERFORMING ARTS MANAGERS AND AGENTS (NAPAMA)
New York: E-mail only: conal@napama.org

www.napama.org

NATIONAL CENTER FOR NON-PROFIT BOARDS
Washington, D.C.: (202) 452 – 6262

www.boardsource.org

NATIONAL ENDOWMENT FOR THE ARTS (NEA)
Washington, D.C.: (202) 682 – 5400

www.arts.endow.gov

NATIONAL ENDOWMENT FOR THE HUMANITIES (NEH)
Washington, D.C.: (202) 606 – 8400

www.neh.gov

NATIONAL THEATRE CONFERENCE (NTC)

www.nationaltheatreconference.org

SCREEN ACTORS' GUILD (SAG)
Los Angeles: (323) 954 – 1600

www.sag.org

SHAKESPEARE THEATRE ASSOCIATION OF AMERICA (STAA)

www.staaonline.org

STAGE DIRECTORS AND CHOREOGRAPHERS SOCIETY (SDC)
New York: (212) 391 – 1070

www.sdcweb.org

THEATRE COMMUNICATIONS GROUP (TCG)
New York: (212) 609 – 5900

www.tcg.org

THEATRE DEVELOPMENT FUND (TDF)
New York: (212) 912 – 9770

www.tdf.org

UNITED STATES INSTITUTE FOR THEATRE TECHNOLOGY (USITT)
New York: (315) 463 – 6463

www.usitt.org

UNIVERSITY/RESIDENT THEATRE ASSOCIATION (U/RTA)
New York: (212) 221 – 1130

www.urta.com

UNITED SCENIC ARTISTS (USA)
New York: (212) 581 – 0300

www.usa829.org

VOLUNTEER LAWYERS FOR THE ARTS (VLA)
New York: (212) 319 – 2787

www.vlany.org

VOLUNTEER MATCH
San Francisco: (415) 241 – 6872

www.volunteermatch.org/nonprofits/gettingstarted

AMERICA'S NON-PROFIT PROFESSIONAL THEATRES: AN OVERVIEW OF FOUR NATIONWIDE ORGANIZATIONS

Theatre Communications Group (TCG)

Theatre Communications Group (TCG) describes itself as "the national organiz-ation for the American not-for-profit professional theatre." Founded in 1961 (the same year as New York's La MaMa Experimental Theatre and the Utah Shakespearean Festival), TCG has provided a national forum and communications network for a field that, in its own words, is "as aesthetically diverse as it is geographically wide-spread." Serving nearly 700 member theatres and affiliate organisations and more than 12,000 individual members, the organisation notes that it offers " . . . a compre-hensive support system that addresses concerns of the theatre companies and individual artists that collectively represent 'our national theatre.'"

TCG's mission is "to strengthen, nurture and promote the not-for-profit American theatre." Through its artistic, management, and international programs, advocacy activities and publications, "TCG seeks to increase the organizational effi-ciency of [its] member theatres, cultivate and celebrate the artistic talent and achievements of the field, and promote a larger public understanding of and appreciation for the theatre field."

TCG's centralized services include publishing the annual *TCG Theatre Directory* of members and resource organizations (a must for every theatre office), the monthly magazine *American Theatre*, the *Artsearch* employment bulletin, *Dramatists Sourcebook*,

Stage Writers Handbook, *The Stage Directors Handbook*, and much more. Available on its website is *Theatre Profiles* online, a grand collection of facts, artistic statements, contact information, and production overviews of all TCG member theatres.

Perhaps most important to theatre leaders and managers, TCG organizes, analyzes, and communicates pertinent, timely, factual information that is extremely useful to individuals and institutions in both their local concerns and national advocacy. Each year its fiscal survey featuring member theatres yields *Theatre Facts*, a compendium of statistics ranging from budget itemizations to ticket sales and attendance figures, to sizes of administrative and artistic staffs.

Membership eligibility is detailed on TCG's website, along with terrific links to membership and advocacy information on the American theatre as well as the international theatre community. Also check out the site for links to myriad programs, services, and America's non-profit professional theatres. (You'll find that many TCG theatres belong to the three following organisations, as well.)

In 2005, TCG received the Tony Honors for Excellence in Theatre in recognition of its impact on the national field. TCG and its member theatres are major contributors to the American theatre sector, which employs more than 131,000 people, produces over 202,000 performances each year and contributes $1.9 billion to the US economy annually. A 501(c)(3) not-for-profit organization, TCG is led by executive director Teresa Eyring and governed by a national board of directors representing the theatre field.

TCG's mailing address is 520 Eighth Avenue, 26th floor, New York City, NY 10018-4156. Its telephone number is (212) 609 – 5900, and its fax, (212) 609 – 5901. TCG can be reached on the web at www.tcg.org

League of Resident Theatres (LORT)

LORT is the largest professional theatre association of its kind in the United States, with over 75 member theatres located in every major market in the U.S., including 29 states and the District of Columbia. LORT Theatres collectively issue more Equity contracts to actors than Broadway and commercial tours combined. LORT administers the primary national not-for-profit collective bargaining agreements with Actors' Equity Association (AEA), Stage Directors & Choreographers Society (SDC), and United Scenic Artists (USA) and also deals directly with personnel and management issues involving Theatre staff, artists, and craftspeople. LORT members communicate collectively via LORT Counsel's office in New York.

LORT is also a forum for sharing information regarding all aspects of theatre. Semi-annual meetings provide opportunities for LORT members to study, discuss, and exchange information on such non-labor management issues as development, marketing, public relations, education, and technology, as well as provide a forum for developing professional relationships. LORT is also committed to the continued training of current and future LORT Managers. All individual LORT member websites may be accessed through links found at the LORT website: www.lort.org

The principle objectives of LORT, as stated in LORT's by-laws, are:

- To promote the general welfare of resident theatres in the United States and its territories;

- To promote community interest in and support of resident theatres;

- To encourage and promote sound communications and relations between and among resident theatres in the United States and between resident theatres and the public;

- To afford resident theatres an opportunity to act for their common purpose and interest;

- To act in the interest and on behalf of its members in labor relations and related matters:

  - To serve as bargaining agent for its members in bargaining collectively with unions representing employees of its members;

  - To establish and maintain stable and equitable labor relations between its members and unions representing employees of its members;

  - To provide guidance and assistance to its members in administering collective bargaining agreements;

  - If requested by a member, to handle disputes between members and their employees and/or union representatives; and

- To represent LORT members before government agencies on problems of labor relations.

- To carry on all lawful activities which may directly or indirectly contribute to the accomplishment of such purposes; and

- To communicate with the Federal Government through the National Endowment for the Arts and the American Arts Alliance and to keep those agencies apprised of the needs and status of LORT's membership.

MEMBERSHIP REQUIREMENTS

The following criteria must be met for new membership into LORT:

- The theatre must be incorporated as a non-profit I.R.S.-approved organization

- Each self-produced production must be rehearsed for a minimum of three weeks

- The theatre must have a playing season of twelve weeks or more

- The theatre will operate under a LORT-Equity contract.

General Enquiries may be made to:
Stephanie Drotar, LORT Management Associate,
Phone: (212) 944 – 1501, ext. 19, Fax: (212) 768 – 0785,
Email: stephanie@lort.org

The LORT Postal Address is:
League of Resident Theatres,
1501 Broadway, Suite 2401,
New York, NY 10036.

The LORT website is: www.lort.org

LORT MEMBER THEATRES
(CITY/STATE)

ACT Theatre	Seattle	WA
Actors Theatre of Louisville	Louisville	KY
Alabama Shakespeare Festival	Montgomery	AL
Alley Theatre	Houston	TX
Alliance Theatre	Atlanta	GA
American Conservatory Theatre	San Francisco	CA
American Repertory Theatre	Cambridge	MA
Arden Theatre Company	Philadelphia	PA
Arena Stage	Washington	DC
Arizona Theatre Company	Tucson/Phoenix	AZ
Arkansas Repertory Theatre	Little Rock	AR
Asolo Repertory Theatre	Sarasota	FL
Barter Theatre	Abingdon	VA
Berkeley Repertory Theatre	Berkeley	CA
Capital Repertory Theatre	Albany	NY
CENTERSTAGE	Baltimore	MD
Center Theatre Group	Los Angeles	CA
The Cincinnati Playhouse In The Park	Cincinnati	OH
City Theatre Company	Pittsburgh	PA
Clarence Brown Theatre Company	Knoxville	TN
The Cleveland Play House	Cleveland	OH

Court Theatre	Chicago	IL
Dallas Theatre Center	Dallas	TX
Delaware Theatre Company	Wilmington	DE
Denver Center Theatre Company	Denver	CO
Florida Stage	Manalapan	FL
Florida Studio Theatre	Sarasota	FL
Ford's Theatre	Washington	DC
Geffen Playhouse	Los Angeles	CA
George Street Playhouse	New Brunswick	NJ
Georgia Shakespeare	Atlanta	GA
Geva Theatre Center	Rochester	NY
The Goodman Theatre	Chicago	IL
Goodspeed Musicals	East Haddam	CT
Great Lakes Theatre Festival	Cleveland	OH
The Guthrie Theatre	Minneapolis	MN
Hartford Stage Company	Hartford	CT
Huntington Theatre Company	Boston	MA
Indiana Repertory Theatre	Indianapolis	IN
Intiman Theatre	Seattle	WA
Kansas City Repertory Theatre	Kansas City	MO
Laguna Playhouse	Laguna Beach	CA
La Jolla Playhouse	La Jolla	CA
Lincoln Center Theatre	New York	NY
Long Wharf Theatre	New Haven	CT
Maltz Jupiter Theatre	Jupiter	FL
Manhattan Theatre Club	New York	NY
Marin Theatre Company	Mill Valley	CA
McCarter Theatre	Princeton	NJ
Merrimack Repertory Theatre	Lowell	MA
Milwaukee Repertory Theatre	Milwaukee	WI
Northlight Theatre	Skokie	IL
The Old Globe	San Diego	CA
Pasadena Playhouse	Pasadena	CA
The People's Light and Theatre Company	Philadelphia	PA
The Philadelphia Theatre Company	Philadelphia	PA
Pittsburgh Public Theatre	Pittsburgh	PA
PlayMakers Repertory Company	Chapel Hill	NC
Portland Center Stage	Portland	OR
Portland Stage Company	Portland	ME
The Repertory Theatre of St. Louis	St. Louis	MO
Roundabout Theatre Company	New York	NY

Round House Theatre	Bethesda	MD
San Jose Repertory Theatre	San Jose	CA
Seattle Repertory Theatre	Seattle	WA
Shakespeare Theatre Company	Washington	DC
Signature Theatre Company	Arlington	VA
South Coast Repertory	Costa Mesa	CA
Syracuse Stage	Syracuse	NY
Theatre For A New Audience	New York	NY
TheatreWorks	Palo Alto	CA
Trinity Repertory Company	Providence	RI
Two River Theatre Company	Red Bank	NJ
Virginia Stage Company	Norfolk	VA
The Wilma Theatre	Philadelphia	PA
Yale Repertory Theatre	New Haven	CT

Institute of Outdoor Drama (IOD)

The Institute of Outdoor Drama, a public service agency, has recently found a new home base at East Carolina University in Greenville, North Carolina. Based at the University of North Carolina in Chapel Hill for the 47 years prior to the move to Greenville, the IOD is the only organization in the United States providing national leadership in fostering artistic and managerial excellence and expansion of the outdoor drama movement through training, research and advisory programs. The Institute serves as a national clearinghouse for more than 101 constituent theatre companies across the nation.

While in transition to its new location at East Carolina University, it may be best to check out the "Institute of Outdoor Drama" on the internet for updated contact numbers and addresses, or to refer to its longstanding website at: http://outdoordrama.unc.edu

The new IOD telephone number is: (252) 328 – 5363.

The IOD represents outdoor theatres in the following categories:

Historical Dramas

(Original plays, often with music and dance, based on significant events and per-formed in amphitheatres located where the events actually occurred.)

Religious Plays

(Outdoor religious dramas are faith-based plays that dramatize significant events in the major world religions.)

Shakespeare Festivals

(Outdoor Shakespeare festivals produce full-length Shakespearean plays, often in rotating repertory with the works of modern and other classical playwrights.)

Musical Theatre

Non-Musical Productions

Children's Shows

Institute of Outdoor Drama Member Theatres

**Each company has a direct link on the IOD website at:
http://outdoordrama.unc.edu/directory/bycompany**

Actors' Theatre Company of Columbus
Actors' Theatre Company, 1000 City Park Ave., Columbus,
OH 43206 (614) 444 – 6888

Airmid Theatre Company
Airmid Theatre Company c/o 844 Bay Shore Ave., West Islip,
NY 11795 (631) 704 – 2888

American Players Theatre
American Players Theatre, P.O. Box 819, Spring Green, WI 53588
(608) 588–2361 (box office), (608) 588 – 7401 (administration).

The Amistad Saga: Reflections
African American Cultural Complex, 119 Sunnybrook Road, Raleigh,
NC 27610 – 1827 (919) 231 – 0625 (box office and administration).

The Aracoma Story, Inc.
P.O. Box 2016, Logan, WV 25601 (304) 752 – 8222 (box office) and
(304) 752 – 0253 (administration).

Austin Shakespeare
701 Tillery St. # 9, Austin, TX 78702 (512) 474 – 8497 (box office)
(512) 470 – 4505 (administration).

Baltimore Shakespeare Festival
3900 Roland Ave., Baltimore, MD 21211 (410) 366 – 8596 (box office),
(410) 366 – 8594 (administration).

California Shakespeare Theatre
701 Heinz Ave, Berkeley, CA 94710 (510) 548 – 9666 (box office),
(510) 548 – 3422 (administration).

The Charlotte Shakespeare Festival
P.O. Box 32875, Charlotte, NC 28232 (704) 625 – 1288 (box office and
administration).

Chesapeake Shakespeare Company
8510 High Ridge Road, Ellicott City, MD 21043 (866) 841 – 4111 (ticket
agency), (410) 313 – 8874 (administration).

The Cleveland Shakespeare Festival
The Cleveland Shakespeare Festival, P.O. Box 93494, Cleveland,
OH 44101 – 5494

Colorado Shakespeare Festival
Campus Box 277 UCB, Boulder, CO 80309-0277 (303) 492 – 0554 (box
office), (303) 492 – 1527 (administration).

Commonwealth Shakespeare Company
539 Tremont St. # 308 Boston, MA 02116 (617) 426 – 0863 (box office and
administration).

Door Shakespeare, Inc.
P.O. Box 351, Baileys Harbor, WI 54202-0351 (920) 839 – 1500 (box office
and administration).

The EmilyAnn Theatre & Gardens
P.O. Box 801, Wimberley, TX 78676 (512) 847 – 6969 (box office and
administration).

Fairbanks Shakespeare Theatre
P.O. Box 73447, Fairbanks, AK 99707 (907) 457 – 7638 (box office and
administration).

First Folio Theatre
146 Juliet Court, Clarendon Hills, IL 60514 (630) 986 – 8067 (box office and
administration).

First For Freedom
Eastern Stage, Inc. 145111 NC Hwy. 903, Halifax, NC 27839 (252) 883 –
7119 (box office and administration).

From This Day Forward
Old Colony Players, P.O. Box 112, Valdese, NC 28690 (828) 879 – 2126
(administration), (828) 879 – 2129 (box office).

The Great Passion Play
The Elna M. Smith Foundation, P.O. Box 471, Eureka Springs,
AR 72632 (866) 566 – 3565 (box office and administration).

Greenstage
P.O. Box 9594, Seattle, WA 98109 (206) 748 – 1551 (administration).

Happy Canyon Co., Inc.
The Happy Canyon Night Show P.O. Box 609 Pendleton, OR
97801 (800) 457 – 6336 (box office), (541) 276 – 2553 (administration).

Harrisburg Shakespeare Festival
605 Strawberry Sq., Harrisburg, PA 17101 (717) 238 – 4111 (box office and
administration).

Heart of America Shakespeare Festival
3619 Broadway, Suite 2, Kansas City, MO 64111 (816) 531 – 7728
(administration).

Hill Country Arts Foundation/Point Theatre
Hill Country Arts Foundation, P.O. Box 1169, Ingram, TX 78025
(830) 367 – 5121 (box office and administration).

The Hill Cumorah Pageant
The Church of Jesus Christ of Latter-Day Saints, 44 Woodstone Lane,
Rochester, NY 14626-1754 (315) 597 – 6808 (box office), (585) 314 – 1681
(administration).

Honey in the Rock
Theatre West Virginia, Inc., P.O. Box 1205, Beckley, WV 25802 (304) 256 –
6800 (box office and administration).

Horn in the West
Southern Appalachian Historical Association, Inc., P.O. Box 295, Boone,
NC 28607 (828) 264 – 2120 (box office and administration).

Hudson Valley Shakespeare Festival
155 Main St, Cold Spring, NY 10516 (845) 265 – 9575 (box office),
(845) 265 – 7858 (administration).

Houston Shakespeare Festival
University of Houston School of Theatre, 113 Wortham, Houston,
TX 77204-4016 (713) 743 – 2929 (box office), (713) 743 – 3003 (administration).

Idaho Shakespeare Festival
P.O. Box 9365, Boise, ID 83707 (208) 336 – 9221 (box office),
(208) 429 – 9908 (administration).

Illinois Shakespeare Festival
Illinois State University, 212 Centennial West, Campus Box 5700, Normal,
IL 61790-5700 (309) 438 – 2535 (box office), (309) 438 – 8974 (administration).

Jenny Wiley Theatre
P.O. Box 22, Prestonsburg, KY 41653 (877) 225 – 5598 (box office),
(606) 886 – 9274 (administration).

Kentucky Shakespeare Festival
1387 S Fourth Street, Louisville, KY 40208 (502) 637 – 4933 (box office and
administration).

Lake Tahoe Shakespeare Festival
948 Incline Way, Incline Village, NV 89451 (800) 747 – 4697 (box office),
(775) 832 – 1616 (administration).

Laura's Memories
Ozark Mountain Players P.O. Box 113, Mansfield, MO 65704 (417) 924 –
3415 (box office), (417) 924 – 3383 (administration).

Liberty: The Saga of Sycamore Shoals
Sycamore Productions, 1651 W Elk Ave, Elizabethton, TN 37643
(423) 543 – 5808 (box office and administration).

Lincoln
Lincoln Amphitheatre, 15043 N CR 300 W, P.O. Box 7–21 Lincoln City, IN
47552, (800) 264 – 4223 (box office), (812) 937 – 9730 (administration).

Little Shepherd of Kingdom Come
Cumberland Mountain Arts & Crafts Council, Inc. 255 Amphitheatre Road,
P.O. Box 1482 Jenkins, KY 41537 (606) 832 – 1453 (box office and
administration).

The Living Word Outdoor Drama
P.O. Box 1481, Cambridge, OH 43725 (740) 439 – 2761 (box office and
administration).

The Lost Colony
Roanoke Island Historical Association 1409 National Park Drive, Manteo,
NC 27954 (252) 473 – 3414 (box office), (252) 473 – 2127 (administration).

Marin Shakespeare Company
P.O. Box 4053, San Rafael, CA 94913 (415) 456 – 4488 (box office),
(415) 499 – 4485 (administration).

Medora Musical
Stagewest Entertainment, P.O. Box 198, Medora, North Dakota, 58645
(701) 623 – 4444 (box office and administration).

Miracle on the Mountain
The Crossnore School, P.O. Box 249, Crossnore, NC 28616
(828) 733 – 4305 (box office), (828) 733 – 5241 (administration).

The Miracle Worker
Helen Keller Birthplace Foundation Board, 300 West North Commons,
Tuscumbia, AL 35674 (888) 329 – 2124 or (256) 383 – 4066 (box office and
administration).

Montana Shakespeare in the Parks
P.O. Box 174120, Bozeman, MT 59717 – 4120 (406) 994 – 9301 (box office),
(406) 994 – 1220 (administration).

The Montford Park Players
P.O. Box 2663, Asheville, NC 28802 (828) 254 – 5146 (box office and
administration).

The Mormon Miracle Pageant
Church of Jesus Christ of Latter-Day Saints, P.O. Box 40, Manti,
UT 84642 (866) 961 – 9040 (box office), (435) 340 – 1075 (administration).

Mountain Play Association
Mountain Play Association P.O. Box 2025 Mill Valley, CA 94942
(415) 383 – 1100 (box office and administration).

Murphys Creek Theatre
580 S. Algiers Rd., Murphys, CA 95247 (209) 728 – 8422 (box office and
administration).

Nashville Shakespeare Festival
161 Rains Ave., Nashville, TN 37203 (615) 255 – 2273 (administration).

Nauvoo Pageant
Nauvoo Pageant Box 267, Nauvoo, IL 62354 (217)453 – 2429 (administration).

Nebraska Shakespeare Festival
c/o Department of Fine Arts, Creighton University, 2500 California Plaza,
Omaha, NE 68178 (402) 280 – 2391 (administration).

New York Shakespeare Festival
New York Shakespeare Festival/The Public Theatre, 425 Lafayette St, New York,
NY 10003 (212) 539 – 8671 (box office), (212) 539 – 8500 (administration).

Oklahoma!
Discoveryland! U.S.A., 5529 S Lewis, Tulsa, OK 74105 (918) 245 – 6552 (box
office), (918) 742 – 5255 (administration).

Oklahoma Shakespeare in the Park
P.O. Box 1437, Oklahoma City, OK 73101 – 1437 (405) 235 – 3700 (box office
and administration).

Old Homestead Association
P.O. Box 10414, Swanzey, NH 03446 (603) 352 – 4184 (box office and
administration).

Opera in the Ozarks at Inspiration Point
P.O. Box 127 Eureka Springs, AR 72632 (479) 253 – 8595 (box office and
administration).

Oregon Shakespeare Festival
15 S. Pioneer St., Ashland, OR 97520 (541) 482 – 4331 (box office),
(541) 482 – 2111 (administration).

Pacific Repertory Theatre
P.O. Box 222035, Carmel, CA 93922 (831) 622 – 0100 (box office),
(831) 622 – 0700 (administration).

The Passion Play in the Smokies
The Passion Play in the Smokies (865) 640 – 8903 (administration).

Pine Knob Theatre, Inc.
2250 Pine Knob Rd, Caneyville, KY 42721 (270) 879 – 8190 (box office and administration).

Pioneer Playhouse
840 Stanford Rd., Danville, KY 40422 (866) 597 – 5297 (box office), (859) 236 – 2747 (administration).

The Promised Land
Walk in the Light Productions, Inc. P.O. Box 260 Bath, NC 27808 (252) 923 – 9909 (box office) and (919) 612 – 2136 (administration).

The Promise in Glen Rose, Inc.
The Promise in Glen Rose, Inc. 122 E. Church St.,Weatherford, TX 76086 (254) 897 – 3926 (box office), (817) 599 – 3022 (administration).

Ramona
Ramona Bowl Amphitheatre 27400 Ramona Bowl Rd, Hemet, CA 92544 – 8108 (951) 658 – 3111 (box office and administration).

Richmond Shakespeare
Richmond Shakespeare, P.O. Box 27543, Richmond, VA 23261 (804) 232 – 4000 (box office and administration).

Riverside Theatre
Riverside Theatre Shakespeare Festival, 213 N Gilbert St, Iowa City, IA 52245 (319) 338 – 7672 (box office), (319) 887 – 1360 (administration).

Salado Legends
Tablerock Festival of Salado, P.O. Box 312, Salado, TX 76571 (254) 947 – 9205 (box office and administration).

Sandstone Productions
901 Fairgrounds Rd., Farmington, NM 87401 (505) 325 – 2570 (box office), (505) 599 – 1140 (administration).

San Francisco Shakespeare Festival
Box 460937, San Francisco, CA 94146 (415) 865 – 4434 (box office), (415) 558 – 0888 (administration).

Shakespeare & Company/MN
Century College-West Campus, 3300 Century Ave N, White Bear Lake, MN 55110 (651) 779 – 5818 (box office and administration).

Shakespeare by the Sea
777 Centre St., San Pedro, CA 90731 (310) 217 – 7596 (box office), (310) 619 – 0599 (administration).

Shakespeare Dallas
3630 Harry Hines Blvd, 4th Floor, Dallas, TX 75219
(214) 559 – 2778 (administration).

Shakespeare Festival of St. Louis
462 N. Taylor Ave., Suite 202, St Louis, MO 63108
(314) 531 – 9800 (administration).

Shakespeare in Delaware Park
P.O. Box 716, Buffalo, NY 14205-0716 (716) 856 – 4533 (box office and
administration).

Shakespeare in the Ozarks
P.O. Box 780, Eureka Springs, AR 72632 (479) 270 – 1278 (box office and
administration).

Shakespeare on the Green
208 N 17th Street, Wilmington, NC, 28401 (910) 399 – 2878 (box office and
administration

Shakespeare on the Sound
Shakespeare on the Sound, Inc., P.O. Box 15, Norwalk, CT 06853
(203) 299 – 1300 (box office and administration).

Shakespeare Orange County
P.O. Box 923, Orange, CA 92856 (714) 590 – 1575 (box office),
(714) 744 – 7016 (administration).

Shakespeare Santa Cruz/Theatre Arts UCSC
University of California, 1156 High St, Santa Cruz, CA 95064
(831) 459 – 2159 (box office), (831) 459 – 5810 (administration).

The Shakespeare Theatre of New Jersey
36 Madison Avenue, Madison, NJ 07940 (973) 408 – 5600 (box office),
(973) 408 – 3278 (administration).

Shakespeare's Associates
P.O. Box 2616, Livermore, CA 94551 – 2616 (800) 838 – 3006 (box office),
(925) 443 – 2273 (administration).

Shepherd of the Hills Outdoor Theatre
5586 West Highway 76, Branson, MO 65616 (800) 653 – 6288 (box office),
(417) 334 – 4191 (administration).

Sleepy Hollow Summer Theatre
P.O. Box 675 Bismarck, ND 58502 (866) 811 – 4111 (box office),
(701) 319 – 0894 (administration).

The Stephen Foster Story
Stephen Foster Productions, 411 East Stephen Foster Ave., Bardstown, KY
40004 (800) 626 – 1563 (box office), (502) 348 – 5971 (administration).

The Story of Jesus
Power & Light Productions, P.O. Box 97, Wauchula, FL 33873
(863) 375 – 4031 (administration and box office).

The Sword of Peace
Snow Camp Historical Drama Society, Inc. P.O. Box 535, Snow Camp, NC
27349 (336) 376 – 6948 (box office and administration).

Tecumseh!
The Scioto Society, Inc., P.O. Box 73, Chillicothe, OH 45601 – 0073
(740) 775 – 0700 (box office), (740) 775 – 4100 (administration).

Texas Musical Drama
Texas Panhandle Heritage Foundation, Inc., 1514 5th Ave, Canyon, TX 79015
(806) 655 – 2181 (box office and administration).

Theatre in the Park, Inc.
225 East Cook St., Springfield, IL 62704 (217) 632 – 5440 (box office),
(217) 241 – 3241 (administration).

Tom Dooley: A Wilkes County Legend
Wilkes Playmakers, Inc., P.O. Box 397, North Wilkesboro, NC 28659
(336) 838 – 7529 (box office and administration).

Trail of the Lonesome Pine
Lonesome Pine Arts and Crafts, Inc., P.O. Box 1976, Big Stone Gap,
VA 24219 (276) 523 – 1235 (box office and administration).

Trumpet in the Land
Ohio Historical Drama Association, Inc., P.O. Box 450, New Philadelphia,
OH 44663 (330) 339 – 1132 (box office) (330) 364 – 5111 (administration).

Under the Cherokee Moon
Cherokee National Historical Society, P.O. Box 515, Tahlequah,
OK 74465 (918) 456 – 6007 (box office and administration).

Unto These Hills
Cherokee Historical Association, P.O. Box 398, Cherokee, NC 28719
(828) 497 – 2111, (box office and administration).

Upstate Shakespeare Festival
37 Augusta St, Greenville, SC 29601 (864) 787 – 4016 (box office and
administration).

Utah Shakespearean Festival
351 West Center St., Cedar City, UT 84720 (435) 586 – 7878 (box office),
(435) 586 – 7880 (administration).

Viva! El Paso
El Paso Association for the Performing Arts, P.O. Box 512351, El Paso,
TX 79951 (915) 231 – 1165 (administration) (915) 544 – 8444 (box
office/ticketmaster).

Will Geer Theatricum Botanicum
1419 N. Topanga Cyn. Blvd., Topanga, CA 90290 (310) 455 – 3723 (box
office), (310) 455 – 2322 (administration).

The Shakespeare Festival Phenomenon and Shakespeare Association of America (STAA)

INTRODUCTION

The bookstores are brimming with new editions. Movie rental firms have dozens of
copies of each title. Copycat film directors and producers are turning the originals
into cute romantic comedies filled with teenage angst. Attendance is up. People are
traveling hundreds, even thousands of miles to see the latest, greatest production.
Indeed, the Bard is back!

Who would believe that as the twenty-first century began, John Updike's latest
novel would feature *Hamlet*'s Gertrude and Claudius, and *Titus Andronicus* would be
on the "must see" new movie list? Did *Shakespeare in Love* really win seven Academy
Awards and gross $100 million in North America, or are pop culture fanatics simply
caught up in the same dream that captured Michelle Pfeiffer and Kevin Kline in one
of the two *A Midsummer Night's Dream* movies still renting on DVD shelves
throughout America? Indeed, new Shakespeare Festivals and timely, sometimes
outrageous productions are popping up throughout America from Maine to
California and internationally, from Tasmania to Tanzania.

BIG BUCKS FOR THE BARD?

Even the world's Shakespeare Festival leaders are scratching their heads and
chuckling over the resurgence of all things linked to the great William. As we
entered the new millennium, England's Sir Peter Hall moved to America to join the
booming Bard-related business in Los Angeles and the Royal Shakespeare Company started farming out Shakespeare to the hinterlands of Great Britain. Canada's
Stratford Shakespeare Festival has consistently played to over 500,000 patrons in
recent years while contributing an estimated $169 million to the local community in
terms of economic impact!

In a world where audiences for serious plays and nonmusical work are often waning, tickets to Shakespeare's plays are hot. Shakespeare Theatre Association of America representatives estimate that there are over 200 Shakespeare companies in America, and over 150 international Shakespeare Festivals and companies around the world (including companies in Australia, Japan, Spain, Australia, South Africa, New Zealand, China, France and Germany to name a few).

In fact, every year for the past decade, over a million people braved America's great outdoors for Shakespeare's sake while millions of others attended Shakespeare productions in indoor theatres throughout the world. In 2010, England's Royal Shakespeare Company sold tickets to over 500,000 patrons and the Oregon Shakespeare Festival sold tickets to a record 410,000 audience members. Add in 500,000 from the Stratford Festival of Canada and that's over 1.4 million tickets to three theatres alone!

SHAKESPEARE IN THE PARKING LOT?

Certainly, entrepreneurs have almost always enjoyed producing Shakespeare. Aside from the diversity of comedies, romances, histories and tragedies, there's a great bonus to budgeting Shakespeare – no royalties! There is also good news for actors, directors, stage managers and production personnel. You don't have to travel to Stratford-Upon-Avon or even Stratford, Canada to belly up to the Bard! America leads the way in Shakespeare production with over 200 Shakespeare companies in operation. It might be Shakespeare-on-the-Rocks or Shakespeare Under the Stars (both in Texas) or Shakespeare in the Park (New York) or Shakespeare in the Parking Lot (Tacoma, Washington). Without a doubt, the Bard is alive and well in the United States and Shakespeare is the most produced playwright in world theatre.

Shakespeare Theatre Association of America (STAA)

STAA STATEMENT OF PURPOSE

The Shakespeare Theatre Association of America was established to provide a forum for artistic and managerial leadership of theatres whose central activity is the production of Shakespeare's plays; to discuss issues and share methods of work, resources, and information; and to act as an advocate for Shakespearean productions and training in North America.

STAA OVERVIEW

The Shakespeare Theatre Association of America was founded in 1991 by Sidney L. Berger, Producing Director of the Houston Shakespeare Festival, and Douglas N. Cook, longtime Producing Artistic Director of the Utah Shakespearean Festival. The first meeting was held on January 12, 1991 in the Library Board Room of the Folger Library. Over the years, STAA has met at the Royal Shakespeare Company in Stratford, England, Shakespeare's Globe in London, the Stratford Festival of Canada, and at Festivals large and small throughout the United States. The STAA quarto is published twice a year and details plans, productions, statistics and strategies related to Shakespeare in production. STAA also assembles a membership directory and holds an annual conference hosted by a member theatre.

The STAA website offers lists of officers, an institutional history, an updated directory, links to over 120 current or former member theatres, and sample copies of quarto. Check out the website at www.staaonline.org for the locations, contact numbers and season plans for each company below:

STAA MEMBER INDEX

A Company of Fools
A Noise Within
Actors Shakespeare Company at New Jersey City University
Actors' Shakespeare Project
Advice to the Players
African-American Shakespeare Company
Alabama Shakespeare Festival
American Players Theatre
American Shakespeare Center
Arkansas Shakespeare Theatre
Artfarm: Shakespeare in the Grove
Atlanta Shakespeare Company (at The New American Shakespeare Tavern)
Austin Shakespeare
Australian Shakespeare Festival
Baltimore Shakespeare Festival, Inc.
Bard on the Beach Shakespeare Festival
Bell Shakespeare Company
Capital Classics Theatre Company
Carolinian Shakespeare Festival
Chesapeake Shakespeare Company
Chicago Shakespeare Theatre
Colorado Shakespeare Festival
Commonwealth Shakespeare Company
Delaware Shakespeare Festival
Elm Shakespeare Company
Fairbanks Shakespeare Theatre
Festival Theatre Ensemble
Flatwater Shakespeare
Folger Theatre
Foothill Theatre Company/Sierra Shakespeare Festival

Freeport Shakespeare Festival
Georgia Shakespeare
Globe of the Great Southwest, Inc.
Grand Valley Shakespeare Festival
Great River Shakespeare Festival
GreenStage
Harrisburg Shakespeare Festival
Heart of America Shakespeare Festival
Houston Shakespeare Festival (a professional project of the University of Houston School of Theatre)
Hudson Valley Shakespeare Festival
Idaho Shakespeare Festival
Illinois Shakespeare Festival
Institute of Outdoor Drama
Ithaca Shakespeare Company
Judith Shakespeare Company NYC
Kentucky Shakespeare Festival
Kingsmen Shakespeare Company
Lake Tahoe Shakespeare Festival
Livermore Shakespeare Festival/Shakespeare's Associates
Los Angeles Women's Shakespeare Company
Marin Shakespeare Company
Maryland Shakespeare Festival
Milwaukee Shakespeare
Montana Shakespeare Co.
Montana Shakespeare in the Parks
Montford Park Players
Nashville Shakespeare Festival
Nebraska Shakespeare Festival
New York Classical Theatre
North Carolina Shakespeare Festival
NorthEast Shakespeare Ensemble
Notre Dame Shakespeare Festival
Ohio Shakespeare Festival
Ojai Shakespeare Festival
Oklahoma Shakespeare in the Park
Oregon Shakespeare Festival
Orlando Shakespeare Theatre in Partnership with UCF
Pasadena Shakespeare Company
Pennsylvania Shakespeare Festival at DeSales University
Philadelphia Shakespeare Festival
Prague Shakespeare Festival

Redfeather Theatre at Holy Cross
Richmond Shakespeare
Riverside Theatre
Rochester Community Players
Sacramento Shakespeare Festival
San Francisco Shakespeare Festival
Seattle Shakespeare Company
Sebastopol Shakespeare Festival
Shady Shakespeare Theatre Company
Shakespeare & Company
Shakespeare at Winedale
Shakespeare Behind Bars
Shakespeare By The Sea
Shakespeare By The Sea Festival
Shakespeare Dallas
Shakespeare Festival St. Louis
Shakespeare Festival/LA
Shakespeare Globe Center Australia
Shakespeare Guild, Inc.
Shakespeare in Delaware Park – Buffalo
Shakespeare in the Ozarks
Shakespeare in the Park Festival Calgary
Shakespeare In the Parking Lot Theatre
Shakespeare in the Valley
Shakespeare in the Vines
Shakespeare on Main Street
Shakespeare on the Saskatchewan Festival Inc.
Shakespeare on the Sound, Inc.
Shakespeare Orange County
Shakespeare SA (South Africa)
Shakespeare Santa Cruz
Shakespeare Theatre Company
Shakespeare Ventures
Shakespeare's Globe
South Carolina Shakespeare Company
Southwest Shakespeare Company
St. Lawrence Shakespeare Festival
Stratford Shakespeare Festival
Tennessee Shakespeare Festival
Tennessee Stage Company/East Tennessee Shakespeare in the Park
Texas Shakespeare Festival
The Classical Theatre Project

The Cleveland Shakespeare Festival
The Colonial Theatre
The Shakespeare Festival at Tulane
The Shakespeare Guild
The Shakespeare Theatre of New Jersey
The Summer Theatre of New Canaan
The Theater At Monmouth
Theatre Arts, Oregon State University
Theatre for a New Audience
Utah Shakespearean Festival
Woodward Shakespeare Festival

A FINAL NOTE

This book promised a "common sense manual" detailing basic arts management strategies and life management tips that would improve your organization, solidify your professional relationships, contribute to your future earnings power, and modify the way you anticipate and plan for your future and the future of your institution. I hope I was able to keep my promises and that you were able to find something useful in this book that made your purchase worthwhile! The text was created "in the field" through myriad consulting adventures, opportunities in education, professional theatre (and beyond); and the knowledge that emerges from a lifetime of "reality-based" success, failure, heartache, and triumph.

My hope for you is a lifetime of artistic, administrative, and personal success helping the arts thrive throughout the world. Your suggestions, comments, or questions are always welcome, and you can contact me at: jvolz@fullerton.edu

Bibliography

Barley, Nella. "*How to Make Your Career Dreams Come True*." Boulder: Bottom Line Personal, 1990.

Byrnes, William J. *Management and the Arts*. Boston: Focal Press, 1999.

Case, Evelyn Carol and Jim Volz. *Words for Lovers: Snippets, Sonnets & Sensual Sayings from William Shakespeare*. Columbiana: WaterMark Inc., 1990.

Celentano, Suzanne Carmack and Kevin Marshall. *Theatre Management*. Studio City: Players Press, 1998.

Drucker, Peter F. *The Drucker Foundation Self-Assessment Tool*. New York: The Drucker Foundation, 1999.

Earle, Dr. Richard. "*Secrets of Successful Stress Reduction*." New York: Boardroom Reports, 1991.

Eustis, Morton. *B'way, Inc! The Theatre as a Business*. New York: Dodd, Mead, & Company, 1934.

Gingold, Diane J. *Business and the Arts: How They Meet the Challenge*. Washington D.C., 1984.

Groder, Dr. Martin G. "*Time to Think Seriously About Consequential Thinking*." Boulder: Bottom Line Personal, 1995.

Jeary, Tony. *Inspire Any Audience*. Dallas: Trade Life Books, 1997.

Kennedy, Gavin. *The Perfect Negotiation*. New York: Wings Books, 1992.

Kennedy, Marilyn Moats. *Salary Strategies*. New York: Bantam Books, 1983.

Kragen, Ken and Jefferson, Graham. *Life is a Contact Sport*. New York: William Morrow and Company, 1994.

Langley, Stephen. *Theatre Management and Production in America*. New York: Drama Book Publishers, 1990.

Langley, Stephen and James Abruzzo. *Jobs in Arts and Media Management: What They Are and How to Get One!* New York: American Council for the Arts, 1989.

Mackay, Harvey. *Swim with the Sharks*. New York: Ivy Books, 1988.

Malloy, Merritt, and Sorensen, Shauna. *The Quotable Quote Book*. New York: Citadel Press, 1990.

Mayer, Jeffrey. "*Time . . . Precious Time. How to Use it Very Wisely*." Boulder: Bottom Line Personal, 1991.

McCormack, Mark H. *What They Don't Teach You at Harvard Business School*. New York: Bantam Books, 1984.

Melillo, Joseph V. *Market the Arts!* New York: The Foundation for the Extension and Development of the American Professional Theatre, 1983.

Moran, Richard. *Never Confuse a Memo With Reality*. New York: HarperCollins Publishers, 1994.

Morison, Bradley G., and Dalgleish, Julie Gordon. *Waiting in the Wings: A Larger Audience for the Arts and How to Develop It*. New York: American Council for the Arts, 1987.

Morrow, Roxanne. *"When 24 Hours Are Not Enough."* HealthBeat, Los Angeles: 1994.

Newman, Danny. *Subscribe Now! Building Arts Audiences Through Dynamic Subscription Promotion*. New York: Theatre Communications Group, 1977.

Peale, Norman Vincent, and Blanchard, Kenneth. *The Power of Ethical Management*. New York: Blanchard, Morrow, and Co., 1992.

Peter, Dr. Laurence. *Peter's Quotations*. New York: Bantam Books, 1987.

Pritchett, Price and Pound, Ron. *The Employee Handbook for Organizational Change*. Dallas: Pritchett and Associates, Inc., 1995.

Reiss, Alvin H. *Cash In! Funding and Promoting the Arts*. New York: Theatre Communications Group, 1986.

Samuels, Steven, Editor. *Theatre Profiles 12*. New York: Theatre Communication Group, 1996.

Schneider, Richard E., and Ford, Mary Jo. *The Theatre Management Handbook*. Cincinnati: Betterway Books, 1999.

Vodde, Ted. *"It's About Time."* Business Alabama, 1986.

Volz, Jim. *Shakespeare Never Slept Here: The Making of a Regional Theatre*. Atlanta: Cherokee Publishing Company, 1986.

Walker, Lou Ann. *"How to Make Time Work for You."* Parade Magazine, 1987.

White, Rolf B., Editor. *The Great Business Quotations*. New York: Dell Publishing, 1986.

Winston, Stephanie. *"Spare Moments Can be Very . . . Very Valuable to You."* Boulder: Bottom Line Personal, 1995.

About the Author

Jim Volz is an international arts consultant, author, producer and professor at California State University, Fullerton. He has produced over 100 professional productions, consulted with over 100 companies, and published more than 100 articles and books on management, arts criticism, Shakespeare and theatre. He served as a longtime critic/columnist for both New York's *Back Stage* and Hollywood's *Drama-Logue* and has published in *American Theatre, Horizon Magazine, Equity News, SSD&C Journal, Theatre Management Journal,* Oxford University Press' *Theatre Research International* and in a myriad of other international publications. He has been the editor of the Shakespeare Theatre Association of America's international publication, *quarto,* since 1991. He is the author/editor of eight books including *A Back Stage Guide to Working in Regional Theatre, How to Run a Theatre* and *Shakespeare Never Slept Here. Buffett and the Bard,* edited with Cindy Melby Phaneuf, *Shakespeare Around the World* with Evelyn Carol Case, and *Working in American Theatre* are books in progress.

Jim is Past President of the National Theatre Conference, an associate member of the American Theatre Critics Association and a longtime voting member for the prestigious Tony Award's Regional Theatre Award. He serves on the National Advisory Council for the Institute of Outdoor Drama, the National Artistic Board of Directors for Florida's Orlando Shakespeare Festival, and the Editorial Board of distinguished scholars for the ISE Shakespeare project, based at the University of Victoria in Canada. He has served as a Strategic Planning/Time Management Program presenter for the National Association of Schools of Music, the National Association of Schools of Dance and the National Association of Schools of Theatre. His loyalties to the Rocky Mountain region include longtime service as associate editor for the University of Colorado's On-Stage Studies, consulting services for the Colorado Shakespeare Festival and continued work as the national adjudicator for the University of Wyoming's National Theatre Essay Competition.

Jim is President of Consultants for the Arts, an international arts consulting service that works with a revolving team of highly qualified theatre professionals contracted to bring their specific area of expertise to each project. Over three decades of service includes work with professional theatres, Shakespeare Festivals, and arts centers in Tasmania, San Francisco, Atlanta, Boulder, Hilton Head Island, Telluride, Sedona, Orlando and dozens of other cities throughout America in areas of

Strategic Planning, Executive Search, Board of Trustee advisement, Producing, Marketing, Fundraising and Institutional Development. In California, arts projects include work with the Cities of Irvine, Cypress, Brea, La Quinta, San Jose, and Fullerton, and arts organizations ranging from South Coast Repertory, the Laguna Playhouse, Marin Theatre Company, the San Francisco Mime Company and San Jose Repertory Theatre to the Irvine Barclay Theatre, Hunger Artists Theatre Company, Irvine Museum, and Arts Orange County.

The Alabama Shakespeare Festival's Board of Trustees recruited Jim to spearhead the ASF's historic expansion from a small summer operation in Anniston, Alabama, to the world's fifth-largest Shakespeare Festival in Montgomery, Alabama. From 1982–1991, Jim orchestrated the tremendous growth of the Alabama Shakespeare Festival as Managing Director in partnership with Artistic Directors Martin L. Platt and Kent Thompson.

Devoted to arts education, Dr. Volz has taught at over a dozen universities, administered MFA programs in acting, stage management, and arts administration and served as Head of the BFA in Arts Administration program and acting Chairman of the Department of Theatre and Dance at Wright State University. He is a Ph.D. graduate from the University of Colorado, Boulder. At California State University, Fullerton, Dr. Volz served for many years on the Board of Trustees for the Philanthropic Foundation and has received honors, grants and recognition for Teaching, Mentoring in the Arts, Publishing, Service to the Campus as a Community, Enhancing Learning in the Classroom, External Community Service, Contributions to Student Leadership, Shakespearean Research, Student Career Planning Service, Professional Theatre Research, and Service to the University.

Over the years, he has served as a presenter at Stratford, England's Royal Shakespeare Company, chair of New York's Stavis Playwright Award for emerging playwrights and a grant reviewer for the National Endowment for the Humanities and the National Endowment for the Arts. As a concerned community member, Jim has served on the Board of Directors of Humana Hospital, the World Affairs Council, the Southeastern Theatre Conference, and the National Theatre Conference. As a civic leader, he has worked on Chamber of Commerce and State Tourism Committees and volunteered services for struggling artists, theatres, arts centers, arts councils, museums and dance companies.

On a national level, Jim has served as a steering committee member for the American Council for the Arts and a longtime member of the League of Resident Theatres, the University/Resident Theatre Association, the American Arts Alliance, the Theatre Communications Group, the Authors Guild, the Dramatists Guild, and the Association for Theatre in Higher Education.

His speaking engagements have covered every area from the Kiwanis, Rotary, Lions, and Optimists clubs to the Volunteer Lawyers for the Arts, Alabama Youth Foundation, Montgomery Business Committee for the Arts, National Conference of State Legislatures, American Council for the Arts, National Society of Fund

Raising Executives, National Business Committee for the Arts, Association of Independent Colleges and Universities, and the Association of Government Accountants.

In the past few years, he has devoted his spare time to community service, travel, basketball and writing. Jim is married to professional actress and award-winning educator, Evelyn Carol Case. As a writing team, they edited *Words for Lovers: Snippets from William Shakespeare*. They have two adventurous children, Nicholas and Caitlin.

Index